Who Is the River

Who Is the River

*Getting Lost and Found
in the Amazon and Other Places*

Paul Zalis

Atheneum   NEW YORK   1986

Library of Congress Cataloging in Publication Data

Zalis, Paul.
  Who is the river.

  1. Amazon River Valley—Description and travel.
2. Zalis, Paul.   I. Title.
F2546.Z35   1986   918.1′10463   85-47638
ISBN 0-689-11594-6

Copyright © 1986 by Paul Zalis
All rights reserved
Published simultaneously in Canada by Collier Macmillan Canada, Inc.
Composition by P & M Typesetting, Inc., Waterbury, Connecticut
Manufactured by Fairfield Graphics, Fairfield, Pennsylvania
Designed by Cathryn S. Aison

FIRST EDITION

This is the spot for dedications, acknowledgments, and epigraphs. Those words seem like bone china, and rather than risk dropping them, I'd just like to say a few thanks along with something else.

First, my sincere gratitude for financial assistance from the University of California, Center for Latin American Studies; the Tinker Foundation; the Wollenberg Foundation; and the University of California, Berkeley, Graduate School of Journalism. Also, for his enthusiasm, time, encouragement, and direction in sending off this small ship, I want to especially thank David Littlejohn.

There is one other thing I would like to say, and it is the most important. Years ago, I read some letters John Steinbeck kept while working on his novel *East of Eden*. The letters actually were a journal in the form of a conversation with his editor. At the beginning, when he sat down to write, he remarked how full of love and happiness his home was. I guess he'd had rough times before, and now, for what seemed like one of the first times in a long time in his life, things were right. I know how he felt. As I said, it was years ago when I first read that and when I did I was a little envious of Steinbeck. I was not in such good shape when it came to matters of the heart then, and the sound of Steinbeck's home had a warmth to it that left me longing. I had a sense of how important it was for him to feel that way to write his book, and I understand that now more than ever. This book, to a great extent, is a book about movement, one I could not have written without a home in which to keep still. I have that now. Barbar, thanks, with all my love.

Who Is the River

Before I left for the Amazon, I had read that it was more than 200 miles wide at its mouth, it discharged 12 times as much water as the Mississippi, an island in its delta was bigger than Switzerland, and it was deep enough for oceangoing vessels to travel a thousand miles upriver. I also had read there were 150-pound turtles in the Amazon, along with porpoises, alligators, piranhas, the world's biggest rodent, longest snake, and largest cockroach. Then, too, I had read there are 20–50,000 Indians still isolated in the Amazon and of the 140 remaining tribes, about 40 still had not been contacted.

This story does not have much to do with any of that stuff.

IN

I

WHEN it ended, I knew it. Everything about the finish was clear. There was a woman outside a hotel bar in New York. We spoke for a minute. I had not seen her before and have not seen her again. She appeared, then was gone, and I knew the story was over.

I suppose everything else about it was that clear, as things only sometimes are. It was just a matter of how much I could piece together. The problem was being on so many rivers. I had gone into the Amazon looking for pyramids but lost myself in a tangle of rivers, and the looking became a search not only for the rivers in the jungle, but also for rivers inside, rivers with currents, rivers of time and memory that overlapped and, at times, mixed with someone else's rivers.

I had not thought of myself as geography, as invisible, internal lines I could chart, but the more I searched, the more things connected, until the rivers and the memories became a story, and also, perhaps, a map.

My first night on the river, I knew only that I was going into the Amazon. I didn't know I would get lost, either in the jungle or in the past, and I didn't know how difficult it would be to find my way through and out. When you are lost in the rivers of the Amazon you look for the strongest current and follow it. Eventually, it will bring you to the sea. It is the same with memory.

Not knowing those things that first night on the river was fine. I wasn't in the mood to put things together. I was content with the way things were, with me on the deck of the *Emerson*, a sixty-foot cargo boat rumbling upriver to the equator.

Early evening there was a half moon, the sky was huge, and the stars could have been asking me to float. To the southeast, a large cloud with a trailing stem of vapor crackled with flashes of heat lightning. The cloud looked like a neon cocktail glass in front of a bar and grill. Between bursts, the glass hung for a moment and swathed the earth in flashcube light. The jungle blinked. It flipped on and glowed, a huge, phosphorescent blanket, then shut off. Behind me, Manaus, the capital of the Amazon, shrank into the river, easing down as we pushed farther away, a jaundiced-colored castle melting into a lump of light.

I emptied a bottle of vitamin B's that in overdose quantities were supposed to give me an antimosquito stench. I wrote a note, sealed it in the bottle, and leaned back over the rail. The cocktail glass lit up and I tossed the bottle and watched it get sucked into the sky and the river and the night. I couldn't hear a splash, only the *put-put-put-put* of the *Emerson* roaring everything into deafness.

From the pilothouse a wiry, high-cheeked Indian we later would call Monkey Man whirled the ship's wheel, guiding us along edges of shadows and into wide ribbons of gray. The river unraveled before the bow, shedding deep folds with luminescent stripes. Monkey Man turned on a searchlight, poked shafts of light at the shore and floating logs, and read the current from partially submerged trees. On the left bank, the shadows opened as a neon cross twinkled on a hill above a leper colony. The *Emerson* slid by, into narrow channels, weaving through what seemed passes between ridges of black mountains. Monkey Man hit the lamp and the mountains became slivers of gray trees crowding the bank. When he switched off the light, I pointed to the moon and gave him the thumbs-up. He smiled and nodded. It was a good night to steer by.

4

II

SEPTEMBER 1979.

Ken Payette slouched in his chair. The collar of his silk shirt slid toward his chin. He clasped his hands, brought them to his mouth, and shook his head.

"This will be difficult," he said. "I only know of one man who does such things."

Payette waved his hand to a boy at the door and said, "Cerveja."

"You like beer?"

He held up one finger and the boy hustled out.

"Well, we'll see what we can do about all this," he said.

Payette was a small man. He was thin and his clothes draped his frame. He spoke with a nasal Brooklyn accent and looked like a gaunt Peter Lorre.

"In the Everglades, I was a guide for years," he said. "But it got to the point where there was a badge behind every bush."

He shook his head, then smiled.

"Yes," he said, rattling the end of the word as if he was hissing and then looking to see if he was understood.

The boy came back with the beer and Payette talked about

5

his boss, Manuel "Bebe" Barros. Bebe and Payette came to the capital of the jungle "years ago" and set up Amazon Explorers. For between $85 and $125 a day, they took groups of gringos, put them on a boat with a dining room and a shower, and escorted them up the Amazon and into the jungle. Their longest trip lasted a week.

"For some people, it's good," Payette said. "They have the money, and we supply them with what they want. On the boat, it's comfortable. They can spend all day in the bush and it's always good to come back to a pleasant place at night. There's beer and pinga and they are well cared for. But ... that's not for everyone.

"Now, for something ... more primitive, there is only one person I know who does such things.

"He's a German, an old man. He's been in Manaus for thirty years, but he's difficult to find. He's always out there. He's gone for months, comes in, and then, zip, he's out again. Crazy. But maybe he'll be good for you.

"His name is Glück [pronounced glick], Kurt Glück. I'll send you to someone who knows Glück well."

Payette scribbled a name on a piece of paper and pushed it across his desk.

"Go to the House of the Hummingbird. It's not far. Ask for this man and tell him Ken Payette sent you. Come back and tell me what happened."

Outside the Hotel Lord, it was midday and the sun pressed as if it would crush anything that moved. People walked along the sides of streets shadowed by stumpy concrete buildings.

At a café along the docks, a waiter leaned over the shoulder of a woman and sprayed repellent on the flies that speckled the pepper bottle. He picked up what was left of a plate of fish and tossed it over the rail. From the eaves beneath the roof of a warehouse, a vulture swooped down for the bones.

The House of the Hummingbird was two cobblestoned blocks away.

"Hello," a slight, dark-skinned man with a smile of gold-capped teeth said as he walked quickly to the door. He introduced himself as Mr. Waldzegar and bowed and waved his hand at walls of shields, blowguns, feathered headsets, and jewelry. "Is there anything we can help you with?"

6

"Richard Melnick?"

"Oh, oh, yes, meester, of course, of course. Boss. He's upstairs. Wait minute."

He clapped his hands twice and a young man appeared. Waldzegar said something quickly in Portuguese, and the man nodded his head and went into a back room.

Waldzegar turned and held up one finger. "Minute."

In a corner behind him, a macaw, perched on a stand, took a nut to its beak and cracked it. "B-e-e-e-a-u-t-y-y-f-u-l, yes," Waldzegar said of the bright red and blue bird.

"Two thousand dollars," he said, and lifted an eyebrow.

"We have other things, Monkey-teeth necklaces." He rushed behind a counter and pulled out a string of tiny teeth.

"Maybe twenty monkeys' teeth on necklace. Take very long to hunt them. Indian hunt them, you know. Very long, very expensive, but I sell cheap, thirty dollars."

The young man came from the back room and waved, and I followed, past long tables covered with feathers and six-foot blowguns, to a stairway at the back, where he pointed up.

At the top, a knock on the door was answered with a loud, "Come in."

A balding, heavyset man took off black-rimmed glasses, loked up from his desk, and extended his hand.

His grip was strong and he introduced himself as "Melnick, Richard Melnick, pleasure." He pointed to a chair.

We talked for a while. He told me he was from Rochester, New York, from the "Polack section of town, but that was years ago." He didn't say his age, but looked like he was in his mid to upper forties. He seemed a little uneasy, but friendly, talking in spurts, with the spurts tied together with "Yeah."

"Hey, who's gonna win the election?" he asked.

It was more than a year away and he said he thought Ted Kennedy would run and win.

"Only thing, who knows what they'll do to him about Chappaquiddick. Poor guy. We all got skeletons in the closet ... You know, people never forgive ... Oh, well. So, what can I do for you?"

I told him I wanted to go up north, along the Rio Negro, maybe into Territorio de Roraima, near the Venezuelan border, or west up past Ilha Grande. Both areas still virtually were unsettled, and Melnick said that a couple years back, a group of missionaries were killed by a tribe of Indians near Roraima.

The incident was reported in the American papers, and I told Melnick I had heard about it.

"Yeah, it was a real big deal around here," he said. "The place was jumpin' after that.

"Fuckin' priests got it, they sure did." He laughed. "But they had it coming to them. Arrogant sons-of-bitches. For years people went up there. We'd traded with those Indians. Not much touble. Then these priests, they go up there and tell them 'No more.' Gotta put their clothes on and come on in. Well, the Indians say no dice. They take everything the priests got and then zzzip." Melnick ran his fingers across his throat. "Sayonara, crossbacks.

"One guy escaped. A Brazilian. He was just up there, helping out with the boat. Matter of fact, he's my neighbor. You should talk to him. He's got good stories.

"Anyways, the kid gets a boat and hightails it back here. Well, Manaus goes crazy. The joint ain't heard news like that in years. But, before anybody knows what to do, Glück's on his way. He's got some German with him and the two of them hop in the dugout and take off. About a week after the massacre, Glück and the German, I forget his name now, reached the village. I talked to the German later and he told me the story.

"So, they get up there and first thing, they see skeletons heaped by the riverbank. Priests are long gone. The river doesn't wait on anything.

"Glück told the German he's going into the village, which is a little ways in from the river. He pulls the canoe up and says, 'If I'm not back in fifteen minutes, go back to Manaus and tell my wife to sell the boat.'

"Yeah, that's what he said." Melnick laughed.

"Well, Glück goes in to see them and fifteen minutes later he returns. They didn't want to do him in and everything's OK now. Indians were just a little pissed at the priests, but everything's all right.

"Going in there and powwowin', Glück's the only guy who could've done that."

Melnick said that a few weeks later Brazilian soldiers went in after the Indians and wiped out most of the village. But many

8

Brazilians were angered by that, and Melnick said the government had developed a new way to deal with Indian insurgence.

"They've hired mercenaries," he said. "Everyone knows they're getting soldiers from Colombia. They're puttin' it to the tribes. Supposedly, it's a secret, but in Manaus, we all know what's going on.

"Ask Glück about this, Glück knows the jungle. He knows it good."

Whether Melnick said it, or I imagined it, I don't know, but the next thing I remember was "the king of the jungle."

I spent the fall and winter telegramming/writing Glück that I wanted to go upriver with him, and in the meantime, I got my partner.

III

I first met Tano ten years before the Amazon. On and off for those ten years, our lives had been tied together by roads and airplanes and boats and plans. The plans usually start in one or another's home where they are clear and easy enough, but once they get us going, sometimes the plans get twisted. You know plans are in trouble when words like yesterday and tomorrow start creeping in, like, "Tomorrow the boat has to come," which is followed by, "It better," or "Yesterday was just bad luck, it'll change," which is also followed by, "It better," or "I know by tomorrow we'll be able to get the hell out of here," which is followed by, "We'd better."

I don't see Tano often, but when I do, there usually are the plans, spoken like chants over a bottle of whiskey and a map. One of us usually has the first plan and has the job of convincing the other, which almost always happens, despite some token resistance. Still, the birth of a plan always will mean a myriad of other plans we have to put together fast to get us out of the trouble the first plan got us into, so whenever someone says he has a plan, it is up to the other one to lift an eyebrow and stay quiet for a second in hope the echo of bad logic will kill the idea. If that doesn't work, and the guy with the plan doesn't back off into an "Ahh, it was just something to think about," then it is usually up to the other person to give the guy with a plan a bit of a hard time, which to my astonishment was not the case when the idea of the Amazon came up.

I only assumed it was fortune, but Tano happened to be in the Southern California desert at the time I was first in Brazil and talking to Melnick. On my return to the States in September 1979, I was going to stop briefly in San Diego where I telegraphed Tano to meet me.

He did, and the plan took shape on the beach.

The woman I was living with at the time, the woman I first went to Brazil with, spent the afternoon lolling in the sun with Tano and me, but late in the day she left. That might have been interpreted as a mistake for anyone trying to keep a grip on either of us, but in that case, maybe it wasn't. Her grip definitely had slackened, so maybe she, too, had a part in the plan.

I think Tano knew what was coming, although he didn't let on.

It was near sunset and almost everyone had left the beach except for a few surfers, but for an hour or so Tano and I thrashed around in the waves, until the sea pretty much beat the hell out of us, the state of being I wanted at least Tano in, so we retreated to the beach. We shook, dropped down, and toweled.

Tano lit a cigarette and I knew the time was right.

Tano was raised in the Midwest, where, as he has told me, socializing is often done over cards after a family meal or during a lunch break at work, the way I suppose English people do it over tea, Parisians over coffee, and Californians over brunch. As Midwestern socializing can be tied in with something more overtly competitive, conversation with someone from that part of the country often can be a ritual of sizing the other person up. Tano has that down to an art. He judges people fast. He might claim that is instinctual—I would agree somewhat as I think that, with whatever else he has got mixed in his blood, he also has raccoon—but I suspect much of it has to do with cards. Cardplayers are by nature suspicious, and Tano has some of that, but also they are guarded, and Tano's got a lot of that. He can be reckless, but he usually keeps his hand close to his chest and his

11

eyes on yours, which is the way he was when I was ready to spring the Amazon on him.

"I got a plan," I said.

No response, but the eyebrow raised, followed by a deep draw on the cigarette, neither of which intimidated me.

"Whatcha got, man?" he asked.

"Well, I think we oughta go to the Amazon together."

I let the pause hang only for a second before quickly launching into an elaborate proposal centering on hiring Glück, taking on the last frontier, and going as deep into the jungle as we could and, for old times' sake, doing it together. I saved my clincher for the end. "You know, man, there's still oogah boogahs down there."

He didn't leap into the air. In fact, he didn't say anything, just sort of half smiled, but I knew I had him. We talked a little about South America.

"You know, I've done my time down there," he said.

I knew, and I was asking him to go back, and I knew he would, and he knew he would, and he did.

IV

OF course, you don't spring the Amazon on just anyone, there being numerous considerations like compatibility, time, money, sense of humor, and toughness, all of which are guesswork unless you have something else, history. Tano and I have a fair amount of that.

This whole business of plans started almost from the beginning with us, just before Columbus Day, close to ten years before the Amazon. Although I am not sure it's right, I would like to remember that the first time I saw Tano was on the street. He was about six feet, thin, with scraggly blond hair that hung like straw from his cowboy hat, blue eyes, and a face that looked part carved, part weathered, with something of a droop to it that looked more timeless than tired, though sometimes it could look a lot of the tired. It was the kind of face in another time you might find on a totem pole, not up top, but tucked in an odd angle in one of the middle segments, like the carver or the tribe figured Tano ought to be up there, but they were not exactly sure where.

If Tano doesn't have to, he doesn't wear clothes, but at the time I met him, he was in the Midwest and it was autumn, so he did—always the same ones, a patched denim jacket, ragged blue jeans, and boots. He wore that outfit all the time. On him, it might be described as western scarecrow, and as to the rest, I took it on faith he changed his underclothes, except I often accused him of never changing his socks.

"What do you mean, they smell like dirty popcorn?" he would say.

Where his clothing was not patched together, it was sewn with stuff you identified by gauge and that made him looked zipped. Underneath the quilting, he had developed an elaborate hobo file system with money and notes sewn into patches and behind waistbands, tiny leather pouches (the kind you might use to keep rings or gold nuggets), fingernail files, GI can openers, roach clips tied together with leather strips at the end of other leather strips with other personal items like a sewing needle, thread, and a tooth of some animal tied to an assortment of fishing tackle dangling on a bobber deep in a jacket pocket, just above a large pouch with contact lens solution and a plastic case. He could draw on any of those things in a flash, but his most accessible possession was a lightweight but long enough to be deadly knife. If he had been born a hundred years earlier, he would have walked around with a six-shooter in a holster, but times had changed and he adapted.

When I first saw him, I didn't know he was a walking tackle box. That came in a series of revelations. What first caught my eye was a bone that dangled from his neck. It was a sliver of a bone, but he wore it like a jewel, and when I got to know him better he told me it was a pork rib.

"It almost choked me to death," he said, "so now I wear it, kind of as a reminder of things."

He did not spill secrets like that easily, and it was only after I knew him a while that he told me, and even then it was only after direct questioning. Like with everyone else, there was the what-you-see and what-you-don't-see side to Tano, but with him there was a big difference between the two.

What you could often see in Tano was a mixture of wildness and hardness, though you couldn't see from where it came. Tano's father was a railroad man and his mother a solid but sometimes fiery-eyed woman, and behind them there were genera-

14

tions of Midwestern blood with an infusion of Cherokee. Tano also had a brother and sister, but the Indian blood surfaced in Tano while more of the Midwest and a touch of the divine found an outlet in the brother and sister. Keeping a tradition going, his sister married a railroad man and already was raising a family when I first met Tano, and his older brother, whom Tano talked little about, was spending a year in Europe memorizing the Bible. Later, his brother wrote a book, in which he claimed to prove the existence of God, and dedicated the book to Tano, which did absolutely no good.

Along with the Indian blood, Tano also got a good dose of brains. Like his knife, he kept that tucked away. His brains might have been his best secret, something he guarded. He channeled most of it into instincts, and he kept those as sharp as his knife, which could split a hair. He didn't show outsiders much. That probably was part of the cardplayer in him. He talked simple and straight, called himself "just a dumb shit," and often told me I was the one with the brains, none of which ever fooled me.

By the time I met him, he already had been honed a bit by the road, though even when he was off it there was something about him that kept moving, even when he was sitting still. It would be easy to say it was his eyes, but it wasn't just that. Maybe it had more to do with how skinny he was and how his clothes hung on him, as if underneath there was not always something as solid as flesh and bone.

When he did move, whatever was underneath didn't always move in the same direction. Like, if he was running for a ride, his elbows didn't stay close to his body but tended to lift up and whirl, and his hat would bounce and he would grab it, and his legs, though they spun in a circle, had a wobble to them, the way a tire might wobble if it was not tight on the axle. Sometimes, watching him, I had the feeling he could fly apart, and even when he was still, I was anxious.

For what reasons, I'm not sure, but when I first met him, he was making a brief stab at university life, a stab that happened to coincide in time and place with a similar attempt of mine. We were both in and out in a few months, and later I would try again, but when Tano was finished, he was finished. After that, he went back to pick up things on the road.

15

In general back then, people read the what-you-see side of Tano as either bum or son-of-a-bitch. Most saw him as the former, but quite a few shared the latter view. Among the first I saw that held that perception was the college football team.

In the dining hall, when he walked past the tables where the football team bulked up, they would turn and sneer, as if they were ready to spit. From my understanding, it was nothing more than Tano's appearance that caused the reaction. "They don't like my face," Tano would say, but then again, he didn't like theirs. Once, when Tano and I got to be pals, his football friends considered rearranging both our faces, a situation I considered involved me less because of appearance than association, something I learned to contend with fast.

At that time, Tano and I already had become friends. We also knew how to keep our distance from each other, which made us into deeper friends, which was what we were doing one night in the dining hall, becoming deeper friends by staying apart. Peaches were served for dessert that night, and Tano and I sat in opposite corners of the room, and though now I have no recollection of what provoked it, we reached dessert simultaneously and almost as simultaneously let it fly at each other across the room. One of the plates didn't make it, and instead landed at the table where the defensive unit sat.

The team had crossed expectations and was doing poorly that year, and when the peaches hit the defense, I thought we were going to be made examples of the team's potential. There were quick apologies on our part, and an even quicker exit, and after that, we limited our cafeteria visits, an adjustment that was relatively easy as our schedules became increasingly nocturnal. Gradually, we managed to reverse things so that breakfast became our dinner, just before we went to bed, and we usually slept late enough to miss everyone else's dinner. The team never seemed to be up in time for breakfast, so we ate in peace, and later on, I got a job at a Howard Johnson's, where I was able to dine nightly on fried clams and microwave spaghetti, so I gave up the cafeteria.

The first time I spoke to Tano, he came to my room with a mutual friend from Nebraska called Biwana, who had achieved a minor reputation as a drug dealer. Biwana looked like a cross between Buddha and the Pillsbury doughboy, and he always had

16

CARE packages from Omaha with staples like beef jerky and carameled popcorn called Screaming Yellow Zonkers. Biwana got his name partially because of his ability to distend his stomach and make it look like he had swallowed a bowling ball. In a way it was kind of fitting that Biwana was the one to bring in the bone man.

It was early autumn and the two had been out sampling the marijuna crop and came in with tales of fallen leaves that if stepped on would talk.

"They say all sorts of things," Tano said, "but usually it starts with 'ouch.' After you step on a few, you learn to walk more carefully."

I had been one of those who, from a distance, classified Tano on the bum side of things, but up close, I changed my opinion. He looked more like a pirate, with his head tilted a bit and one eye squinting in the light as if it had spent the day behind a patch. He sat on the edge of a mattress with a Sears sleeping bag that served as my bed, and immediately noticed a pair of wing tips with wooden shoe trees in my closet.

"What's that in those shoes?" he asked.

"Shoe trees," I answered as matter-of-factly as I could.

"Do you water 'em?"

"Oh, a little bit," I said, "that and a little fertilizer—dirty socks, toenails, bandages, that kind of thing."

"They look pretty healthy, like they been growin' good," he said, shaking his head. "How big's them things they're filling?"

"They're thirteens."

He had a long look that said "Goll dang," but he didn't say that, only, after a second, he asked, "Do you ever take them for a walk?"

"All the time. They were out today. You could take them for a walk sometime, if you want."

I don't remember much more of it, but the conversation rambled on in the same vein for some time, to the apparent annoyance of others present, including my roommate, who was from New Hampshire, chewed Dentyne, and combed his hair every fourteen minutes. He was silent, which was meant to tell me Tano was crazy and should be treated like a fool, which was not the way I took him.

The following Sunday I went to church. Catholicism was

17

hanging on by a thread with me and it turned out to be the last time I would attend a mass, except for my grandmother's funeral seven years later. It was 1970, the sixties just were arriving in Iowa then, and there were folk singers, guitars, and English instead of Latin at the service. I didn't sing, but I didn't mind some of the songs, and after the service I bought a honeycomb at a variation of the after-church bake sale.

On the way back to my room, I ran across the bone man and invited him to share the honeycomb. We sat on a knoll surrounded by dormitories, got our fingers coated with honey, and talked.

Although it was autumn and I spent Mondays through Fridays in classrooms, I thought that because of a little bit of movement the summer before, I had begun to get out on the road, a practice I intended to develop. Tano, too, had been on the road some, more than me at least, so we hit it off immediately.

When I was eighteen, it did not take much of a mental leap to see that there were a lot of people and things that could tie you up, a way of looking at things that Tano shared, so that was another reason we hit it off.

"I gotta get outa here, and back on the road," he said, "else I'm gonna go crazy," which I understood as the bad, locked-up kind of crazy and not the devil-be-damned, kick-up-your-boots kind.

I liked the way he talked. His words mostly had a Midwestern twang, but there was a good pinch of cowboy to it and something else, something he might call "olden." He used words that most people didn't use anymore, like "two bits" and "jack" (for money), and when he sat down, he would "sit a spell," and when he was sitting, he would "cogitate" or "jaw on it," and when he was finished sitting and "smokin' a boge" and "resting my bones," he would "up and poke around and get some wind through my hair."

It was like he tried to ignore modern lingo and instead used a dead or dying part of the language that no one was going to mess with anymore, so it was more, just his, and if he wanted to, he would add a little poetry, like the wind through the hair.

When later he married a Frenchwoman and she came to the States, she picked up some of Tano's way of talking, so that when it was around four or five o'clock in the afternoon, she might say

18

something like, "Reckon I'll feex some taters for chow, man," which came out coated in a thick French accent that left you in a lurch and wanting to answer something like, *"Oui,* ma'am."

So, I liked the way Tano talked and after he told me about not wanting to go crazy in that place, and I said the same, we talked about escaping, which we planned to do with pizzazz by tying sheets together and climbing down from my third and his second story windows while we blared Jefferson Airplane's "Volunteers" from the roof. We thought that was a hell of a plan. We talked about escaping from college and the Midwest and the States and any other forms of incarceration we could identify. We both worried about going crazy, but Tano's idea of escape was perhaps more pure. First, I had a someone and a someplace I wanted to go.

I had a girl in California (different from the one who later walked away from Tano and me at the beach). I had met her the previous summer in Maine, where we both worked and both were apparently at a stage where we were ripe to fall in love for the first time, which we did. By September, she was back in California and I was in Iowa. That did nothing but fan flames. By October, passion had knotted itself into a bit of madness and I was ready to bolt. So I put together a plan.

On an upcoming Saturday, our school was to play its homecoming football game. If it won, tradition called for the president of the university to declare the following Monday a no-school holiday. I didn't have classes on the Friday before the big game, so my plan was to leave Thursday night after supper and hitchhike straight through to California and return, on a standby flight, Monday night. On my hitchhiking gauge, I figured it was about thirty hours of driving to San Francisco, and since hitching usually meant double the straight driving time, I also figured if I stayed on the road, day and night, I could make it in less than sixty hours, or sometime Saturday night, if all went well.

I was worried about two things, weather and money. The snows already had hit the Rockies and I only had $50, enough to catch the flight back Monday and nothing more. I had no money for food, so going out meant going hungry, which I hoped to keep to the two days. That, it seemed to me, mostly depended on the weather.

Inspiration often must be acted upon quickly, which with

that plan, was not the case. I conceived of it on the Monday before the on-the-road weekend, thereby giving myself more than seventy-two hours either to be encouraged or to chicken out. By Tuesday night, the weather began to shift from Indian summer to howling winds over the plains cold, which shook my resolve enough that I mentioned my plan to a few rational beings, who did the rational thing and told me it was stupid. Despite that, I hung on, and the plan was still in the balance the next night, Wednesday night, twenty-four hours before takeoff, when I ran into Tano. I told him I didn't care about not eating for a few days, told him I'd risk getting caught in a blizzard, told him I felt lucky about rides, and told him I was desperate to see her.

He asked me if I knew what the coming Monday was. I remembered Columbus Day, and he said, "Well, they told Columbus he couldn't do it."

I was off.

Ever since, he always has called or written on Columbus Day.

V

TEN years later, and the week before I went to the Amazon, I flew to New York and stayed in Hoboken, across the Hudson from Manhattan, with a woman I had spent two years with in San Francisco, the same woman who had walked away at the beach in San Diego. Although she and I still had some bright moments, dark clouds were on the horizon, and five or six days before I left, when the clouds were closer than the horizon, Tano sent me a note.

It had been a gray, drizzly, spring day and I had spent the morning in Manhattan looking up some turn-of-the-century books about the South American jungle. By early afternoon, I gathered the books I needed, and took a bus back to Hoboken. The flat was empty and in the mailbox I found Tano's note.

Zalis—

As we were laying around on Willoby Fenton's boat in Bluefields, I scratched out a little poem. Even tho I had my shit stolen in Peru, by then I had it memorized & so it be-

21

came my only memento of our trip. As a send-off for our next fateful trip south, (the end of) it goes like this:

> Been burned out and beat up,
> Kissed by the sky,
> Forgot how to quit,
> Learned how to lie.
>
> Ain't writin no letters
> Receivin no mail
> A monkey on a limb
> Just swinging by his tail.
>
> Blowin on the breezes
> No time for what's tame,
> Scrounging for somethin'
> That ain't got no name.
>
> I'm playin at blackjack
> Gamblin my bail,
> Got 19 and hit me,
> There ain't no way to fail.
>
> I'm a hunter of fortune
> Ridin the gale,
> I'm out on the road,
> I'm hittin the trail.

See ya on the river!

Tano

It was still raining when I went outside and walked about three blocks to the waterfront, where I could see New York. The skyline had a garland of clouds and smoke and mist, and the Hudson River was black. I walked north until I reached a playground with a swing set. It looked like the one in the scene from *On the Waterfront* where Marlon Brando played with Eva Marie Saint's glove. Even if it wasn't the playground, I imagined it was, and it felt good to be walking there, in the rain, with the swing set glistening, and the black, leafless trees, and me with stuff inside my head about the end of things with a woman, about Tano and his poem with the line about "scroungin for somethin that ain't got no name," and the times Tano and I had been through, and the river ahead, and the movie, where the ex-boxer says, "I coulda been a contenduh." It was funny to be walking there, in the rain, and all that happening at the same time.

I didn't know it then, but the afternoon in Hoboken was a tip-off. Forces were loose and moving things around, lining them up for one of these moments when reality, or whatever it is, stops, and your mind clicks into a space that is a key to a picture. Then you could step out and see things that previously made little relative sense, but suddenly appeared connected and made sense, like they were meant to be.

VI

AT midnight, I arrived in Manaus, a city of more than half a million near the confluence of the Rio Negro and Rio Solimões and at the heart of the Amazon. Before I left New York, the last thing I did was reread Tano's letter.

On the flight, I had tried to get some sleep, but I was too nervous and found myself daydreaming about troubles I was leaving back in the States and unknown troubles I was asking for by going to South America again with Tano. At the time, I thought going to the Amazon was in part a personal kind of French Foreign Legion, a slate clearer I hoped would solve some of my troubles. I sometimes have used the whitewashing effect of moving to simplify and clear up history, something it seems capable of doing until I get back. There, you always can find someone who has kept the ledger straight, at least someone who will tell you whitewash is whitewash and it wears off fast.

I whitewashed some on the plane, but when we arrived I passed the brush to Manaus, which did a good job of letting me know I was in someplace different. Walking off the plane was like walking off a submarine on the bottom of a swamp. The air was hot and wet, and breathing was a cross between gasping and gurgling.

Manaus may be the capital of the jungle, but inside the terminal, immigration people already had computers to search records, so in terms of the last frontier, maybe I was too late.

A mobile wall separated the customs area from the rest of the building, but I looked over a partition and saw an old man in short pants and sandals pacing outside the airport windows. He stopped every few seconds to press his face to the glass and look for what was described in a letter to him as a tall, skinny guy with dark hair.

The old man looked like the picture he had sent me. He had a khaki cap, the kind skippers on fishing boats wear, and silver hair and thick shocks of black eyebrows that could have used trimming. When I got closer, I could see his eyes were a mixture of blue and aluminum, and never stopped moving, sweeping back and forth like a radar beacon.

"Kurt Glück?"

"Yes, yes, pleased, pleased" he answered, while looking me over, which mostly was looking up. He was short and his skin was brown and creased and his handshake was strong. When I was finished looking him over, which mostly was looking down, I looked up and saw behind him a smirking face.

Tano's hair was tied in a pony tail, he had a mustache, a clean khaki shirt and shorts and sandals, but he didn't have on the earring he got when he first crossed the equator. I hugged him and told him he looked good, which was my way of telling him in company I was surprised how clean he looked. I introduced him to Glück, who said he had seen Tano sitting on a bench, but "I not know this was your friend," which might have been Glück's way of telling me in company that he was surprised, too, but for different reasons.

As we walked to a bus ("a taxi is too expensive," we all agreed), Glück wasted no time. He took out his wallet and flipped through a packet of pictures that he said were about a place in the jungle where there were pyramids. His English was good, but edged with a thick German accent that seemed to give his sentences more weight. I listened, but only with the recording section of my brain, and in a minute I had to ask him to repeat what he had said about the pictures. I only had part of the story, not because I wasn't paying attention, but because I was paying too much attention to the lines outside of his words, the lines on his face and the tone of his voice and how many words he used to say things that didn't need saying. I was looking to see if I was going to get screwed.

I had come to the lower side of the world to pay him what was for me a hefty chunk of money, and since I usually don't have hefty chunks of money, I wanted to be sure of things. Of course, there was little way out at that point. I had all but committed myself to Glück and he knew it, and I knew it, but still, I was looking for assurances.

The only other time I was in the Amazon, the time I met Payette and Melnick, I got burned. I was with the woman from San Diego–and–San Francisco–and–Hoboken and we had hired a guide to take us for a week up the Rio Negro. It was a disaster. The guide's name was Marcos, and I hired him because Glück was gone at the time. We spent most of our time with Marcos at a hidden fishing camp about six hours upriver where he had arranged to meet with some of his family and friends. They spent most of the time drunk while my friend and I stayed sober and fumed. What was particularly maddening was that much of the revelry was at our expense. Marcos had convinced me before the trip to buy plenty of pinga, the local rum, to keep the natives along the way happy. It did. His family and friends toasted us continuously.

We tried to keep our protests tactful. We had heard, or maybe imagined, stories of guides taking their clients upriver and then relieving them of whatever they had of value, or if that wasn't enough, making it a one-way trip. So I waited until Marcos had a particularly bad late morning hangover before managing to convince him, surprisingly easily, to make our trip a round trip. But all was not finished. On the way back he decided to show us that besides being a guide, he was an acrobat—although he had to work up to that.

By midafternoon a storm began to follow us, about the same time Marcos's hangover began to wear off, so he opened another bottle of pinga. The Rio Negro is as much as ten miles wide as it nears Manaus, and if you are caught with a small boat out in the middle when a storm hits, you had better have something going for you. We didn't have much. The waves churned and grew to surfable size while the clouds caught up with us and curtained off the sun. By then, Marcos had to tip the pinga bottle up pretty high to get something to come out, so whatever the weather was going to do, he was ready. Lightning cracked, but Marcos was undaunted. He took a last swig, rose like Christ ready to walk across the water, at least slowly if not majestically, stepped up, stood across the keel and stern, and steered with his feet.

I probably would have been impressed if I wasn't distracted by four-foot waves growing to five-foot waves crashing across our bow, lightning that was getting close enough to halo Marcos, thunder that had speeded up from three seconds after the lightning to no seconds, and rain that didn't have to improve at all, it just started falling in sheets.

Marcos refused to be relieved of his responsibilities and instead refueled himself with pinga. To combat his bravado, I planned an intelligent response.

"Just ignore him," I said to the woman from San Diego—and—San Francisco—and—Hoboken. "He just wants our attention."

Her response was "Asshole!" which I think was directed at Marcos, who never did sit down, but matched waves and lightning and thunder with shots of pinga; and in the end, he beat it. We weathered the storm, which rather than drown us made us cold and wet and miserable and, for about an hour, a little scared, but justice did prevail.

When we arrived in Manaus, Marcos had to maneuver through a jam of other dugouts, skiffs, floating steel drums, and assorted junk. He almost managed. Still standing on the keel, he swung us through, but just before he shot to shore, he clipped a piling that left a four-foot gash in the bow, but unfortunately somehow left him standing.

On shore, I regrouped. I suppose the Bogart thing would have been to have knocked Marcos unconscious and taken him and the dugout home myself, but I left the final solution to reason and the wallet.

I had not paid Marcos in full before our trip so I still had bargaining power when we returned. We went to pick up our

27

baggage at Marcos's home, and he called a taxi to take us back to our hotel. We should have waited to call the taxi. By the time the cab arrived, we just had finished pulling the luggage from his house. The time of reckoning had arrived.

In good liberal fashion, I told Marcos he had "disappointed us," then in good conservative fashion, told him we would pay only half of what we owed him. In good wounded fashion, Marcos's eyes turned red and then watery.

"There is no justice," he said, and told us he had to support a wife and four children. The pinga was wearing off and I thought he was about to cry. It was early evening and we argued for a while, until a small crowd of neighbors had come to watch (had they seen this before?), and I felt I was about to be a character in one of those police brutality scenes you read about, where the tables turn and the cop gets stoned or shot. Somehow, I had the cop–bad guy role, and I didn't like it. This guy could have killed us, I told myself. I also didn't like the swelling tears, I was embarrassed for him, and if I was reading the signs right, they were telling me to exit, which I did. We compromised. I agreed to half of the disputed amount. That restored his honor and mine and allowed me to leave.

That was what Glück had to measure up against, and just to make sure, whatever appeared romantic or adventurous or professional or intelligent about the old German I seized.

While Glück and Tano and I waited for the bus outside the airport, I mentioned to Glück the trouble I'd had with Marcos. Glück "Yes, yes"-ed my story away, but I wanted more and asked him if he brought pinga along on his trips.

"For what?" he said, which was enough for me. Then Glück showed us more pictures of the pyramids and I listened.

The pictures were of a long, green valley, taken from almost but not quite an airplane's point of view. In the center, nubs of triangles poked out of the jungle floor.

Glück said he recently had returned from near the pyramids and described them as looking "like the things from Egypt." They were overgrown with vegetation and lay near the Venezuelan border. He said he did not reach the pyramids, but only got as far as an overlooking ridge of mountains from where he took the pictures.

28

"To get there and back, it took thirty-four hard, hard days," he said, "and we would need at least forty to do it right."

"It would be a good adventure to go there," he said.

Tano and I didn't say anything, but out of the corner of my eye I saw he too was smiling.

"Tomorrow, we talk," I said.

Glück asked Tano if he had found a place to stay, but before he could answer, Glück offered a "tourist room" in his house for $10 a night. Tano said he had a room for $1.50 in a downtown place called the Pensão Universal.

"Zis is cheap, good," Glück said, with something like disbelief or mockery in his voice, I wasn't sure which, though knowing Tano I knew what to expect.

A rehabilitated school bus picked us up and bounced us into town with the buzz of insects as backdrop. The bus probably had carried kids across the Appalachian trail, using the trail for twenty years before it was driven down across the States and along the Pan American Highway, using the shoulder, and over to Brazil. At least it felt that way. We didn't talk much on the way in, but when I seemed to be more on than off my seat, I took out a gift I thought a German might like—wursts: brat, knock, and liver—which Glück thanked me for, but not that profusely.

As we entered Manaus, Glück leaned over and looked out the window and mumbled something about being uncertain as to where he should get off. It was odd he seemed unfamiliar with his home turf, but at the time, I thought nothing more of it.

"Aqui, aqui," he shouted to the bus driver, and we stopped and said good-bye and Glück said he would come by at nine o'clock the next morning, to "let you sleep."

The bus left Tano and me off northwest of town, near a pair of water tanks that reminded me of a couple of dynamos near the New Jersey shore. There were no taxis, so we walked, which felt good after all the hours on the plane and after bumping along on the bus. The streets were deserted, with only stray dogs and steam from a recent rain breaking the stillness.

When Tano and I get together, it is always a little jumpy getting the talk going. There already were enough shared times, and on the verge of adding some more, we didn't know where to begin. For a little while, we just let our feet do the talking—a

29

rhythm of pavement and leather we had played on and off for ten years. It seemed to smooth us into an opening.

"God damn it," he said.

"God damn it," I agreed.

On our first long road trip together, Tano and I went to Florida. His name was Corky then, but later he changed it, when he said he had to. He was getting out of the States and had women trouble, so he started looking for a new name. The connection between those two things, women and names, I didn't question, other than I suspected it probably was a good deal of trouble. He was on the road and went home to Illinois to see his folks and told his mother he needed a new name. Apparently, she didn't question things either. She recently had seen a movie version of John Steinbeck's "The Red Pony," and an old Mexican in it named Jetano reminded her of her son. Jetano meant gypsy, and Corky trimmed a few letters off to make it a little more lightweight and then he thought it fit just right.

Going to Florida, though, he was still Corky. (The roots of that name I never questioned, and now it's too late. It's part of a past he keeps to himself.) He swung through New Jersey in an old Ford station wagon and picked me up. Between us, I think we had $60. It was cold and damp and March and we wanted to make it to sunshine and oranges, which we knew we couldn't do on $60, so the plan was to dump the car after spending $20 on gas. That would get us as far as Savannah, Georgia.

Going down, we were a Mississippi riverboat on wheels, and picked up the appropriate cast of aces, jacks, and spades. We picked up anyone we could squeeze into that old station wagon, which had holes in the seats and holes in the body and a hole or two in a window or two, and we packed them in and played loud music on the radio and smoked and shared packs of bologna, which we curled up and dipped in jars of mustard, and laughed when "Magic Bus" came on the radio and we turned around in the front seat and saw that we couldn't have squeezed in another body.

Near the beginning of the trip, we picked up a black kid who said he just had got out of Rahway Prison that morning. He was supposed to get out of the car somewhere around Camden, but the outside world seemed to take him by surprise and he might have missed where he wanted to get off by a state or two.

Once, around dawn, in a back-road gas station in North Carolina (we avoided the main drags because of tolls), a potbellied attendant in suspenders said our driving machine "smells like a polecat." We kind of took to that. We got to moving like a polecat and took most of the day to get through North Carolina, so we ended up that night at Duke University. Schools, then, were the Motel Six of the subculture, and usually meant a guaranteed flop on a floor in someone's room or lounge or hallway. But the sixties were fading into just a blip on history's radar screen, and in Durham, they faded fast.

We cruised the campus until we found a corner of a lounge that seemed an appropriate suite, then found the campus theater, where we watched the movie Z. Connections get fuzzy here, but the next thing I recall, Tano and I were in the upper limbs of an oak tree that crowned the center of a square between dormitories. The stars were out and we sang verses from a James Taylor song, bellowing lines about monkeys liking fruits and bananas, which is why they spend their time in the top of trees. That managed to attract a crowd which did not applaud. When we finished, someone said, "Get the campus police." So we climbed down.

Sometimes we talk about monkeys singing in trees, and we talked about them in Manaus, but walking into the city after midnight, my back soaked with sweat, the talk was about pyramids.

That afternoon, Tano had met a twenty-eight-year-old Italian anarchist named Ilhio, who had read about the pyramids in the Manaus newspaper. He said the pyramids lay in a mountainous region controlled by the Yanomari Indians. Years ago, so the story went, German missionaries lived there, and the Indians attacked and killed the German men, but took the women. Now, supposedly, there were Indians with blond hair and blue eyes. One of them had come down from the mountains and lived in a lower village. His name was Tatunka Nada No Se, which means Watersnake Nothing, and was the man interviewed in the paper, a man Tano and I eventually would meet.

In the article, Tatunka Nada said there were people from outer space living underground beneath the pyramids, and he talked of jewels and El Dorado, but great danger if one goes to the area.

Tano and I had known each other too long to react directly

31

to the possibility of that kind of adventure, so instead we talked in sideways language, being calm enough not to pounce on the idea of finding pyramids, but clear enough to let each other know that was what we wanted to do.

"Forty days is a good amount of time for a trip," I said.

"Real good," he said.

Halfway into town, we flagged down a taxi, took it to the market, walked the remaining few blocks east to the Pensão Universal, where a royal blue neon light directed us in and Tano directed me through a narrow hallway ("Wait till you see this place we got, man"), around a bend, then proudly used a key to open the door to a seven by seven foot turquoise concrete room, etched with graffiti, hot, sticky, without windows, with a corrugated tin roof, and filled with the stench from a nearby toilet. Still, there was some class; the hole had a fan.

In the face of such things, I did what needed to be done: tossed down my bag, and pulled out a bottle of twelve-year-old Scotch I had bought in the airport duty-free shop, and said the first thing that came to my mind. "Let's get out of here."

We woke up a man passed out on a folding chair near the doorway ("He's the hotel clerk," Tano said), borrowed two cups, went outside, and sat on the curb. In no time we were drunk.

In the time I had known Tano, stoops and curbs had been our thrones in a roving court. We had slept on sidewalks in Mexico, under piers in Florida, and in cemeteries in Nicaragua, but nothing anywhere took a curb. We had reigned over curbs, but the one in Manaus was perhaps the best.

"The last edge," Tano said.

Across the street, vines reclaimed a wall, gilded the cracks, and snaked across telephone lines. Tano had arrived three days before me and during that time he said he had talked to people who complained that Manaus was like any other South American city, overcrowded, polluted, sweltering, with mangy dogs and sidewalks like tumbled dominoes.

"Not me," Tano said, clenching his hands. "I feel the jungle here all the time."

Some power must have heard him say that because as he finished, a moth the size of a robin spiraled down from a street

32

lamp and touched the pavement, just as a Volkswagen sped through the intersection and mounted in on the tar.

We took a drink and sang.

When you share time with someone, often, particularly if it is a long time, you begin to share a common language. Certain events tend to mean the same things to you, words or jokes or expressions can get stamped as your own currency, and depending on how much time you've spent together, other nonverbal things become common property, like a particular kind of afternoon sunlight, or a fog, or even less obvious things like the way your insides can feel mixed up if the wind shifts, meaning the weather is going to come in from a direction it rarely ever takes. Usually, to be able to share that kind of thing is good. It breaks the loneliness. Then again, most times it is not so much of a surprise, because you usually build up to things like wind shifts with some people, realizing you were seeing things in the same way, or hearing them, or smelling them, or feeling them, then reacting to them. Sometimes, though, you can get spooked. Someone you hardly know will say something or do something in exactly the way you would have, like they know a secret. That doesn't happen too much with me, but I keep a watch for it and when it does, I probably tend to overreact and start spilling things until I realize I might have made a mistake and I want to take back what I said.

What all that helps to do is filter the world. With Tano and me, we both were spooked in the beginning, but the more things we shared and the more things we spilled, the more things got firmer. Then we got wild and went charging around as if we had aces up our sleeves, which in our case got to be something we both thought was pretty extraordinary. We could count on each other.

I mention that here because, in trying to show what happened in the Amazon, there is a problem with the language. Although sometimes Tano and I try to do it with the outside world, between us, we don't move in a very linear direction. We've got shared things and we've got other things we want to share, and often we get too excited, so we end up skipping around. I suppose that is a way of claiming territory together, but rather than immediately heading for four-cornered boundaries, we just go,

33

sometimes half-assed and blind because we never have been able to tell what the boundaries were. That was part of the reason for the jumping. We talked that way. One second the Volkswagen hit the moth, then we took a swig and lurched into singing the doggie national anthem.

The anthem was composed on a trip across the northwestern United States in the spring of 1979. On that one, we kept our thumbs in our pockets and, instead, packed ourselves like highway astronauts in a Volkswagen Tano described as "filled with so much energy the seams in the chassis were about to bust."

It is sung to the tune of "Winter Wonderland."

> It's a doggy, doggy's world,
> It's a poochy woocher's life.
> We're so happy to be,
> Doggies and free,
> Living in a doggy-catcher's land.

Seeing ourselves as dogs and most of the rest of the world as crawling with dogcatchers might seem paranoiac, but Tano and I had thought that way and known each other long enough that dog visions had less to do with an emotional reaction and more to do with our way of thinking. Whether or not this was psychotic, it was ingrained. We tended to see things in a similar way. One reason we stuck together was that we saw the same hourglass. Time seemed to be running out in most places we dogs hoped to go; but then, as the land was going, something else was going, too. It was as if there was a land grab going on for spirit and adventure and other things, things you couldn't see, things that had meaning. As those things disappeared, more and more we felt cornered.

I wanted to be long gone before it was over.

"Not me," Tano said. "I want to see it all come down. It's gonna be a helluva show."

Once, a few years before, when I was living in San Francisco, I got a postcard from Tano. The card had a picture of a pair of oil pumps on the prairie, with the caption, "Double Header Pumping Oil in Wyoming," although the caption had been altered with a pen to read "Double Headed Monster in Wyoming."

34

On the back, the card read:

Frank,

Howdy partner. Well, you once sent me a picture post-card (from Wall Drug) of a dinosaur, so I thot I'd send you one. Hurry ice age!

Jess

We sang "Doggy-Catcher's Land" again and we laughed and drank to our ditty and I told him how things were going with me in the States, and I showed him a talisman that was supposed to keep witches away. A woman I liked gave it to me, and she got it from a witch, so I trusted its power.

"You'll need it."

VII

GLÜCK gave us less time than he said and knocked at our door at 8 AM. I climbed out of bed, out of a dream and into a hangover, before pulling on a pair of pants and greeting him. Tano had not moved yet, though I heard him breathing, so I told Glück to have a coffee at a café in front of the Pensão, and we would be out in a minute.

When Tano gets up, he does it like he has spent the night fighting. It's worse after he has been drinking. He moans first, then sometimes he'll sigh, prop himself up, and almost immediately drop back down again and start all over. That happened about three times, until he finally threw himself out of bed. I wasn't much better. I moved slowly, trying to keep the alcohol undisturbed while also trying to shake the sleep free, though I wanted that to happen very slowly. I didn't want to be fully conscious until I was outside our room.

Tano stunk and I told him. He answered by sticking his nose in the air and splashing Scotch into his armpits, and when he came back from what was called a banho, but what wasn't much more than a hole in the concrete floor, he sprayed Off insect repellent under his arms, and finally added Desenex antifungal powder.

When Tano was properly dusted and the level bubble in my head was crisscrossing the middle mark at regular enough intervals, I took a package from my gear and went down to have cafezinho with Glück.

Walking around a corner and down a hallway was tough, but we made it, though standing at the counter, sipping glasses of saccharine coffee, we had to hang on to stand up. Glück was buzzing. He said he had been awake since five and anxious to get things started, so as much for ourselves as for him, we skipped breakfast and rolled along with, or after, him.

We walked back toward the free-trade zone, near the marketplace, to the Casa do Beija-Flor, the House of the Hummingbird. Glück pounded on Melnick's door, just below a wooden name plate that said "Kurt Glück," the same kind of tag Glück wore on his shirt when he was in Manaus. The tag acted as his personal billboard, though I suspected it also had something to do with his needing a name in the city, a name he was always quick to give. If people asked, he would hand them his business card, his name and address handwritten on a fish scale the size of a clam shell, which doubled as a fingernail file.

Melnick grumbled as he unbolted the lock and sounded upset about being awakened, but when he opened the door, he beamed.

He invited us in and we exchanged how-do's, and I gave him a gift of liverwurst and Polish and Lithuanian bread and kielbasi. When I met him the previous year, he'd told me the only thing he missed from the States was kielbasi, and I told him if I ever saw him again, I would bring him some.

"Up until today, I thought the Pope was the greatest Polack in the world," he said.

Then Melnick remembered something. He spun around, ran upstairs, and brought down Sunday's newspaper, slapping his hand against the paper as he pounded back down the wooden steps. The paper had the story Ilhio told Tano about the pyramid story, but it also had references to Glück as a journalist explorer who had been searching for the pyramids. Melnick and Glück said they didn't like the guy who wrote the story. Glück called

37

him a liar. The writer apparently had given Glück trouble and told him he was not permitted near the pyramids. Glück's answer: "What? There are no signs. The trees are not posted."

The journalist threatened to get Glück arrested if he ever went back.

"Ahh, makes nuhzing," Glück said.

We had pre-trip business to knock off in town, so we told Melnick we would see him later. He said that when we returned from the jungle, he would make us a fish stew, and I tried sounding cavalier and said that if we made it back, beers would do.

Glück invited Tano and me to his home for lunch—an invitation Tano and I understood was for both food and business. Though it was only a little after nine, Glück wanted to start home.

We went to catch a bus near the cathedral, which, along with the market and the old customs house, formed a triangle—the Times Square of Manaus. The market and the customs house, an old Victorian building erected during the rubber boom, anchored the city to the river, while the cathedral anchored everything to the heavens. It was as if the three buildings were part of a Manaus pantheon honoring business, government, and God, but within their parameter, it was a mess. In front of the cathedral there was a small zoo with a handful of exhausted jungle animals, like an ocelot and a monkey, and in front of the zoo, a small plaza where most city buses stopped.

The plaza was a bus port, with series of concrete islands stretching in the road and no safe way to get through traffic but to run. Everything seemed to be at high speed, the buses downshifting to the islands while billowing clouds of exhaust, a screech, and then a tumble of flesh out the front door, followed by a shove of more flesh back in the bus. It all happened so quickly you expected a vacuum behind the bodies. It was as if we had stepped into an early newsreel with everything going a little too fast and time and frames of reality skipping beats.

It was one thing to step off a plane from New York into Manaus time, which by the clock was one hour faster. By everything else, it was either just behind or a century behind, and all the time it seemed to want to catch up.

In the free-trade zone, disco music blared from import shops selling everything from digital wristwatches with illuminated faces the size of hockey pucks to gourmet delicacies like synthetic cheese spread in aerosol containers and geometrically uniform potato chips packed in tennis ball cans.

"Shtoopid shtuff" was the way Glück described it.

Luncheonettes featured "cheesebuggahs," "Fanta," and "Bebsi"; overcrowded buses and taxis jammed the streets and ignored traffic signals, and above it all was the equatorial sun. By ten in the morning it was London in tropical reverse. Engine exhaust blanketed the city in a steamy fog and people condensed. Even the birds in Manaus must sweat.

Although there might have been shades of it, Manaus wasn't much of a Sodom or Gomorrah, even though the locals left room for divine intervention. A few years back, a freak hailstorm struck the city in September. Glück said people ran outside and scraped the ice off car windows and shouted, "God must be Brazilian, he has sent us ice cream!"

Tano and I would have settled for pity from above, but we were ignored. On the bus to Glück's house, our heads just bobbed in our hangovers. Glück took that as a sign to keep talking.

"You know Santa Claudia, the mineral water?" he asked.

I did. The last time I was in Manaus I drank gallons.

"It's booshit," he said. "How you say? It's shtinky. Polluted. I took it to German scientists and they tested it and said it had shit in it.

"And the ice cube plant."

I tried to stop my head from bobbing.

"It is just below where the sewer goes into the river." Glück laughed. "Such shit, this city."

We bobbed.

It was a Brazilian holiday and all the supermercados were closed except a Japanese one near Glück's home, where we bought $70 worth of canned meat, powdered milk, rice, and noodles, which Glück said he had "calculated" for a month-long trip. I suggested some garlic and sardines, which I had calculated for unknown reasons other than an excuse to talk and make it

39

evident that despite the previous night's binge we still were alive, and Glück agreed, adding, "I think we have plenty."

Three dogs greeted us at the gate of his house, and we walked past a small front yard, with avocado, hyacinth, and cinnamon trees, through an empty garage to a backyard patio where Glück pulled up chairs beside a hammock. Glück's wife, a still beautiful Brazilian woman in her sixties, came out and brought a pitcher of cold maracaju, passion fruit, and we settled into small talk.

Glück's pet toucan strolled across the patio, climbed up the arm of my chair, glanced at me, then stepped down. He picked up a baby's pacifier and rolled the nipple around his beak.

"Would make a good photograph," Glück said.

For a moment I thought of Marcos, but naaah.

After a lunch of grilled some-kind-of-meat, and rice and beans and manioc, we adjourned to Glück's study, a dark, paneled room with Venetian doors that opened to a small patio.

"I leave the doors open for my turtle," Glück said. "He like going in and out."

Shelves, filled with books on the jungle and his diaries, lined the walls. Glück sat at a desk shadowed by a wall-sized map of the Amazon.

He took books down and showed us pictures of himself in trips he had made, including an account of a 1949 expedition up Chimborazo, the highest peak in Ecuador. In the book, he had a picture of a young man with blond, wavy hair, wearing khaki shorts, shirt, and a scarf. The man looked like a cross between Don Juan and a Boy Scout.

"Yes, me," Glück said and nodded.

Glück was letting us size him up, which we did, not so objectively, by letting him talk, which he did, by starting from the beginning, and then making big jumps.

"I was born in Bavaria, in 1914," he said. "In 1936, I was in the Luftwaffe. I was a mechanic."

In 1938, when he finished his stint in the Luftwaffe, he told the government he wanted to be a diesel engineer and he wanted to learn the skill on an American boat. The authorities questioned why he wanted to go on an American ship, and Glück said he told them Germany needed dollars, which he would be paid in, which for unknown reasons the government bought. They gave him a ten-month passport and he hopped on a Standard Oil boat. So, Glück said, he got what he wanted, a way out of Germany and into the world.

When the war broke out, about ten months later, he was in Venezuela. He had finished his tour and the ship he was booked to return to Germany on was about to leave when the news broke about the invasion of Poland.

The ship was supposed to stop at Port of Spain, Trinidad, and Glück was sure he would be taken there and "forced to pick bananas until the end of the war."

He made a plea to Standard Oil to keep him away from the Nazis and they accommodated him, setting him up at the Miramar Hotel in Caracas, all expenses paid, with a monthly stipend.

"Beautiful, no?" he said.

The next six years he was stationed in Venezuela. In Germany in his youth he had learned to play tennis, a sport that would supplement his income in South America, as he spent the war hustling tennis matches while making trips into the jungle and mountains.

Forty years later, he sat beneath his wall map and pointed to the west, in an area between the Rio Negro and the Rio Solimões, where there were few markings, but where there was said to be a crater four kilometers wide.

"I've tried to find it three different times," Glück said. "But every time, the flies."

On one of the trips, the flies and mosquitoes drove two Austrian television men close to madness. They fought with each other, and then they threatened to attack Glück. But they held off, because "they said I was an old man."

Glück pointed to another spot on the map, just north of Manaus, where a German woman was raising three-toed sloths, supposedly the only ones in the world.

Then he pointed to the north, near the Venezuelan border, to the territory of the Yanomari. We were getting down to business.

"That is where the pyramids are," he said. "It is very wild there."

Glück knew when to throw in the right word.

When he went there with another Austrian, Glück said he

had to go through three waterfalls, and was able only to reach the mountains above the plains where the pyramids stood. Because they were short of time, they had to turn back without ever descending into the valley.

The Brazilian expedition, reported in the paper, got close and supposedly found Phoenician pottery. That was what the paper said.

"There is much mystery there," Glück said. "There are stories the Indians tell, that at night they can hear motors beneath the ground, and they believe it is from the underground city where lives the people from the heavens."

Getting more to the point, he said, "We will need forty days to make the trip."

Glück charged a per diem fee and Tano and I originally had planned for thirty days. The additional ten days meant we would have to scrape for the extra cash. Glück noticed our hesitation and said he had "professional and wealthy people, even nobility," who have the money but not the time to do a trip with him. "Then I have students who have the time but no money."

We were somewhere in between.

Would he negotiate? He suggested a reasonable compromise. We suggested an even more reasonable compromise, and he nodded. "OK."

I asked him if Tano and I could talk briefly, alone—why I did that I don't know. There was no doubt with all parties involved. Maybe it was just that things were happening too fast. So, we retreated to Glück's living room. Tano and I looked at each other, and one of us said, "Why are we doing this?" and the other one must have shrugged, because we turned around and went into Glück's study. Tano pulled his side of the deal from one of his hidden pockets, and I pulled mine from a belt under my shirt, rolling out enough soggy $100 bills to cover my share before shaking Glück's hand.

Probably because things were happening so fast, on the bus back to town Tano and I didn't talk, though he was quick to agree to join me at the mercado café above the docks. We would talk there.

The Manaus market looks like an iron lawn tent, the kind

the navy might have built, although it actually was built in the late nineteenth century during the rubber boom. Inside, I imagined, things really had not changed much. Butchers carved fly-covered carcasses on stone slabs beside small boys who scaled fish one-and-a-half times their size. Between crates of puckered fruit and either rotting or hard vegetables and sacks of black beans and rice, there were stalls where old women sold black magic potions and candles and incense and packets of herbs with Indians on them, each packet promising things like romance, or health, or tranquillity, while across were stalls with brooms and straw hats, and in a corner a picture of Jesus Christ. The market was high-ceilinged and dark, with narrow side aisles that made you feel as if you were in a cave, except at the back, where the iron grating reached the river. That was the café. There, waiters in white shirts and black pants paced between tables, taking orders and swatting flies. An iron trellis let in fresh air and kept the vultures out, and from the back tables, along the edge, you could watch dugouts and rambling wooden passenger boats chug up and down the river.

The café was a good place to dream. The river spread five miles across from where we sat, but a green strip on the opposite shore was an invitation. Manaus was a city with half a million people, but it was an island city in the middle of a jungle bigger than the Mediterranean. Even with all those people and skyscrapers and pavement and cars and buses, the jungle, as Tano said, was always there. Insects and heavy air and sun suggested it was everywhere, but it was an unrevealed truth. For most people, the jungle can be seen only at the river, and then only at the other side, as if in a vision. In a way, that's good. It keeps things separated. You don't ease into that jungle, walking out some back dirt road, out where the houses stop. You get to it by going on the river, which is both a barrier and a passage.

"We could change history," Tano said. I never had heard Tano give two cents for history, so the words threw me, but I was almost as quick to follow him into that mess. We talked about Phoenicians, and El Dorado, and Indians, and jaguars, and forty days. We weren't being so restrained as the night before, but then again, we didn't believe completely what we were saying, so it was all right to say those things. I understood what he was getting at. It was like salt over the shoulder, or spitting in the devil's eye.

We drank coffee while across the river clouds dragged a curtain of rain over the vision. We kept saying crazy things out loud, but underneath, there was a layer of conversation going on that went like this:

"OK. We've just shelled out our fortunes and there may or may not be things he's calling pyramids up there. In fact, chances are there aren't, but we're doing this anyway, just to finish it out. That's fine. But still, it's about time things went right for us, and maybe this time they will. I'm tired of getting the shit kicked out of me. Maybe this is the time we cash in, but I'm not counting on that. What I am counting on is that, one way or another, this is going to be an adventure, and God damn it, I'm glad it's us together."

"Me, too."

I was glad Tano was saying the things he did, mostly because I knew how badly things had gone for him the last time we were in South America, in 1977. We had split up in Colombia and Tano eventually ended up in Argentina, where he lived for a while until his money ran out. Then he headed back for the States. He went overland, taking second-class buses along the west coast, but by the time he reached Peru, he had contracted hepatitis, which he figured he must have got from drinking bad water somewhere along the line.

"That changed me," he told me some years later. "Up until then, I was an arrogant bastard and thought I couldn't be broken. We're fragile, man, and we sure as hell can be broken.

"I had to get back and scam some medical help. I couldn't do that there. Day and night I took those buses, I didn't have the money to stop. Halfway through I got delirious. I had a fever the whole way, but then stuff started getting fuzzy and I couldn't control things anymore. Once, it was night, I was on a bus and we were bouncing along and my insides felt like they were coming out and I just started peeing. I couldn't stop. I couldn't do anything. It just started coming out and soaking me and running down my leg and onto the floor. It was awful, soaked with your own piss and not being able to do a damn thing about it. It taught me a lot though. Someone could've stepped on me and ground me into the ground. I didn't have anything left."

When he told me that, we were at his cabin in Illinois. It was way past midnight, and we had been drinking, and I asked him about a talisman he'd had on that trip to South America, something we both had got in the beginning of the trip, and something I knew that if it was found, he would have been busted.

"Yeah, I had it around my neck," he said. "It's a powerful thing. When I got into Colombia, soldiers stopped the bus I was on and they dragged me off. They tore me down. Went through everything. First my gear. I didn't have much left except my bag. All my shit was stolen in Peru. Then they stripped me down. One piece of clothing at a time, until they got me down to nothing except the pouch around my neck. We were standing under a streetlight and they had guns on me, then when it was just me standing there with the pouch around my neck, the head honcho comes up, walks right up to my face, stares me in the eye, and with his finger lifts the pouch an inch off my chest. I was sick then and I couldn't hardly see and I thought I was finished, but I looked that fucker dead in the eye and he looked at me and kind of jiggled the pouch and looked at me some more and I stared back at him, and then he dropped it and told his boys to let me go."

After that, Tano made it to an island off the coast, where we had stayed months before. He was too sick to go any farther and had to hole up in the hotel where we had been. He stayed a few days, he wasn't sure how many because he pretty much had passed out. He told me he had been too sick even to get out of bed and get water. It wasn't like him to tell me about any of that stuff. He always kept bad times to himself, but I had asked him about it, and maybe since it was late and we were a little drunk, he told me. I told him I wished I had been there to help him out, and he said, "I wish you had, too."

VIII

GLÜCK returned the next morning. He always seemed out of place in our room. He would sit at the end of one of our beds and look like a Prussian field marshal in a porto-potty. I knew most of his clients came from the upriver, uptown, $100-a-night Hotel Tropical, but he never mentioned anything about our quarters, other than they were "cheap, yes."

Our second day with him was one of preparations. Tano was worn out from heaving during the night. We had gone to dinner for pizza Portuguesa, a gooey, oily version of the Italian pie that required two cooks, our waiter, and ten minutes to pry it out of the pan. Then about half an hour later, it took Tano about ten seconds to get rid of it, saying,"Man, that banho of ours is great. It forces you to puke."

Since we were tacking the ten days on to the trip, Tano had to change plane reservations, knock-on-wood, so he opted to pass up the Glück express. I would go with the old man.

First item of business was money. Dollars were gold in Manaus and there was a robust black market in greenbacks. Brazilian inflation was running about 40 percent and the banks, in establishing the exchange rate for cruzeiros, were weeks behind the decline. American dollars were security and people hungry for them were easy to find, but Gluck's contacts in the money-changing world all had offices above the eighth floor in buildings scattered across town. It was only 7:30 AM and many of the currency dealers weren't at work yet, so our attempts to find a broker in pre–business hours took on the heavy breathing and sweating of training for a mountain expedition. Up and down stairs we went with Glück running a soliloquy on jungle and city life.

"Manaus has much more danger than the joongle," he said, waving his hand as if to dismiss the city.

"I was hit by a car here once," he said, and added a "Yes," without looking at me to see if my assumed surprise deserved a Yes.

"Crossing the street . . . "

He cut across heavy traffic to a median, saying over his shoulder, "The car just sped away. Crossing the street has more danger than anything in the joongle. Is crazy."

Melnick had told us he'd recently read a newspaper story about a Brazilian ship striking a Norwegian freighter in the Atlantic. The Brazilian ship never stopped and the Norwegian freighter struggled into Santos in southern Brazil, where they took pictures of the damaged hull and made a complaint.

"It's the Brazilian way," Melnick said. "You're guilty until proven innocent. People go and get lawyers to defend themselves and then return."

"So, as much as I can, I stay in the joongle," Glück said. "I have taken many people into the joongle."

Most of Glück's trips were one- to three-month expeditions, like the one Tano and I were planning with him. But in between major trips, for extra scratch, he made day-long excursions up the river for people willing to pay through the nose.

He once took Ali Khan's wife out for a sojourn at night, promising to give her the classical and the private. He picked her up at the Hotel Amazonas, then took her by launch to a church in the jungle, where he lit candles and played a tape recording of Beethoven's Ninth Symphony.

"She loved it," he said.

The church and the Ninth proved to be good advertisement. Glück said that when she returned to cosmopolitan life, she told

47

her friends to take the trip. Among those who bit, Glück said, were John and Mary Lindsay. On their trip Mary Lindsay asked Glück how he knew where to go. He said the boat steers by itself.

" 'Really?' she said." Glück laughed. "Ah, *sheiss*. Elizabeth Forester, too," he said. "You know, the famous bird-watcher."

I didn't know, but nodded my head for him to continue.

"Torture," he said, his eyes rolling at the memory.

"She drank tea and ate biscuits"—which didn't sound like much torture—"and at night, covered herself in cold cream. Then she complained about the cold at night." He shook his head again. "Ach. I had to put hot water bottles in her hammock, but that didn't work. Finally, I get a small cat from an Eendyun. I put the cat in her hammock at night, then she sleep like a baby."

As if to verify his credentials, Glück rattled off names of other people he had taken out, King Leopold of Belgium, a nephew of Richard Nixon—"you know, the president." "Yes, I know, the president." One of the Kennedy clan—"You know, the other president with the brothers." "Yes, I know ... "

We found a businessman who changed dollars for me, then we were off to the German Rowing Club, where Glück kept his boat.

"The Club," as Glück called it, boasted only one German member, our guy, and if there were a Manaus Monopoly game, the Club would have occupied the four-dollar real estate spot right after "Go." The Club wasn't much more than a barn with some lockers in a sewage-filled estuary east of town. Years ago, a German rowing team used it as its dock and base, but when we were there only a dusty silver trophy attested to possible championship days.

Glück kept his four-meter skiff moored at the Club, and all his expedition gear in two lockers. Two cabocolos (Amazonian peasants of mixed white and Indian blood) in their late thirties, whom Glück always addressed as boys, kept the forty-odd lockers and a couple of dozen boats at least secure, if not in some kind of order.

Glück and I took his boat and motored upriver to an inlet, northwest of town, where we hoped to find the *Emerson*. Our plan was to tie our boat to the cargo ship and take it to Barcelos, about three hundred and fifty miles up the Rio Negro. It would cost $60 for the three of us and would save time and, more important, fuel, which we otherwise would have had to carry.

The *Emerson* was supposed to be docked near the Brahma Chopp brewery, but when we got there, no *Emerson*. An Indian told us it had gone to be fueled and wouldn't return for an hour. We decided to wait. We tied the skiff to a piling and walked up a mud embankment to a hut that passed as a cantina, with a pool table without felt, two wooden tables, and a few chairs.

Glück ordered two guaranas, the local soft drink that tasted like cream soda and originally was made from the bark of an Amazon tree, and launched into more stories. He said that ten years earlier he went on a trip covering the length of the Amazon, from one of its supposed sources in the Andes to its mouth in the Atlantic, with a staff writer from *Reader's Digest* magazine. "You know this *Reader's Digest?*" "Yes, I know." After it was completed, the editor apparently was pleased with the trip and story, and wrote Glück to see if he would undertake another project, surveying a hundred people in Manaus to find what was the most important thing in their life.

"The *Reader's Digest* makes these questions."

"I know."

Glück said it took him three days to complete the survey that included everyone from the mayor to shoeshine boys and taxi drivers. Glück laughed and turned his palms up and dropped his hands.

"Ninety-five of the people answered, 'Nada,' nuhzing," he said. Of the remaining five, a German missionary said health, a lawyer industrialization, an old woman and a nun, God, and an old man, rice and beans.

The story was meant to explain how even if we waited the full hour for the *Emerson* it probably wouldn't show, and although the boat was supposed to leave the following night, Wednesday, we could not be certain.

"It's better to go back to the Club, and we'll find out about the *Emerson* later," Glück said.

That night, I met Tano's Italian friend Ilhio. A short man, with a dark beard, sandals, and white muslin pants and a shirt, he came to our room to visit Tano and brought a copy of Sunday's newspaper, with the pyramid story.

49

"It's fantastic," he said, and proceeded to retell everything we had heard three times. Glück had warned Tano and me not to tell anyone we were planning to go there, which was fine with us as it added intrigue. We listened and Ilhio continued with hands-waving-in-the-air flourishes, and described the pyramids and the Phoenicians and the underground space people, all of which we listened to with open mouths until he was finished, and no one said anything and Tano rolled cigarettes and I said I was going down near the docks to write letters at Mandy's Bar, where the whores hang out.

IX

WE woke to what sounded like an attack of marbles, but was only the pounding of rain on the tin roof. Glück came by at the same time as the day before, 7:30 A.M., and said he had been up since the same time as the day before, 5 A.M., then gave us bad news that was good news. The boat to Barcelos would not leave until Thursday, the next day. That was OK by Tano and me. Glück stayed a while and told us stories of the jungle, stories that were a variation on the theme, "It will not be the same in twenty or thirty years, but at least the Americans or Japanese or Germans are not here. They would use bulldozers and it would take even less time." Not necessarily because of his analysis, the rest of the day Tano and I spent in Cannery Row fashion, shuffling between the hotel luncheonette, market, café, and naps.

We had dinner with the Italian. We tried to persuade a Swiss couple to join us. The Swiss stayed in a room next to ours. We had met them the day before. They told us they had been travel- ing in South America for eight months. The woman had dark skin, blue eyes, and brown hair. In another time she could have posed for Vermeer, or in just another country, for Coppertone. I had to avoid looking at her to keep my heart steady.

Her bearded, sandaled, white-pajamaed, blend-into-the-culture boyfriend said that after working their way through much of South America, the "maybe mañana" efficiency was beginning to make him crazy.

"Oh, you are too Swiss," she said, which gave Tano and me hope, but after Tano said, "You just have to get to accepting it for what it is," they went back into their room together, so we sagged.

Tano and I figured it would be nice to sit across a table from the "You are too Swiss" girl, nice enough that we thought it would be worth putting up with the too Swiss guy, but none of that made any difference as after we knocked on their door and asked them they said they already had eaten. So, we redirected our efforts more aggressively at one of the locals.

We found an open-front Lebanese restaurant by the docks and sat near the lip of the sidewalk, strategically positioned a few feet from a lovely young Brazilian woman waiting for a bus. She had dark hair, long thin legs, and a red dress. If she were from the south of Brazil, she would have come from Ipanema and they would have written a song about her.

Between hunks of pita bread and sips of Brahma Chopps, we all flirted with her. Ilhio tried the Italian-cosmopolitan approach, calling her in Portuguese from the table. She giggled and said "No." I tried the American approach and walked up to her, and in sign language beckoned her to sit with us. She shook her head, No. Tano tried the international cool approach and just sat back, which she didn't seem to notice, so she didn't have to say no.

We retreated to a strategy of trench warfare—arching eyebrows, winks, and long-range sniper attacks of *"faça favor"*—all rebuked by a smile that rose and set behind a newspaper she handled like a geisha with a fan. When her bus came, she took a last look our way, which I suppose said, "Too bad," and climbed on and sat in the back and faded away behind clouds of exhaust.

So, then there was the beer. We talked about our trip and Ilhio said he never would pay anyone to take him into the jungle. He said he would get a canoe and go back alone, learning survival skills as he went, which I told myself was the kind of talk to have at a café in Manaus, and which was also meant to shame us, which it didn't. Tano and I had had enough of half-assed trips, and for once, from start to finish, we wanted to do it right.

In the morning, I went to one of the wristwatch–cheese spread stores and bought a bag full of postcards with naked Indian kids spearfishing and guys with bones in their noses, and scribbled good-byes. When I went back to the Pensão, I shaved at a sink in the hallway, and the Swiss woman came by to wish me luck. While she talked about "What a great adventure you will have," I got enough shaving cream off my face so I could talk without spitting. I took my time, because I couldn't find the right words for what I wanted to say, which was something frivolous, something that should have told me the jungle already was affecting me. I wanted to tell her I thought she was beautiful. I mentally worked it into a "You're a very beautiful woman," then changed to, "I don't mean anything by this, but I think you're very beautiful," which all sounded as stupid in my head as it does on paper, so I finally settled for, "Anyway, you know you're beautiful, so I don't have to tell you," which worked and I didn't tell her, though later I told Tano I wanted to tell her and he said it was stupid, so everything still was making sense.

Packing, I felt nervous for the first time, the pre-trip jitters. Once, after Tano and I had holed up for a week on the island off Colombia, the same island he went to after he got hepatitis, when we were ready to go back on the road, Tano stopped me while we were packing.

"Man, how come every time we go on a trip together, it's like going to war?"

I didn't know then, and I didn't know in Manaus, but he was right.

"Well, here we go again," Tano said and took out the bottle of Scotch. "To what we've made it through before, and to whatever's on its way."

He took a deep slug, followed it with an "ahh," and passed the bottle to me. I took a shot, wiped my mouth, smiled, and shook his hand.

"Let's go, bro," he said.

We went to Melnick's and left passports, money, some gear, and the rest of the Scotch in his safe, then took a last look at his wall map. We figured we would be going about nine hundred miles, but because there were other people in the shop we didn't point.

Glück met us at the Pensão. We squeezed our gear, food,

53

and the three of us into a Volkswagen taxi that didn't have a front passenger seat, drove to the Club, bought three hundred liters of petrol, loaded the boat, and motored across the harbor to meet the *Emerson.* It was early evening, and we loaded our gear on board and the boat in the hold. The skiff was too long, so we had to leave the door of the hold open, with the bow of our boat sticking out like a white pimple.

Glück took a picture of us beside the *Emerson,* then mounted the steps to the cantina to buy guarana. He walked slowly and teetered in a waddle. His legs were rickety and he looked stooped and old. It was sad to see him slowly climb up into the dark sky, and I wondered how many more of these trips he had in him.

At exactly 8:00 the engine turned over with a *rat-tat-tat-tat* as we heard every piston bang in its cylinder, and at 8:10, we cast off, on our way upriver.

Glück held up his thumb and shouted over the engine noise, "This is good."

He had told us before that when he leaves Manaus, the first moments out are the best. "Then all I have to think about is all the time I will be away."

By midnight, the moon perched above the bow. The water was like polished obsidian speckled with galaxies, and the *Emerson* pushed through reflections.

X

BETWEEN the roar of the engine and the excitement of leaving, I couldn't sleep much. I felt pinched in the mesh of my hammock, which seemed like it was strung in a carburetor above the pounding of barrel-sized pistons. On board you didn't talk, you cupped your hands around your mouth and shouted, unless you went to the bow where you didn't need your hands.

At 5 A.M., we docked at Airão, a small village about 110 miles up the Rio Negro from Manaus. I remember some places and times exactly because Tano and I were traveling in the company of a mobile Big Ben. I haven't worn a watch, except an occasional pocket watch in a vest, since I was nine. Glück made up for whatever time I might have lost. He rarely missed announcing fifteen-minute intervals and always tagged any change of events with the time.

I didn't notice it at first, but on the boat, and then through the time we spent in the jungle, he slept with a flashlight he flicked on periodically through the night and seemed to switch on more, the deeper we went in the jungle. He was checking his watch. Times when I couldn't sleep, my restless hours would be marked by the click of the flashlight. In the jungle, the click and

55

the light often silenced monkeys and birds and bugs, as if Glück's time check somehow stopped jungle time. That only seemed to encourage him.

Our stop in Airão was brief. We let off a passenger as the first of our on board meal bells rang and we ate a breakfast of sweetened coffee and biscuits at a wooden picnic table near the stern, just in front of a banho, so it felt like home.

The *Emerson* was something like a floating carport without the cars. Between the pilothouse at the bow, and kitchen and banho at the stern, a long, low roof protected forty feet of open space middeck. A dozen passengers hung hammocks between rafters and piled their baggage around wooden support beams.

We stayed only a few minutes at Airão, but our next stop was only a few minutes away, at a sawmill three hundred yards upriver. It was dawn by then and we watched a truck loaded with timber pull back to the shoreline then get stuck in the mud, just as everyone on deck had predicted, a prediction made with hand signals. Our crew of four went down and, knee-deep in the river, set up a fire line with some of the wood cutters, using their shoulders as rollers and hauling the logs from the truck into the boat's hold.

We left two hours later. Glück had gone off the boat and bought two hundred oranges at the lumber camp, and I whiled away the morning eating the fruit, writing in my journal, and watching the shore.

Being on the *Emerson* was something like being on a float in an endless parade. The jungle was a line of green spectators leaning forward. Trees draped in nets of vines pushed for the sky or out into the river in a struggle for light. Our privilege was movement and space. Occasionally, we passed another boat, but mostly that world as it was seemed to turn in private review. Drawings in clouds floated above us while the water swept gainst our bow, carrying limbs and mud and rocks and bones to the sea. We moved against the grain of the world, defeating its current and, even in the heat of the noon sun, stealing breezes. River travel was deluxe travel.

"The life," Tano shouted over the engine.

The life.

At exactly noon, a bell rang signaling lunch, though it was more like the Last Supper. As soon as the first gong sounded, eight men bolted to a picnic table meant for six. By the time the bell finished ringing, in a pair of "Come and get it" jingles, the table was full. Tano and Glück and I never failed in our speed.

Meals were a stitch of wings. The men lined the table, shoulder to shoulder, with the elbows flapping just above our plates, belonging to whoever was sitting on either side, so we ate as if we were picking things out from under a ledge, only the ledge was arms. Platters of rice and black beans and noodles in yellow oil and some kind of meat mush and another kind of fish mush swirled around the table, once around, enough to empty them. Plates were mounded as high as gravity would permit until a halo of grease dripped on the table. Then, even though elbows blocked the view, you hunched over your mound, the way a dog would, dropped your mouth down under the elbows to the lip of the plate, and shoveled and scraped and tipped things down the pipe.

Eight private worlds sat at the table. No one ever spoke. Once, after I looked to my right and saw a cabocolo silently drooling fat and manioc off his chin, I looked across at Tano. His cheeks were packed, but he still had his right wing lifted and his head was down and he was ready to open his mouth for another push of beans. His eyes lifted up at me, leaving a lot of white under his pupils, the way he might look if he was caught stealing. I could have been looking in a mirror. I tried to gag a smile, but I choked on it and was afraid I would spit out whatever I had jammed into my jowls. It was like laughing in church, which I beat when I was a kid by thinking of the Crucifixion and tried to beat at the table by thinking of starving people in India and swallowing slowly and closing my eyes. The roar of the engine obliterated the rest.

There must have been ten kilos of food on the table and in five minutes, all of it had moved. One by one, diners left, after wiping their mouths with the backs of their hands and their hands on the tablecloth, then taking a wedge of goiabada, a sweet, jellied fruit. Then the women and children and, no doubt, weaker men approached for the next seating.

During the six meals I ate on the *Emerson,* all of which Tano, Glück, and I enjoyed at the first seatings, I never heard a word exchanged.

"Jeezuz," Tano said as we staggered to our hammocks. "That was something else. A thieves' meal."

I was food shocked and passed out. My mind was too leaden for dreams, but one of my senses unanchored as I felt someone staring. My eyes opened, and a young Indian woman standing above me smiled and handed me a glass of what looked like egg-nog and tasted like cool, runny tapioca. When I looked back up, she was gone, but there still was a glass in my hand and when I sipped it again, it tasted the same, so I didn't question anything and didn't want to look over the edge of my hammock at Tano or Glück. Sometimes it was better to keep things as they seemed.

Midafternoon a storm took chase. Glück said all the weather moved northeast. We watched the clouds race to our stern, then overtake us. A young Indian deckhand, with a round face like a pumpkin, slid barefoot along the rails and pulled down a canvas tarp that transformed us into a floating tent. Thunder shook and wind threw up the bottom of the tarps and hosed the deck with rain.

The rain made the jungle look as if a screen door separated us. It rained hard for forty minutes, then quickly faded to a light veil of drizzle before the sun cracked the sky and spread it apart, a jigsaw of clouds disassembling.

I was at the bow and Glück came up, as the rain seemed to have moved him to talk. The rain had pushed me inside myself, where I didn't feel like going at the time, so I was glad to oblige. Tano joined, too, and the conversation centered on teeth, of which Glück only had two.

"I lost my teeth on one of my trips," he said.

I didn't know whether to smile and prod him on or say I was sorry, though neither was necessary as he continued.

He said he'd had a bad toothache and was too far out to return to Manaus and see a dentist, so he got a pair of pliers he used for the motor on his boat and pulled out the tooth himself. Then he said he got to thinking, "Why bother with these teeth?

58

They always give me trouble. So I pulled the rest out, leaving only these two"—he pointed at a top and bottom incisor—"to hold my pipe."

He told the story without embellishment, as if he were explaining how he painted his boat. I figured that meant he either told the story a lot or it was simply the truth, so I couldn't help but believe him.

"But now, I no smoke the pipe." He shook his head. "Ahh, *sheiss.*"

His ability for dental work apparently gave him confidence.

"I was out in an Eendyun village once and an Eendyun had a toothache."

He got his pliers and then had four of the strongest members of the tribe hold the Indian with the toothache down on the ground.

"I told them not let go until I give the verd," he said.

The verd didn't come right away. He had to pull, wrench, and finally yank the tooth out while the fellow on the ground screamed.

"Then, I said, 'Let go,' and the Eendyun leaped in the air and went rooning into the joongle. Two hours later, he came rooning back with a gift for me and said the pain was gone."

Glück told more joongle stories, which passed the time until the six o'clock dinner gong struck. The performance was a repeat of lunch, though since lunch was so quick, I timed dinner. It edged out lunch by a minute.

Tano and I sat at the bow that night, retelling Glück's stories and watching the stars. The night before, near midnight, I had seen the Southern Cross just above the horizon, but in the early evening we only saw the Big Dipper.

"Down here, it's like being a child and looking at the sky for the first time," Tano said. "All the stars are different. You just take it for granted, looking at the sky that the stars are a certain way, but everything's different ... everything's turned."

I said something about being on the other side of the world without the north star to anchor us.

"Only the Southern Cross," Tano said with a sneer. "That'll anchor you."

Tano's feeling about religion focuses on Christianity, particularly Catholicism, to which he probably attributes the Fall.

For the most part, the Church has been a dead horse for me, but for Tano, it can always stand another kick.

During the day, Glück had told Tano about taking nuns on a trip, and that night, he retold it to me.

"Glück took some nuns up the river for a day outing. Two of the nuns were from southern Brazil and they had the head nun."

"The mother superior," I said.

"Yeah, right," Tano said. "Well, they're going up the river and it's getting hot and Glück says, 'Why don't we go in swimming?' and they say, 'We didn't bring any swimsuits,' and Glück says, 'Well, do you think I brought mine?' So, what's he do? He pulls off his clothes and jumps in and goes swimming. He shouts back at them, 'Come on in, come on in, it's really nice in here.'

" 'Oh, nooo, we can't go in.' " (Tano did the nun's voices in falsetto.) "But finally, they decide, 'OK, we'll do it.'

"So, they take off their big outer garments and get down to where they don't have any bras on, but they leave on their underwear.

"Then, Glück says, get this, I never knew this," Tano said, his voice cracking with laughter, "but nuns wear boxer shorts. God, isn't that a gas?"

I laughed, but then got defensive.

"I hope you don't have anything against boxer shorts," I said. "I wear them."

"Yeah, but nuns . . . can you see all these nuns in the world running around in their boxer shorts?"

At that point, Tano was doubled up at the thought of it.

"So, then the nuns get into the water," he said, "but they're afraid to go out swimming. Glück says, 'OK. Just hang on to the boat.' They hang on to the edge of the boat and he starts up the motor and goes down the river dragging these nuns along the side. They're just bouncing up and down in the waves, having the greatest time. Can you see him, dragging these nuns up the Amazon?

"Then the current and stuff starts pulling their pants down and they all scream, 'Stop, stop, stop' "—Tano again in falsetto—

"while their pants are now down around their ankles, but they loved it.

"Then when they get out, they make Glück promise not to tell ... what do you call the head priest?"

"The mother superior," I said.

"The Baby Jesus," Tano said, laughing. "Or the head priest ... the mother superior, that was it."

The night got warmer as we talked and the moon drifted toward the bow. It was near full and bathed us in blue-white light. The *Emerson* curled through channels, past humps of islands. Monkey Man switched on the light and caught a bird, maybe a crane, its eye gleaming as it swept downriver.

During the day the jungle had been as real as store windows along a sidewalk, yet always kept from us by the river. At night, the jungle was unreal and it was on us. As much as I liked it in the day, the jungle was better at night. With the darkness, you could slip off the boat and venture into shadows.

The waters felt familiar. Maybe they had touched me years ago. I spent part of my childhood in Titusville, Florida, a small town on the west side of the Indian River, about twenty miles from Cape Canaveral. Florida, then, was jungle and sun, but in the late 1950s missiles began to rise out of that jungle.

My father worked at the Cape. His job was to guide telecommunication satellites. On summer afternoons, we would meet him at the beach when he finished work at five o'clock. My mother would pack our 1949 Pontiac sedan with however many younger brothers I had at the time, a dog named Prancer—a boxer who drooled so much my father had to stuff paper towels in his jowls—and a picnic dinner.

To get to the beach from Titusville, you had to cross the Indian River, then twenty miles of swamp that also skirted the missile base, and then the Banana River, before finally reaching the ocean.

I am not sure why, but crossing the Indian River scared me. Maybe it was being afraid of falling in. I remember slumping, often with Prancer, into the foot well in the backseat when we crossed the bridge. I was deft at the maneuver, polishing my dive in town when I would see kids from school who had ridiculed our Pontiac as the "pink bomb."

Once over the river, there was a half-hour drive through swamp and jungle, where, I had been told, Hollywood had come to film some of the Johnny Weissmuller *Tarzan* movies I watched on Saturday television. Although I knew Weissmuller and oogah boogahs had come and gone years ago, I knew the alligators, rattlesnakes, and mosquitoes were still there, along with stories about people who went into that stretch of jungle and were lost forever. It was the same kind of place King Kong came from, and even driving through in the pink bomb, I never felt completely at ease.

It was different at the beach. I don't recall time lagging, but there were some slow moments and they are the ones that stayed. It was an easy place to drift, and standing at the shoreline, at the point where the ocean and sand touch, was like straddling a dreamy tightrope. Behind me were palmetto trees, and a ready-made Hollywood jungle, and missiles, and the edge of space, and out in front of me was water, and on the outer edge, places I had begun to read about like Africa and China and the Amazon and Ireland.

Ireland was exotic because of my teachers. I went to school in the back rows of St. Theresa's Catholic Church, where an Irish nun, Sister Margaret Mary, taught everything from the times tables to the lives of the saints to diagramming sentences, from behind the pews, where we had set up our desks.

She had come to Titusville with a group of nuns and a priest from Ireland, and she gave me a pen pal from County Cork. My pen pal, Michael, had been a student of Sister Margaret Mary's in Ireland, and she would describe him and his family and the school in County Cork to me, which all sounded green and faraway and slightly magical.

I suspected Sister Margaret Mary might be enchanted, something the Church seemed to allow room for by having saints. In the winter she wore a heavy black habit with rosary beads dangling from her waist and in the summer the habit was white linen. She spoke with an accent that sounded half song and told stories about the Crusades, and Saint Michael and the snakes, and miracles and rainbows and pots of gold and tiny underground people called leprechauns. The stories promised passages and one of my early goals in life was to capture a leprechaun and have him take me to his underground kingdom.

Mysteries opening up to me then weren't only fairy tales. Instead of a globe in my room I had a map of the planets. Like many kids in Titusville, my father's job in the space program was my own link to the stars, which even in daylight didn't seem that far away. The Cape was close enough to school that when we knew of an upcoming launch, Sister Margaret Mary would take the class outside to watch.

Lining up in alphabetical order or according to size—either way I was last—we marched outside to the corner of the church parking lot where home plate was at lunchtime. It was an easy way to keep an eye on your father's work. The missiles came up over the palms, past left field, out beyond the Indian River. They arced like deep fly balls that no one would catch, their flames burning holes through the sky before sailing out into my map of the planets.

During one of those launches, one that I knew my father was working on, I watched with Mark Pittman, whose father was a lawyer. When Mark asked, I told him, "Yeah, my dad's guiding it," and then I felt sorry for him to have a father like Perry Mason.

I could think about those things at the ocean, with my feet sinking in the wet sand, but usually what interested me most at the beach was the horizon, where once I saw the beginning of China. Even now, I remember what it looked like.

XI

THE sky was crisp blue, the kind of blue you usually see only in the desert, when we arrived in Barcelos, an old mission town. As the *Emerson* glided to dock, a white church shimmered on a bluff, producing the effect that maybe it was supposed to produce, looking like a host stuck halfway between the earth and sky. At noon, it talked.

A dozen people had come to greet our boat, and after we tied on to a pair of pilings and the deckhands had begun unloading the hold, the air exploded with calliope music, the kind you would hear on an old merry-go-round, only it was deafening. The music bounced off and shuddered things, so at first you couldn't tell from where it was coming. In sounded unearthly in part, because despite the volume no one except Tano and I paid any attention.

"What the hell's that?" Tano said.

We were the only ones on deck, and hell if I knew. Down below, the men continued to unload. Everyone looked like they didn't hear a thing.

When the song stopped it immediately was followed by a *thhumph ... thhumph* like a phonographic needle bouncing at the end of a record. Then a deep, echoing voice, how Cecil B. De Mille might have a Portuguese God sound if he was talking through a barrel, came on and spoke in incantations. In a minute, he gave way to a supplicative woman's voice, and the two then carried on a twenty-minute chitchat interlaced with lots of Deuses and Jesus Cristos and Nossa Mães. With the voices, you could hone in on the source, which of course came from the church steeple. The Word was carried a mile, and with help from the wind, maybe two into the jungle.

We unloaded our gear and packed Glück's skiff. After we paid our fare, the captain invited us to a last lunch with the crew. Again it was silent, even more so than the others as there was no acompanying engine noise, although comparatively leisured as we ate for at least ten minutes. After lunch, Tano bought cigarettes from one of the crew and we took a snapshot of each of us standing with Glück in front of the *Emerson,* a kind of "The way we were" shot, then we climbed into the skiff and pushed away from the shore.

"It's good to be free," Glück said.

I didn't even have to look at Tano.

Glück took the tiller, on which he had mounted a 20-horsepower engine. We kept a pair of forty-liter gasoline tanks and our gear in the front third of the boat, while Tano and I sat on a metal plank in the center. Glück let out the engine and we cut a pyramid of waves in the center of the river as he whistled "The Daring Young Man on the Flying Trapeze."

A half hour out, the river broke into four channels with the strongest current to the far right.

"Which one would you choose?" Tano said.

We took the second from the right, the one I would have taken because it looked the widest. Twenty minutes up the channel we hit shallow water and sheared a propeller pin. Glück had a jar full of extra pins and in minutes he had the broken one replaced, then suggested, "Let's go for a shwim."

Swimming in April in the Rio Negro was like taking a bath in warm coffee. The Negro is what its name says, black water, and Tano's and my skin was white from the American winter, so to the birds we must have looked like birch trees blowing in an underwater wind. It was the rainy season and the water was high, but the sun was bright and we found shallow pools where we slid, stomach up, and poached.

The sunny-side-up life was short-lived though, as for the next couple of hours the channel we originally took went through exponential tricks, splitting into twos and fours and worse, with the up-channel current fading with the depth of the water down to a trickle. Several times we dead-ended up lagoons as the current completely died out and only the wind rippled the surface. We followed an egret that looked like a white ghost rowing in the air, but he, too, took us nowhere. Forced to stop at the end of another lagoon, we backtracked, then caught the first inlet we could find north, assuming that as we moved up the Negro, the main branch of the river was to the right. Glück said he chose the channel we took to avoid wasting gas fighting the main river current. Now, in an attempt to find that main current, we always went right, but the only thing we found was the realization we were lost.

To be lost our first day on the river, actually our first few hours, was not a good sign. True, we had, according to Glück, more than a month's worth of supplies and enough gas to wander aimlessly for a couple of weeks, but, as they say, ventures are started after a first step, which for us was in the wrong direction.

Glück seemed unperturbed. He whistled nearly all the time, mostly, except for the "Daring Young Man," unrecognizable but melodious warbles, while the boat hummed in and out of stilled passages.

"Makes nuhzing," he would say as we would turn back to look at him and shrug after we hit another closed lagoon. Still, we noticed he decreased the accelerator to conserve gas.

We turned right, then swung west into another lagoon that looked promising as stalks of grass cut ripples in the water, suggesting current, but again we were wrong. It was only the wind. We dead-ended into a cul-de-sac of black, stagnant water that looked like a tar pit.

Glück checked his watch and announced four o'clock. "I think we should camp."

We eased the skiff through a clearing on the south bank. The wind died and shadows draped the lagoon. There was no noise, only the echo of our voices against the circle of trees.

66

"Just out and we're lost in the joongle," Tano said.

"Makes nuhzing," Glück said.

Actually, it didn't make a difference to us, only the time and gasoline it would take to backtrack out, which our triumvirate of minds felt reasonably certain we could do. The emptiness of the spot passed when we found trees that had been cut down and an old fire pit with bones from a large fish and a tapir.

After unloading the kitchen, Glück gave us our first jungle lesson, how to string a hammock. Stringing a hammock basically meant stringing a bow between two trees you trusted. On the trip to Barcelos, Glück had warned us, "There is little danger in the joongle, only shtoopidity."

"Shtoopidity Lesson Number One" was not stringing your hammock beneath a Brazil nut tree. The nuts come packed in a hard shell the size and weight of a croquet ball.

"I know people who have been killed, hit by a nut," Glück said.

When we strung our beds, we made sure the trees were benign. We stretched our hammocks, leaving a slight sag, between a pair of trees that could handle our weight. The narrower the trunk, the better, as long as it was strong enough, as we had to wrap the rope several times around each tree. Next, we knotted either end, which Tano and Glück always handled easily and I fumbled, a failure that has haunted me since boy scout days when I blew the knot-tying merit badge. Finally, we strung a taut guy line an inch above either end of the hammock and draped a plastic tarp over as a makeshift fly sheet with its corners tied to nearby bushes. The plastic sheet was folded down halfway, like bed sheets turned, and the total unoccupied effect was of a sleeping bag floating in air. We added security by sticking our machetes in the ground, just to the side, but within arm's reach. "Shtoopidity Lesson Number Two" was not to put the machete directly beneath your hammock.

Our sleeping arrangements officially were not christened yet, but they would come to be called pods, partly because that was exactly what they looked like, and partly because that gave them the outer-space spookiness the movie *Invasion of the Body Snatchers* had given the word "pod."

After bedding, I moved to preventive medicine. To repel

67

any mosquitoes that might find me during the night, I popped four vitamin B pills I had bought by the hundreds in New Jersey; if that didn't work, at least I'd heard that vitamin B was supposed to combat depression. I understood it was safe to down handfuls of the pills, as you discharged what your body didn't use, a discharge that was supposed to include stench, a stench mosquitoes didn't like. I only half-believed that. For added protection I wore army fatigues. I got those at an army-navy store in lower Manhattan, where the sales clerk, an old guy with a cigar, told me the pants were "'Nam tested. No skeets gonna bite trew dem." I didn't believe that. I bought a half-dozen vials of mosquito turpentine that was guaranteed. To get it I drove two hours to a camping supply store near the Catskills where a salesman told me the repellent, which came in tiny bottles with the picture of a bearded, smiling man on the label, was the "strongest in the world." I got to believe him. The stuff gave me first-degree burns. I also bought a couple cans of standard supermarket aerosol instant mosquito death. No one told me about that, but the label on the can promised annihilation of anything that was an inch or smaller and moved. I hoped things wouldn't get to the point where I would have to see if I did or didn't believe that.

Glück fried potatoes and Spam for dinner and we washed it down with tea from cinnamon leaves Glück brought from his backyard in Manaus. By the time we finished supper, the crickets, frogs, and night birds had come out, and the jungle turned shades of gray, then black. We sipped tea and leaned back as the moon began to rise and Glück told us another story, and perhaps because of dinner, it was food related.

"Above the mountains north of Manaus, there is a German missionary. The Eendyuns love him so much they ask him if they could eat him when he died."

Glück said that after a man whom the Indians believe is a good man dies, the Indians take his remains into the jungle, burn the body, pulverize the bones into powder, mix them with grain or meal, and eat the mash.

"They believe a man's power is in his bones and the power can be passed on if you eat the bones."

The priest, whom Glück said he knew, had not died yet, but

68

the Indians told the priest of their plans, saying they would invade the consecrated grounds of the Catholic cemetery and steal his bones at night.

"The priest, he said, 'That's OK. You can do that if you like.' "

Glück always had stories. He had bookshelves of journals and said that between trips, he was using a tape recorder and typewriter to build them into a book. Actually, typewriters had been Glück's ticket to freedom. Often in camp, Glück would sit on a wooden stool the Indians had carved for him and read a book published in 1921 and titled *Der Liebe Augusten,* by Horst Wolfram Geissler. When I asked him what it was about, he said, "It's my life story. It's about a German music box maker who travels until he runs out of money and then stops and makes a music box, sells it, and picks up again."

Glück read it the way a preacher might read the Bible, before and after bed, and he had been reading it for years. It was given him by Heidi, the woman who raised the three-toed sloths near Manaus.

"In many ways, my life has been like the music box maker," he said. In Germany, Glück had learned to repair typewriters, a skill that along with tennis, brought him security in South America. After the war, he left his passport in Venezuela and, with his trade, headed south.

"There was nuhzing left in Germany," he said. "It was all gone. My family wanted me to return, but I wrote them there was nuhzing in Germany for me. It would be better if I stayed here and sent them packages, food shtuff and things, to help them survive."

Glück had come to use his book as a litmus test.

"Now, I give the music box maker book to people who come with me on a trip. If they like it, they are good people. If they don't, the trip is finished."

He never offered Tano or me the book, but we weren't offended, and later, in an unusual moment of solemnity, Tano and I agreed we wouldn't mind doing like the Indians and eating each other's bones, which was a good enough litmus test for both of us.

After the stories, I went to my mosquitoes. We all had sleeping bags, which despite the heat during the day were good to have in the predawn hours. My bag was compact, but not exactly lightweight, as it had been capable of keeping me warm in snow, and every night I had a choice: whether to wake up sweating or itching. Most nights I at least started out choosing sweat, and I chose sweat the first night. I took off my clothes, climbed into the pod and the bag, and rolled the tarp down. Inside the bag I kept the mosquito turpentine, and if worse got to worst, a knife.

I watched the moon arc through a grate of trees and I began personifying sounds, but by the time I was listening to muezzins on stalks of grass, a crack of branches and a thump beside my hammock woke me. The moon was high and I must have been asleep for a couple hours. Above me, a monkey screeched, shook branches, and dropped small, pulpy fruit that looked something like rotten plums, "Shtooopidity Lesson Something-Or-Other" Glück had not yet taught us about. My monkey kept it up for a half hour or so, but I got to be pretty good at dodging his shots, slipping the tarp over my head when I heard a rustle of leaves that signaled another assault. He never hit me, and finally gave up and swung to another tree and back into the forest.

The pod did a good job on me. I slept as if I was knotted. I dreamt I was buried alive in a narrow grave, and I was unable to free myself, my arms folded like they were held by a straitjacket, the position I was in when Glück called "Hello," after sunrise.

We ate breakfast and broke camp quickly after deciding to retrace our route and return to our first bad turn. A gray dawn got grayer as we pushed off, and it began to rain. Tano and I pulled our hats down to above our eyebrows and wrapped ourselves in the tarps we had used as flies for the pods. Glück covered himself in clear plastic wrap and put on his cap.

We sweated under the plastic to keep dry from the rain, so by the time the rain faded to sprinkles, we were as wet as if we had sat out in the downpour. Between mornings like that and nights in the pod, in no time, we would mildew.

It took less than two hours to return to our mistaken turn. The sky was clearing, though the sun stayed behind clouds, and to celebrate, we took Sunday morning baths on a sandbar.

We turned up the main river and fought the current as well

70

as a prop plane would handle the jet stream. We moved, but the shoreline passed at walking speed.

Glück whistled. Tano and I watched. When we began, the river and jungle and sky boxed us in and it felt like we were driving through a tunnel. The stroke of the engine stitched everything in an echo. Only thing, I heard different things. If the river was narrow and the sky slim, my thoughts were thin, or maybe just clearer and tied in with the landscape. There wasn't much room for daydreaming. Everything was on you. If the river widened and the sky opened, I was more alone and spaces, distance and time, long. When the jungle was close, I worked more out of instinct, but when the jungle was far, the way it was by midmorning that day, other things got going.

At times cruising the main river felt like crossing the prairies in a semi on one of those days that are mostly sky. When you were lucky enough to catch a ride with a long-distance trucker, chances were it was for company. He wanted someone to talk to and keep him awake. Sometimes, if you were very lucky, the engine was too loud for talking or the trucker was the quiet type, and the time would pass with the landscape, which sometimes was as blank as that day on the river. On my nineteenth birthday, I figured I had hitchhiked more than 10,000 miles the previous year. I made the tally at the time not to boast, but because one of the airlines had established a 10,000-mile club, and I thought there should be a similar group for people who used thumbs instead of tickets. Most of the miles on my odometer I clicked off alone, but a few jaunts were with Tano.

Trips, then, were destined for women or wildness, which at the time were exclusive entities. The wildness rearranged your soul while the women patched your heart. Luckily, Tano and I had good women, who if they didn't understand what we were after—I wasn't always sure we did—at least they put up with our chase.

Hitting the road was something almost sacred. We were lizards, running in spurts, and shedding our skins as fast as we figured where we were, which sometimes took a long time. We took knocks, and sometimes they came hard and fast and we felt them cut and shape us. Every time you stood on a highway and stuck out your thumb, there was a chance you would go through

71

the wringer, but it was like the first time you kissed a new girl. You remembered what happened the last time you went through this and got your guts kicked in, but you still did it again.

My grandfather once told me I didn't know what traveling on the road meant because I never rode the rails. He had, and told stories about hard times and beatings some men got, but also a story of revenge about a Chicago rail yard dick who used a bulldog to prey on hoboes.

"He got it though," my grandfather said. "It was a week before they found the dick and his dog in a cornfield in Iowa. Both of them had a pipe up their ass.

"Ha, haaaah," my grandfather laughed. "Those were hard times. You don't know hard times."

Maybe not. I had breaks. One was being born in an easier time. I wasn't force blown by the times in a chase for a buck and a meal, though I have had to chase both. Then again, I told myself, I was after different currency. I was dealt certain cards and at least knew it didn't do any good to dwell on what you did or did not have. It was how you handled the cards that counted.

That was why it was good to have a vision. The road never was completely open-ended for me, even when I wasn't sure where I was going. The first time I pulled up anchor, it was for something, and usually it has been that way since.

The first time I went to California, after Tano reminded me of Columbus Day, was not the first time I hit the road, but it was for the same reason and the same girl.

Out of idiocy, I attended classes that day, and it wasn't until after supper that I launched. As I said, I went with the finances of a bum, enough money for a standby flight back to where I started, so I tried to make sure my last supper would last and I ate a lot quickly, under the assumption that I could put food down my throat faster than my stomach could signal my brain the storage tanks were full. It seemed to work, in that I felt full and nauseated when I left and hitched out to the interstate. Otherwise, I traveled light. I left my sleeping bag on my bed (I had abandoned sheets and blankets as too much maintenance), but used the sleeping bag duffel as luggage for a change of clothes. I figured that without a bag I wouldn't be tempted to stop and sleep, as I had no time for that.

Throughout college, I attended classes zealously, less out of a quest for knowledge than a cheapskate's sense I was paying those guys to perform, so I might as well be there to get my money's worth, which was why I stayed to the end of the day. Also, the delay was in hope that the rain, which began in the morning, would stop. It did. It changed to snow.

I stood beneath an overpass and held out a cardboard sign that said CALIF. The last time I had made a sign I was fourteen. The sign was in honor of Mickey Mantle, and I took it to Yankee Stadium where he responded by going 0-for-4 while the Yankees got shut out.

If I were more experienced, when I stuck my thumb out I would have felt trouble. I was leaving at the start of the season's first snowfall, I was broke, knew I would be hungry and tired, and had a better than even chance I would end up a frozen piece of litter by the time I reached Cheyenne. None of that impressed me as much as the ache in my stomach, though, which I hoped would not wear off too fast because then I would have to start thinking about those other things.

I stood beneath the underpass about twenty minutes and the ache was still aching when a Volvo sportscar pulled over and I ran up and swung open the door.

"You're pretty lucky," a young guy in the driver's seat said. "I'm going all the way to the coast."

For the next two days we drove like they were going to be our last two days. I had my girl at the end of the line, and the driver, whose name was Donald, had a Belgian wife and a kid whom he hadn't seen in months. Donald had been working on a federal housing project in Michigan and the pressure and long distance and consequent trouble with keeping his marriage going had driven him near a nervous breakdown, which, he said, he had suffered before.

"One day, in the army, I just couldn't take it anymore," he said. "I was with this black dude and we were in a jeep. I was driving and we were waiting at a railroad crossing for an oncoming train. Then, it all seemed to come down and I drove the jeep out on the tracks and yanked the key. The black dude begged, 'Donald, Donald, please. You can't.'"

Donald didn't or the black guy didn't let him, I don't remember which, but I didn't sleep much when I drove with Don-

73

ald and I kept my eyes on him and the oncoming lane of traffic. It was easy to stay awake, though, as he had good stories, especially about California.

Stories were one of the best things about being on the road. When you were in a car with someone, and since you didn't expect to see each other again, it was like walking into a bar you never would return to and unloading on the bartender. Driving stories were often half confession, half dreams, and most of the time they were good.

Donald told me he had been away for six months and couldn't stand Michigan, and through the distance, the West Coast had developed a halo. My only contact with the place had been with this one woman whom I was willing to go halfway across the country and through a snow storm for, so I tended to believe people who put a halo on the coast.

I would ask Donald questions about California and he would tell me stories, mostly about people there and compare them to people in Michigan.

"One of the last weekends I spent in Marin," he said, "I went to the beach with Julienne"—I am not sure if that was her name, but it was something like that—"and a priest. We were nude and walked along the sea talking about philosophy and classical music." He laughed. "The people I worked with in Michigan wouldn't have been able to tell the difference between Tchaikovsky and Chopin."

When I was eighteen, I knew Tchaikovsky played the cannons, but I wasn't sure about Chopin. I felt reasonably certain he wasn't R&R, but not knowing, I just huffed a bit, a good, Brahmin snoot at the rubes in Michigan. Donald told more stories, some about his wife and a crazy father-in-law artist from Europe, some about hopping Southern Pacific freight trains, and others about taking peyote and living with the Hopi Indians.

The image of the priest and Donald and his wife probably would have been lost in the basement of my brain if it wasn't for Donald's Tchaikovsky-Chopin remark. My ignorance has been a great blaze for retracing memories. Even at the word "ignorance" my mind lights up. Once, on an otherwise meaningless summer night of drinking with the boys, including one who at the time was attending an engineering/architecture school, I stopped con-

74

versation with the remark, "Yeah, the house"—a vacation home my family rented in New Hampshire—"was really nice, one of those circa architectural types."

I have left enough of those sorts of things strewn in my past so that a good portion of my memory is illuminated.

What driving on a freeway across the western United States for the first time lacked in spectacle, it gained in imagination. Actually, it was imagination that had lopped off some of the grandeur I expected the West would grant at first sight. I didn't know whether I should blame Walt Disney or *National Geographic* or bank calendars, but the Rockies in Wyoming, along Route 80, didn't rise up like pictures I had seen of the Grand Tetons. I didn't see cowboys herd cattle across the highway and I didn't see a wooden Indian in Cheyenne. What I did get was a sense of space. In Nebraska, stubbled cornfields frosted with snow rolled endlessly into a gray sky, the stalks looking like masts of ships sunk in an arctic sea. Through the prairie states, you began to feel the openness, but by the time you reached the Rocky Mountains, you knew distances the size of states back east could be gobbled up in a matter of hours. The land was vast, but that four-lane highway shrank the place. Miles, divisible by higher speed limits the farther west you went, shortened until you reached Nevada, where there was not a speed limit, only the limit to the capabilities of your machine.

The snowstorm hung over the mountains as we crossed, and a single pair of tracks in the right lane soon were buried.

When we stopped at a truckers café, a waitress told us, "You two must be the last ones through. They're closing the road right behind you."

The West was being zipped tight, and it felt good being just ahead of the zipper.

At that and similar stops, I kept to my fast, even though Donald offered to buy me food. Water, cigarettes, and stale car air suited me fine. They seasoned the adventure, though I did accept capsuled nutrition. Donald had a jar of pink and yellow pills he said were vitamins for pregnant women (I don't remember why he had them), which I accepted gratefully, took four times

75

a day, and later thought it was a good joke to cross the West eating nothing but "pregnant ladies' pills."

We stopped twice to sleep in motels, a luxury I did not expect. Donald had driven straight through from Michigan, and late that first night, he stopped in Rawlings, Nebraska, and got a room. He offered me the choice to try and sneak in and sleep on the floor, or stick my thumb back out and see how much ground I could make that night. I actually thought about it for a few minutes, but I blamed the snow, which was still falling, for relieving me of choice.

Our nerves demanded the second stop. We were up early in the morning in Rawlings and drove hard throughout the day, much of it through a blizzard. I had to shake my head to keep from being hypnotized by the swirl of snow in the car's lights, but at least the snow kept cars out of oncoming lanes.

When I wasn't staring in the lights and shaking my head, Donald or I was talking, which I did little of for fear of a Chopin slipup and because his stories were more interesting than mine. When I did talk, I tilted the converstion toward women and then to my girl, in hope that what was driving me might infect him and keep us both going as long as possible.

It worked. By 3 A.M. the next night, we still were moving, listening to a song, "Cocaine," on the radio and roaring down from the mountains and out of the storm and into Salt Lake. The road was icy, and with the continuous hours of driving and the end of the snow, Donald's foot had become heavier. Then, as he whirled around a curve, the adventure and stories and our world looked like they had reached curtain time.

A truck had jackknifed across our two lanes. On the left, the mountain walled the highway and to the right, a narrow shoulder stopped at a cliff and dropped into a shadow.

"Get down, we're going under," Donald said, his voice raised, but not panicked.

With the ice and our speed, we couldn't stop. He slumped in his seat and I dropped but didn't go all the way to the floor. I didn't say anything, but understood he was aiming for an underpass in the truck's rubber and metal, where the cab coupled to the trailer and now was lifted like a fault from the jackknife. Getting on the floor meant he planned to decapitate the top of the car and hoped we would blow on through.

76

That thought happened in an eternity that must have been only a half second. In the next half second, I don't know how or why, the truck moved, down to the left, toward the wall of mountain. The hole we had aimed for had been in the far right lane, and Donald just turned the steering wheel so that we swung off the road, near the cliff, caught the skirt of the shoulder, our rear wheels spinning in the gravel, then roared past.

Neither of us said anything for a long time, then Donald said, "I can't believe he moved. I can't fucking believe he moved."

I slowly closed my eyes and Donald began singing "Cocaine."

West of Salt Lake, we got a room with a Mormon Bible in it, and when I took an extra blanket and rolled it out to sleep on the floor, it was five o'clock and I could see the false dawn.

Next day, Donald didn't say anything about the truck or his demolition derby idea, only now and then he would sing a verse from "Cocaine," and I would think he was a hot shit.

I made fewer references to my girl, or time, or speed, but by midnight Saturday, I saw white bridge lights sparkling over San Francisco Bay.

I never saw Donald again, although we exchanged addresses and said we would try to get together. He said he hoped I would find love and whatever else I was looking for met my expectations. I wished him luck in patching things up with his wife and family and trying to get something going again in California.

The following Christmas I was on the road, and in California, and made a brief stop at his home in Sausalito. His house was dark and had lots of big pillows on the floor and felt like a houseboat dry-docked. He wasn't there, but I met his wife, who was not as pretty as I imagined, but was warm and spoke with a soft accent. She offered me tea and we talked and she asked me about the woman I had come to see in California. She was fine and we were doing well then, and Donald's wife said, "Good." A year later, when I was back east, I got a letter from Donald asking me to send him a copy of the Sunday *New York Times* classified sections, so then, I assumed things weren't going well with him, either.

The sun came out and I forgot about echoes, and to give the day a sense of beach holiday, I greased my face and arms with sun screen, tipped the brim of my hat down, and wandered in and out of sleep.

Midafternoon, we crossed out of a no-man's land lattice of channels and on to a part of the river covered by a set of aerial maps Glück had somehow confiscated from the military in Manaus. The maps were five-year-old aerial photographs and showed the river and jungle in a black and white maze. I never understood how Glück got them, only that he shouldn't have them, but I didn't have any complaints. Part of Glück's appeal was he had little respect for authority.

He relished confrontations with authority and told a story about one between two of my naps. A local tourist agency, run by Brazilians, could not understand why Glück was taking foreigners in a canoe up the river. The jungle trips the agency offered included a large houseboat, martinis, showers, guns, music, and servants. The tourist agents could not see why people would go with Glück and willingly spend days cramped in a canoe and nights suspended by hammocks in trees. The tourist agent's thinking went, "Glück must be up to something, maybe digging gold." (The El Dorado myth persisted: often Tano and I and Glück were asked if we were Oro hombres, or in an updated version, pilferers of Indian artifacts.) Glück's competition complained to local military officials, and Glück was called on the carpet. His appointment was with a person known as the General, and was set for a Monday at 10 A.M.

When Glück arrived, he looked the way he always looked, like he had just climbed out of his boat. Along with his cap and sport shirt, he had on a pair of shorts and sandals.

"What are you doing?" an officer asked him as he entered army headquarters.

"I'm here to see the General," Glück said.

"You can't see the General when you are wearing short pants," the officer said.

"Listen," Glück said. "I didn't ask the General to come and see me, he asked me to come see him. I come the way I am."

"But you listen," the officer said. "You can't go in to see the General dressed like that."

78

"Good," Glück said. "I did not want to see him anyway."

"But the General wants to see you."

"OK, I'll go in and see the General."

"You can't go in dressed like that to see the General."

"But the General wants to see me, I don't want to see him."

"Well, it doesn't matter. The General is not here on Mondays. He leaves Fridays and does not return until Wednesday. You come back Wednesday."

"Ach, this is crazy," Glück said, but on Wednesday, he returned, dressed in the same shorts and sandals.

"I'm here to see the General," Glück told the officer. The two engaged in an echo of Monday's conversation, until Glück finally asked, "Who is the General?"

"We don't know," the officer said.

"Ach, this is *sheiss,*" Glück said and then went up and down hallways trying to find the General.

"I asked a dozen people, 'Who is the General? Who is the General?' but no one knew," Glück told us.

Finally, they told him to return Friday.

Same thing. " 'Who is the General?' 'Who is the General?' 'No one knows who is the General?' " Glück said. "Then I gave up."

What made some of Glück's stories funnier than they were, was that at the time, Tano and I didn't realize Glück's trouble with some English words, like how he almost always got the word "where" confused with "who."

The encounter with the General taught the old dog a new trick. The following year, at tax collection time, Glück was called to the city assessor's office to pay taxes he owed on his boat for the preceding six years. Glück came promptly but once again in shorts and sandals.

When the front desk bureaucrat looked up and asked Glück why he was there, Glück told him he had come to pay his taxes. The tax man told him, "You can't come to pay your taxes in short pants."

"Why, I did not want to pay the tax anyway," Glück said.

"You go home and change."

"I don't have anything else," Glück said, but he left and did not return.

The following year, boat tax time returned, and so did Glück, once more in his jungle finery.

"You can't come and pay your taxes with your short pants on," the tax man said.

"Fine. You want the taxes, I did not want to come here and pay the taxes." Then he went home.

Glück said to us. "That happened for six straight years, and I never paid the boat tax."

When it came to the aerial photographs, Glück only told us they were *"verboten."*

With our compass, we followed the main channel, counted islands we passed, and judged distances until we were certain we had emerged deep in a quadrant covered by the map. Bolstered, we decided to take a side channel and break from the gas battle with the main current.

A spiral of egrets, maybe a hundred, lifted and swirled to the sky as we took a close turn in the river and passed a low-hanging tree speckled with mud packs the size of cantaloupes. The tree was filled with oriole nests and they in turn were surrounded by wasp nests, an arrangement that speckled the jungle.

Glück decided we should have fish for supper, so he tied a three-inch lure to a line as thick as telephone wire, threw it behind us, and trawled. In no time we had an eighteen-inch tucunare, a wide-bodied fish with yellow spots on its side. It bit Glück on the thumb when he pulled it aboard.

"Sheiss . . . The cabocolo, he says that the yellow spots are Jesus Christ's fingerprint," Glück said.

We camped at a deserted, palm-thatched hut on a ledge above the river, the first of many rubber workers' huts we would use. They were uptown. You could string your hammock quickly from rafters, and thanks to the government's chemical spraying program, many of the huts had a white dusting that looked like talcum powder, but was DDT, which did the job on rats, roaches, and most everything else that moved, even mosquitoes.

Staying in a hut was a double-edged sword though, like smoking cigarettes, but at the thought of pods and a tarp at our nose, we always were ready to bargain away the future. The further out we got and the closer to the pyramids, the more we craved the huts that dotted the shoreline the way boarded-up gas stations do on old, abandoned county roads back in the States. Glück got to calling them Hiltons, or actually, "Heeltones," and around three thirty in the afternoon, he would begin singing, "Who is the Heeltone? Who is the Heeltone?" again mixing up the "who" and the "where."

Most of the rubberworkers were gone. With the boom and bust of the rubber trade, rubber collecting presently was in a forty-year bust cycle. It peaked near the turn of the century, just before rubber trees were planted in the South Pacific to avoid their predators in the Amazon. Still, some rubber workers tried, but for every occupied hut there must have been a hundred empty.

Glück cleaned, filleted, and cooked Christ's fingerprint while Tano and I went for a swim. The sun was almost down, and Tano kept his hat on as he walked out. He went about fifteen yards, to where only his head was above water, and in the glare of the sky and river, he looked like a planet. He stayed awhile, not saying much, and when he came out his body glistened bright red. He didn't complain though, only gooked himself in grease and walked without bending his elbows or knees.

After dinner, we washed pans, reloaded the gas into smaller containers, sat near the edge of the cliff and watched darkness slide over the river.

"You know, Tatunka Nada No Se"—the upriver pyramid connection—"he says that the end of the world will come in 1981," Glück said. "The Eendyun here, he also predicted the coming of the Vikings to North America, and the coming of the Spanish and World War II."

I assumed that was Glück's way of leading up to something.

"So, what do you think about the end of everything next year?" I asked.

"It's boo shit," he said.

Glück sat on his stool between us, and Tano and I laid on the ground. The moon rose over Glück's shoulders, and he told us about how he was in the Luftwaffe and how he was thrown in a stockade for laughing at a German colonel who wore a monocle and a sheathed sword. Soon after, Glück developed his philosophy to end war. "All captured officers above the rank of major should be hanged. Just hang them up. Hang them up. Then no one would want to be an officer and that would be it."

"Right on," Tano said, which I don't think Glück understood.

Two riverboats with red and green lights passed below us, dragging ribbons of reflected light in the water.

"Christmas packages," Glück said. "Ah, yes, . . . I had a Tarzan go on a trip with me once. He was from Brooklyn, in New York. I took him north of Manaus. He wore a cloth around his parts and carried a rifle and a tranquilizer gun. He shot anything that moved. I was afraid he would shoot me, or maybe himself, but that didn't happen.

"He stayed for a few weeks, and all day, every day, he would go into the joongle with his machete and cut trails. He cut miles of trails, but he only cut the trees and bush down to the height of his shoulder. After he was finished, I don't know if he liked playing this Tarzan."

82

XII

I had bad dreams I could not shake in the morning. The buzz of cicadas only made things feel more stuck, but when we were back out on the river, movement blew the dust out of my attic. The sun warmed my skin and Tano pointed to yellow-speckled trees that looked as if someone had sprinkled them with saffron, and the world again was a paradise. The land peeled back and the river widened to an inland sea and Tano and I slumped in the boat and watched the sky and the Negro become two oval mirrors reflecting each other, with a ribbon of green as a frame. Soon we could not see the horizon, only the edge of the river melt into a wash of blue.

The December after my first trip to California, I quit college and again headed west, and again caught one ride, with a guy just out of Vietnam. We had the same trouble with snow, but he had a big, souped-up Mustang and we drove straight through.

I spent Christmas and New Year's with my girl's family in Oakland. It was the longest stretch of time we'd had together since Maine and it made us feel like a normal couple. We went to movies and went to visit Jack London's home, where I signed the guest register and put my address as "Amerika," the spelling of which I had picked up from reading Jerry Rubin and Abbie Hoffman that fall. We also went to what for me was the biggest supermarket I had ever seen, with aisles so long and wide you could have used a car to drive around, and took rides to Santa Cruz and San Francisco during which she would talk about things like Beethoven and Bobby Seale and Eldridge Cleaver and *The New Yorker,* and then she would speak in Spanish and talk about going to an Ivy League college the next fall. I was young and she was younger, but she drooled brains. I occasionally thought I had a few, too, but maybe it was to balance her, or because I was through with education then, I talked about other things I was learning, things I thought were more important, about desolate places and risk and what you might be forced to do to hang on to your heart. She was flowering and I thought I might be beginning to go to seed, and we both used the other for balance. We clung to one another until there were claw marks.

After New Year's, I figured my welcome was up with her family, so early one morning, I packed up and went to Berkeley, where I became, as they say, a street person. I had thirty-seven cents in my pocket, but survived on what remained of goodwill from the previous decade. I anchored myself in a place called the Free Church, which reminded me of the caddy shack at a golf course where I used to work when I was fourteen. At the caddy shack, I would arrive as soon after dawn as I could, but would have to wait a few hours before tee-off times and then still count on the caddy master being in a good mood and noticing I had arrived early before he would line me up with a job. At the Free Church, the wait could be as long as all day and it was for a place to sleep. The church was actually a small room with some card tables and wooden benches. Two guys sat behind a desk with a phone and made calls during the day and kept a book, like a real estate agent's, with listings of homes where streets could sleep at night. Around 8 PM, the guys with the book would begin calling names and handing out cards with addresses and referrals for places to crash. If after all the addresses were gone there still were people looking for a place to sleep, the dregs were told to try a hostel near Telegraph Avenue, where you could spend the night, but had to even the score by doing work around the building in the morning. I spent one night in the hostel.

I had an upstairs room without a door, but with two bunk beds. I took a top bunk and below me a black guy slept and never woke while I was there. On the top bunk across from me, a red-haired kid whittled a stick and asked me where I came from. He said he was from "California, man, land of the flower children, man, the greatest place in the world." I worked up a smile and lay down.

It was about ten o'clock. I took my shoes off and rolled my jacket around them and used it as a pillow. I had heard from other streets that a lot of things got ripped off at the hostel, including shoes. Mine already had holes in the soles, but if I lost them I thought I would be as good as dead. I slept with my arms around the pillow, and underneath, I kept my pocketknife.

I woke in the middle of the night when something bumped against my bed. It was dark, but a fluorescent light in the hall gave voices form. I looked down and saw a woman who was maybe five feet six and 200 pounds pull a short, skinny guy with a goatee over to the lower bunk across from me. "Come on," she said, as if she were yelling at a dog. She pulled off her pants and I could see rolls of white hanging like a towel over two thick legs. The guy didn't or couldn't take off his clothes, but she said, "I'll do it," and then the sound of a zipper. They smelled like liquor and cigarettes and she laid on the bed, and yanked the guy on top of her, and then said, "Let's go." He didn't seem to get going quick enough and she said, "Come on, get it up, you fucker," which I wasn't sure was meant to praise or ridicule, but soon I heard her rocking and the bed going *kathump, kathump, kathump,* like a slow jackhammer. She said, "Keep going," and he must have, because she kept up a steady grunt for a while.

I had watched the beginning of things with one eye from the corner of my bed, but when they fell on their bed, out of decency I turned and just listened. She kept him going for quite some time, long enough so that I almost got used to it and began to fall asleep. Then I heard a thud and a bang on the floor and looked down and saw the guy and figured he got the boot.

I got up early in the morning and saw that he was back in her bed, his head curled up on her chest, and at the other end, two stumpy, hairy ankles and feet and a pair of ankles with socks and men's shoes sticking out from an army surplus blanket.

85

I mopped the floor in a bathroom for the privilege of sleeping in that flophouse and I did a good job, too.

Another night I got an offer of a place on a floor with two guys who wore earrings and motorcycle jackets. They drove a station wagon and gave me a ride to their home. One of them, the driver, talked about the day before, when his daughter had come home early with her boyfriend from school. Both kids wanted to give sex a try but were virgins, so the guy driving showed them how. I was sitting in the front seat while the story was being told and the driver's companion was behind me. Once, the fellow in the back seat patted my hair and said something about having nice curls, and I leaned away and said something like, "Oh, shit." Then they said I could sleep on their floor and they wouldn't bother me, but when I got to their house, I met the driver's eighty-year-old mother who got upset when she heard the word "heads" used by one of the motorcycle-jacketed guys to describe some people in Berkeley. I smoothed things out and told her heads were people with long hair and then told her boys I was going out on the road and hitching out of there, but the driver was so grateful to me for calming his mother down, he drove me back to the Free Church.

While the Free Church took care of lodging, another church, I think it was Lutheran, took care of board. Every night at six o'clock, dozens of streets lined up outside a kitchen behind the Lutheran church for a free meal of stew and rice and old bread that came in cardboard boxes. The stew came splashed on paper plates and people ate in the church basement at long picnic tables. After a while, I began to recognize faces, and sometimes we talked, but mostly people kept to themselves. What I remember clearest about those dinners was one night sitting across from a veiled young woman who carried a child wrapped in a blanket. The woman had skin like cream and blue eyes that were too open, like they didn't focus, but stared beyond things. I watched her throughout my dinner and wanted to say something but didn't, mostly because I didn't know what to say, but partly because there was something about her that made me afraid. Later, I wrote about seeing her and made up a story about chasing after her, but that never happened. When she left the table, I saw a tiny plastic arm stick out of the blanket she cradled and I was glad I kept my mouth shut.

Since those dinners were the only thing I would eat during a day, I ate slowly. Most everyone else panhandled and had breakfast at the House of Pancakes, and lunch at burger joints, but I couldn't bring myself to beg, at least not on the street.

Eventually, I did beg to get out of there. On a rainy after-noon I sat in the Free Church talking to a thirty-five-year-old Navaho from New Mexico. He told me how the past winter had been bitter in the Southwest, but when the government sent in prefabricated houses and supplies to freezing Indians, they piled them up and burned them. While he told me the story, someone brought a box of used clothing into the church, and the dozen streets who were there tore through the box like raccoons in a garbage can. The winter in Berkeley had been cold and wet, and those people were forced to take whatever was in the box to keep warm and forced to the Free Church for a roof over their head, while I told myself a series of choices had brought me. I had chosen to wear my hair long, had chosen my $1.50 trench coat because I liked it, and chosen my boots because they fit (though by then they had holes the size of fifty-cent pieces). The choices were slipping away from me though, and soon my boots would be completely worn and someday there wouldn't be a free dinner. Besides, I still thought there might be ways I could change things.

XIII

IN the afternoon, the rains came. Tano and I dropped under the tarps while Glück wrapped himself in plastic, pulled down his cap, and plugged on. I slept, curled up like a snail, until the boat jolted me into a vague wakefulness. I looked at Tano and the river and the old man and slowly pieced my reality together, but the break left me disconnected.

We passed a series of islands, cut to the right across smaller channels of curent, and slipped into a lagoon on the south shore of the main river. We pitched camp and took a swim, but as Glück made dinner, the rains returned, hard, and we took cover in the pods.

The showers passed in a few minutes and we had dinner, then Tano and I went out and sat by the edge of the river. Our camp looked more like a South Pacific beach. We had tied the boat to a tree stump in a shallow lagoon and strung our hammocks to feather palms. Across the lagoon, a swamp had sunk a swatch of jungle and in the clearing the sun set and flocks of colored birds, mostly parrots, squawked and crisscrossed the sky as if it were a loom. One bird I couldn't see sang in a voice that

88

sounded like a stream of water dripping from the top of trees into a cistern that echoed the rapid *ploploploploplop.*

The river was wide and smooth and looked dead, like a lake frozen black in winter, but when we threw in a stick, it was swept down and out of sight.

Glück came down to talk. He had taken out his false teeth so his words hissed through his gums.

"I'm always happy when out of Manaus," he said. "When I first went there in 1959 it was a beautiful city, but now it is terrible. I asked the mayor to ban cars from the city, but he didn't listen."

Glück told stories about Indians who lived like monkeys in trees and then said he was tired and went back to camp. It was the first night of the full moon, so Tano and I stayed by the river. Behind us, trees dripped from the rain.

"I've felt so comfortable out here in this jungle," Tano said, "I still do, but today, I started getting an eerie feeling."

"Yeah, I felt that, too. Maybe it's us being between this big, open river and sky. There are fewer and fewer people."

"And fewer rubber worker huts."

"We're pushing out farther toward an edge, and today I felt sort of lonely."

"Lonely?"

"Well, outside of everything, my past, the States."

"That makes you feel lonely and not good?" Tano said.

"Well, lonely in the sense that it makes me feel alone," I said, trying to define a blank, dreamy afternoon in a word I couldn't find.

"Well, alone, OK," Tano said. "I get the feeling, too, as there are fewer of these rubber worker huts, one of these days we're going to see people standing on the shore, staring at us, and they're going to be oogah boogs. We're getting out there, now.

"This river suits me fine," he said.

It felt good to me, too, even if it did make me feel alone that day; then again, most places outside the States felt good. When I was younger, when I was first out and taking trips like the one with Donald, the perfectness of moving seemed like it had come into my life on schedule. I expected things would stay in motion awhile, then fade into something else, though I didn't know what the something else would be, but it had not shown any signs of that. As much as it had on me, I thought moving might have had an even stronger hold on Tano. He had dropped out of college when I stayed, had changed his name a few times, and made a point of not getting yoked with a definition. When we traveled together, and met people who asked what we did for a living, Tano always answered, "I'm just a laborer," and later, after I had asked, he said, "No matter what I do, that's all I'm ever gonna say."

But that night, by the lagoon, he surprised me and made me sad.

"I don't know, man, sooner or later this traveling is going to be burned out of me. I'm gonna want to settle down, maybe get a piece of land, maybe do something like raise horses."

"I still get the itch pretty strong," I said. "I thought maybe I would have got over that by now, but I guess not."

"Oh, I'll still want to take trips now and then," he said. "It's just sometimes you get tired of the constant shit you have to go through."

I tried to keep myself from thinking about it, but I wondered whether the Amazon would be our last trip together.

Once, after Tano and I first met, we spent most of one evening walking. When it was about three o'clock in the morning and we had walked a long way, we ended up on an overpass above the highway that connected New York and San Francisco. It was windy and cold, but I had my coat open and we stood there and watched the cars speeding in both directions. Even at that time of night, they still were out there. We didn't say much, just watched the lights and cars roar by in an echo of rubber and cement and spinning metal that began as a distant hush, the way wind sounds in pine trees, then whistled louder until it broke beneath us and crossed from the past into the future. Then it died, to the same kind of whisper it had when it started and then it was gone. We stayed and listened a long time. It happened again and again, and I knew even when I left, whenever I wanted to, I could always hear those whispers.

My parents tell me that when I was four they could keep me

90

quiet in the afternoon by turning on the television and having me watch "American Bandstand." As they say, I would sit there for a half hour or whatever it was and be captivated by all those bodies swinging around inside that box, bopping to that rock-and-roll music. I do remember some years later when Chubby Checker hit. I loved watching the twist.

When I first hooked up with Tano, we were terrible about movement.

"I can't stand stopping," he once told me. "It takes me a week or something to get across the country and then when I'm there, maybe a day or so, I'm crazy again to get going. Somethin's in my bones."

I knew what he meant. When we first knew each other and we were mostly stopped but taking midnight walks, once in a while we would say being stopped was like "stagnant waters"— joe college for going stir crazy.

"In a way, I hope some of this stuff burns out," Tano had said. "Or else, I'll really go crazy."

That was only half true, as we both loved the going. When I thought about it then, I thought that might have had a lot to do with death.

"When you're dead, you're dead-stopped," I once had heard. Somehow it became important not only to keep going, but to keep going faster, and then even more important to go even faster. Then again, the faster you went, the more of a risk you took in dead-stopping.

I once met a French climber in Peru. He was nineteen years old and we met at a Peruvian trading camp in the Andes, north of Lima. The Frenchman was there to climb Huascarán, the highest peak in Peru, and then hang-glide down. When he told me what he planned to do, I laughed, and he laughed, and when I ask him how dangerous it might be, he shrugged. He said he had been climbing since he was a boy and never had been in a serious accident, and besides, he thought he was lucky. His face did not have a line on it, and when he spoke, his eyes were as open as a fish's. He was tall and lanky and when he walked, he took big, swooping steps that hit the ground as if he had suction cups on his feet, the way Spiderman would have walked. When you

watched him, you had the feeling he never had stumbled. He reminded me of what a friend who ran a mountaineering school in
Wyoming told me.

"Sometimes these young bucks come here and they never
have taken a fall, and they go around like they can walk on water.
They have no idea that sooner or later they're gonna die, and for
a while, that works."

I met the French climber the day I turned twenty-five. I felt
a lot older than he, which felt both good and bad, but mostly
good. I knew what it was like to be scared of dying and what it
was like not to be scared. It was more fun not to be, but I didn't
mind hanging on to some of the being scared part. That kept an
edge on things.

Two or three weeks after I met the Frenchman, I returned,
after a trip south, to Lima. When I walked into my hotel, I noticed the front page of a newspaper lying on a chair, and a front-
page picture of the Frenchman floating down out of the mountains on his hangglider, Icarus on a kite. Inside the paper, there
was an interview with him, and a close-up picture, and there he
was, smiling that same broad, twinkly smile.

"Remember that first trip we took together to Florida?" I
asked Tano on the river.

"Oh, man . . . Somehow that one set a pattern for all the
others. We were arrogant sons-of-bitches and then got our faces
slapped down."

Florida was a turning point. After the night at Duke, the one
I talked about earlier, the one in the tree, we drove to Savannah,
Georgia, where we found an empty lot beside an apartment
building, parked Tano's car, and hitchhiked south. Hitching in
southern Georgia was clear-cut. People either gave us a ride or
they gave us the finger. My hair was long then and Tano's was
past his shoulders, which I guess accounted for the fingers and
once for a group of kids in the back of a pickup truck who gave
us the peace sign. It took us long enough to get through Georgia
so the fingers outnumbered the rides by ten to one, but fast
enough so that none of the fingers could double back and give
us something worse, which in those *Easy Rider* days, I feared.

In Florida, the tone of welcome changed from animosity or
goodwill to indifference as carloads of sunglassed faces raced

past, pretending not to look at us, which left us feeling transparent and pining for Georgia, where at least we felt alive. Originally, we had hoped to go to southern Florida, possibly the Keys, but the state was deceiving in its size and to get as far as Miami would take more than a couple of hours from the border. After three hours at the same on-ramp north of Jacksonville, we decided to cut the rest of the trip in half and shoot for Daytona. It still took most of the day, but by late afternoon we walked onto Daytona Beach and threw down our bags.

The next few minutes could have risen from a college kid's fantasy about a trip to Florida, but I am pulling it out of the side of my brain that catalogs memories of real things. As Tano and I emptied sand from our shoes and took off our shirts, a pretty twentyish, bikinied girl with blond hair, white teeth, small breasts but nice legs, and a tan that meant she had been there awhile, bounded over to pick up a volleyball that had rolled to my feet.

"Hey, where you guys from?" she said.

I looked around to see if we were going to be part of one of those "Muscleman rescues girl and pounds skinny guy into sand" scenes, but the volleyball didn't seem to come from any game as far as I could see, so it felt safe to answer, which we did. We exchanged names and she told us she was beginning her second week in Daytona and then said, "Have you got a place to stay?"

When I was in high school in New Jersey and the guys and I went to the shore, I had her lines in the beach scene, but I never got much farther than "Do you have a light?" which was worse than it sounds as I didn't smoke much then and if they ever did have a light, I would have been forced to choose between choking or pretend smoking. Only once did I get as far as getting a match, and my victim said, "Here's a pack of matches, keep 'em," and turned around and continud reading her book. Things seemed a lot easier in Daytona.

"No, we just got here," one of us said, then before Tano or I could look at each other, she said, "I've got room, come on up," and she picked up her ball, and kicking sand behind her, ran toward a motel with palm trees and a pool.

Very, very slowly, Tano turned and said, "I don't believe this," then very, very quickly we put our shoes back on, repacked our gear, and followed her.

Her room was poolside, had an open cooler with ice and beer, women's clothing on the floor, a wet bikini hanging from a lampshade, overflowing ashtrays which dotted the floor, and one large, made double bed.

"It's not much, but I've been here a week and so far the hotel manager's been cool. Put your stuff down," she said as she walked into the bathroom.

I made a move to drop my bags on the bed, but Tano's eyes caught fire and he pointed to the floor where he had dropped his sleeping bag, which was supposed to mean I should drop mine in the same place and we would settle the other thing later. I did, drop my bag, and later, we did, settle the other thing.

"There's no key," she said as she came out of the bathroom, "but everyone around here's cool."

We weren't complaining. Then she said, "Well, back to the beach, see you guys later," which deflated us a bit, but then there was always the later.

It was getting late in the day and we were hungry so we walked toward the boardwalk and tried to figure out the thing we said we would figure out back in the bedroom.

"You son-of-a-bitch," Tano said.

"Well, I was standing right next to the bed."

"Well, golly, I was standing right next to the bed," he mimicked. "So what? I was standing on her underwear."

"Then you could've slept in it." I shrugged.

"Well, you ain't getting away with it that fast, man," he said.

We argued through hot dogs and orange juice and later we argued when we sat on a bench on the boardwalk, beside a guy who had an American flag sewn to the seat of his pants. We kept arguing after two cops with billy clubs hauled the guy with the flag pants away, and when Tano mumbled "pigs," I thought the cops were going to decide the argument in my favor, but thankfully they didn't hear him.

When we got back to arguing, which wasn't really arguing, just expressions of who really deserved the bed, with deserved being based on abstinence and raggediness, qualities that had us running neck-and-neck, we decided to flip a coin. Tano flipped, I called, and I won.

"Sheeeit," Tano said in a way that as I got to know meant

he was trying to spit the word. "She still has a say in this," he said, which was the right thing to say as it was an element that had eluded us.

I don't think I gloated, but if I did, I shouldn't have. We got back to the motel in the early evening, but it already was too late. The door was open and someone had a tape deck blaring and inside there were about fifteen people, mostly male, with our friend sitting cross-legged on her bed, a beer in one hand, a joint in another, and face-down bodies of undetermined sex beside her.

"Hey, everybody, here's two more of my friends," and a show of hands waved through the smoke. "C'mon in, you guys,"

It was a long night. At some point, I fell asleep at the corner of the bed where for what seemed hours I kept vigil in hopes that the world would leave. It didn't. Tano had staked out a piece of the floor and, with his head in the closet and his feet stretching into the room, passed out long before most of the crowd. I woke before dawn, tapped Tano on the shoulder, and convinced him, not easily, to leave. Later that day, we heard the hotel manager had lost his legendary cool and got the police and cleared everyone out, so at least, we said, we felt a step ahead of things.

I spent most of the morning on the beach, catching up on the sleep I missed, but near noon, I decided to take a jaunt and visit an aunt and uncle who lived close to Daytona. I started hitching out, and by midafternoon I had traveled about five miles, all on foot.

After I gave up and was walking back through a black shantytown, still with my thumb out, I passed a couple of kids, about twelve or thirteen years old, playing basketball at a netless hoop on the side of a garage. They stopped when they saw me and the shorter of the two yelled the obvious.

"Man, you ain't gonna get no rides 'round here, white boy."

I wish I could remember I made a quick reply, but it took me a while to piece together an answer that wasn't much of an answer at all.

"Maybe," I said, "but neither are you gonna sink a basket from right where you're standing," which was about fifteen feet from the hoop, and which he turned around and did.

"Man, white boy, you shouldn't be talkin' like that in this

95

part town," which probably was true. "You're a big boy, but you ain't big enough," which no doubt, was truer.

"Why don't you come over here and take us on," he said. I stopped and thought about it, but only for a second or two.

After I sank a few, I told them my cousin was Jerry West, and after they sank a few, they told me their uncle was Wilt Chamberlain, so we all understood each other and things went well.

We split two games of 21, which was how I decided to leave things, and out on the street, I started walking again with my thumb back out and they waved and then flashed me a peace sign and doubled up, laughing.

"Come back sometime, white boy," the little guy said, "and bring Jerry with you."

It was almost dark when I got back, and Tano was asleep with his hat covering his face, and just about alone, except for a few nearby cars.

"You've been doing what?" he said, after I woke him and told him where I had been. I repeated what I had said and seeing the conversation was going nowhere, changed the subject to our erstwhile lady friend and her room full of friends and Tano gave me the news about their getting the boot.

"Well, we'd better find us a place to stay," he said, and checking our resources, which had gone from not much to hardly any, we made the quick decision to head south and camp on the beach. Daytona, then, as it was when I was growing up in Florida, and maybe still is today, was famous for permitting cars on the beach. People drove just above the water's edge and during the day, if you wanted to take a swim, you were forced to look both ways. I found that annoying, but I got used to it, and then after we decided to camp, I even appreciated the traffic as for the first and probably only time in my life, I hitched on the beach. Even better, the guy in the first car to pass stopped and gave us a lift.

I don't remember the guy or his car, but I do remember a few miles down he stopped and we made a fire and he took out what he said was a "bong," a water pipe he stuffed with seaweed and hashish.

A full moon crept out of the ocean early that night and I

96

took off my clothes and went swimming for what seemed like a long time, which took nothing off the edge of my bong, which was the way the guy with the car described what the bong was supposed to do for you. When I came out of the sea, Tano was on a sand dune, his arms outstretched at the ten and two o'clock positions, as if he was going to fly. The moon was shining on him and he was glistening and he was howling and I ran up and did similar things. Gradually our howls became words the world of the God-fearing would describe as sacrilegious or blasphemous. They were the kinds of things I remembered hearing the Archangel Michael said when he decided to take on God, only I think ours were even more arrogant. We stayed on those dunes awhile, at least it seemed that way, until the moon was nearly above us, then we called for whomever or whatever to strike us down if they dared, which whomever or whatever, being smarter than that, didn't do just then. They stretched out our punishment. For years.

"Man, we were so fucking young and stupid and arrogant," Tano said, taking a last drag from his cigarette and flicking the butt into the river, which immediately swept it into the night.

"I know," I said, something we could have said years earlier, because we already knew, and even if we didn't say it to each other, because we never talked about the night on the sand dunes, we each had at least said it to ourselves.

I don't remember going to sleep that night in Daytona, but I do remember waking up. It was a couple of hours before dawn. The sky had clouded and a harsh wind came off the sea. I was in a sleeping bag, a thin, Dacron-filled one with mobile Dacron that had shifted and clustered in pockets and left major sections of the bag an empty polyester shell. I curled into fetal position to keep warm and ducked my head down into the bag. I still felt the wind whip through and I started to shake. That might have been the aftereffects of the bong, though I attributed it to the cold. The wind got stronger and my shaking started to take on a rhythm I developed into a burrowing technique as I turned, twisted, and gradually began to sink in the sand. Finally, after hours of squirming, while the wind only got stronger, I lifted my head out of the bag, half out of disbelief and half out of surrender.

As things sometimes happen, at the same moment, Tano,

who was about four feet from me, did the same. I first saw his hair, then the top of his head, then his forehead and his eyes and his whole face which was about the way he might have seen me. It was like we were jack-in-the-boxes on slow springs. each of us lifting out at the same time, then for a moment, staring at each other. Sand blew all around us and we had to squint to see, which Tano did with his nose and mouth shriveled, the same way I knew I must have. The wind was so strong, we would have had to shout to talk, but there was no need for that, anyway. Tano had a stubble of beard and his hair was in knots and there was sand on his face, and for all the world, he looked like a rat. He must have seen the same thing, because we both started laughing, then ducked back into our holes and weathered the rest of the night.

I will never forget the way he looked and the way I felt when we stuck our heads into that night, and remembering that, I suppose, is something like keeping the corner of a sole of a shoe you were forced to eat.

XIV

THINGS continued in the same vein for the next day, and for that matter, the following few days. It rained the first day, which we spent in, or actually beside and under Daytona, with our backs against wet rocks beneath a pier. We met two other guys beneath the pier. They spooked us. One looked like Tano, only five to ten years older, and the other looked like me, aged the same amount. One of them took a picture of us and said he was going to use it for a hobo calendar and he would send us a copy, but we never saw them again.

Occasionally Tano or I would wander out from under the pier and go on reconnaissance missions and come back with food, which, because of finances, primarily consisted of Fig Newtons. Somehow I had been convinced, and managed to convince Tano, although he took it somewhat reluctantly, that Fig Newtons were the most life-sustaining food we could consume, so they became a staple of any traveling we did together. Wherever we went after Daytona, Tano would kid me about making sure that no matter what happened, we would hang on to enough money to buy a box of Fig Newtons.

When we left Daytona, it took most of a day to get to Jacksonville, where we decided to find the state university and its resident hippies, who in turn, we believed, would give us a place on the floor for the night. We were wrong. If Daytona was how we saw Our Fall, Jacksonville gave us a glimpse of other things to come.

By the time Tano and I reached Jacksonville, our hitchhiking experience had given us confidence to make generalities about traveling. One was that no matter where you were, a hippie, if he had room in his car, always stopped and gave another hippie a ride. That may say less about Tano's and my ability at making generalities than it did about our lack of understanding human nature. Still, until Jacksonville, it mostly had held true.

I don't know how many cars, but it was at least two hours' worth, with dozens and dozens and dozens of long-haired and bearded faces with a lot of empty room beside them, passing us before Tano said, "Man, what is going on?"

I certainly didn't know other than I knew I was getting depressed, which Tano apparently was getting, too, as enough beards and ponytails had driven by to warrant our slipping them the finger when it was obvious they weren't going to stop.

Eventually, we did get a ride, from a short-haired, hot-rodding high school kid whom Tano immediately asked, "How come no one stops around here to give rides?" to which the kid replied, "I don't know. I did."

He drove us to the front of the university, we thanked him, then mumbled to ourselves as we walked to the dormitories and looked closely at each other in case we were missing something obvious. Whatever it was, it hung with us.

Inside, no matter where we went, from lounges to laundry rooms to empty corners at the dead end of hallways—the sure places—we were told we could not stay, and told, more often than not, by people we would say looked like hippies. Tano even got so desperate as to make friends with some hippie types in the snack bar, and after an exchange of cigarettes and rock 'n' roll small talk, asked them outright if we could sleep on the floor of their room or if they knew a place we could stay for one night. The answer did not come in a direct and simple, "No," but in an "It wouldn't be cool" kind of lingo that turned the color in Tano's face and had him longing for the Midwest.

100

"Makes me want to puke," he said later. "At least folks back where I come from, when they don't like your face or don't want you or whatever, they tell it to you straight."

It was near midnight when we gave up, and just after midnight when we gave up hitching out. It hardly seemed we had walked out of sight from campus when we came to a wooded area, climbed a fence, then walked to what looked like an open meadow where we unrolled our sleeping bags. It was cloudy and dark and the ground felt like someone's lawn, though we couldn't see a house nearby, so we didn't worry much about it, and since we were exhausted, fell immediately to sleep.

In the middle of the night, drops of water began to splat on my face and although I didn't look at Tano, I mumbled, "Here we go again. All we needed was rain," and once more, slipped my head down in my sleeping bag and curled up. It was a miserable night. By morning it still was coming down and my bag and I were soaked. I knew it was morning because the sun was shining through the parts of my bag vacated by the Dacron, which at first didn't strike me as odd because I was more concerned with how cold I felt. Finally, around the time I decided I'd had enough, the question of rays of sun passing through my bag during a continuous downpour rose to a conscious-enough level to demand an answer. I stuck my head out, and with water spraying my face, laughed.

"What are you doing?" Tano said from somewhere in the middle of his bag.

"We're on a golf course, in fact, we're on a green," I said. "It hasn't been raining. The sprinklers have been on."

The trip through Georgia went almost as fast as the one down, though we both wished it could have gone faster. We spent one afternoon at the northern edge of a town, I think it was called Riceboro, where a pickup truck with three middle-aged men in the front cab passed us and gave us the finger and yelled out something hospitable like, "Get de fug outta hair, hippuhs."

We half smiled, as politely as we could, and hoped someone would help us do exactly what the three gentlemen suggested. For ten or fifteen minutes a few cars passed, but no one stopped, then the three guys in the truck drove back in the opposite direction, toward town.

"Kenchya heeyuh?" they said, their voices trailing into a "fug out."

"Oh, man," one of us said. "They're gonna be back in a while and it's getting dark."

There maybe was an hour of light left and Tano and I began to yearn for Florida, where people ignored us. For a few minutes, we thought about quitting hitching for the day and crawling out of town and hiding the night in the pines, but I had a vision of those three guys with suspenders and Redman Tobacco pouches sticking out their shirt pockets, Jack Daniel's on their breath, dogs in front of them, a mob behind, and guns and a rope under their arms, so more out of fear than bravery, I said, "Let's stick it out until dark."

As soon as I said that, we saw in the distance, maybe a third of a mile away, the blue pickup truck coming, and as it got closer, I thought I saw extra pairs of arms waving out the back. Before it reached us, it had to pass through a stoplight. That gave us a moment to panic. One of us said something about running when I turned around and saw a car parked about thirty yards north of us, with some guy blowing its horn and waving us to come. We never ran so fast.

I didn't remember seeing the car pass, but it must have, I guess. Two guys in their mid-twenties were in the front seat and we quickly climbed in the back and they, not so quickly, got back on the road before they asked us where we were going.

"North," we said, looking back at the pickup, which was one car and 50 yards behind. Tano and I didn't tell our driver about the posse, for fear we might be thrown out, just watched out the back window until the pickup pulled off the road. They had followed for about ten minutes, enough time, I imagined perhaps romantically, for us to reach the county line.

Early in the evening, we stopped at a fast-food joint where, because it was St. Patrick's Day, they were serving green milk shakes. It seemed to be a good time to have a green milk shake and I ordered one, and a black kid, about sixteen, served me. He had on a derby and a shamrock on his chest that read, "I'm glad to be Irish." I smiled when I read it and he caught my eye, shrugged his shoulders, and looked over at a burly young white guy who obviously was the boss. I paid for my shake, then as I

102

was walking out, flashed him the peace sign, which he returned, holding his fingers beside the cash register where the boss couldn't see.

Two days later, we and Tano's car were safely in Washington, D.C. We stopped to visit a friend of Tano's, whom he had spent some time with the previous summer. It rained the two days we were there. We stayed in an apartment that had high ceilings and foggy-colored walls, and in the gray light of dismal days the place felt cold and like a cave. Tano's friend was rarely there, he seemed to spend most of his time at a university, like a real student, studying, which thankfully made me feel like less of a real student. Tano and I spent most of our time in the cave, smoking cigarettes and listening to old Beatles' music. I don't remember anything else about the cave and Washington except Tano talking about another friend he had met in Washington. The friend's name was Joe.

Joe was about our age, Tano said, and he lived in and roamed the Washington sewers. Somehow, Tano and he hooked up, I think through the friend who rented the cave, and for a while Tano and Joe cruised together through the underground tunnels of Washington. Tano said little about Joe and what adventures the two had, other than saying, "Joe is the freest guy I know," which at the time was the highest accolade I could imagine. The guy who rented the cave didn't know where Joe was anymore, but that didn't bother Tano. He already had plans to see Joe the upcoming summer, in San Francisco, in front of City Lights bookstore, on June 1 at high noon.

Tano made it out there on schedule. He stayed with my girl, the one I had gone running across the country after, and he half fell in love with her. She was an old girl friend by then as, à la Joe, I was trying to achieve a freer state of being, but Tano said, "Man, she's as honest as a dog. She's still nuts about you. Why? I don't know." I never thought I got the whole story from Tano about his visit with her, and back then, if there was more of a story, it was probably better I only got a partial one. I was trying for the freer state of things, but there definitely was an underside of things where I was vulnerable.

Anyway, Tano stayed with her, and on June 1, he crossed the Bay into San Francisco, about two hours ahead of schedule, and waited for Joe. By midafternoon, Joe had not arrived, so Tano went inside City Lights and asked if there had been any messages, but there were none and he went back to Oakland.

I always felt bad for Tano about the business with Joe.

"Did you ever find out what happened to him?" I asked Tano on the river.

"Never."

XV

WHEN we went to our hammocks there were only wisps of clouds in the sky. Maybe I slept an hour before a mosquito biting me on the shoulder woke me and in the distance I heard what sounded like a locomotive. For ten minutes, I listened to it get closer, then crickets quieted and the mosquitoes stopped whining and the rains came, rumbling across the track of trees.

It was a deluge. I pulled the tarp over my head, but it wasn't taut and my left side leaked and the down in the bag soaked up water. Gusts of wind rocked my hammock, and the trees bent, sounding like creaking in the hull of a ship.

In the morning, it still was raining. My skin was wrinkled from sleeping in the sponge, and when I moved, my pod squished. Glück got up before us and had coffee going, but we decided to pack and try to eat on the river. We shoved off, with Glück singing some German "la da dee da daa" song, and for the next couple of hours, moved in a light drizzle. By afternoon, the sun returned and we quilted our gear across the boat to dry, while beside us porpoises broke the water in a puff that sounded like distant shotgun blasts.

We stopped for a swim on a sandbar and found big cat

prints leading back into the jungle. If it is the bear and particularly the grizzly who reigns over North American forests, it is the big cats—the panther and jaguar—who rule the forests of the Amazon. A friend who worked in Alaska for a year said conversations there, from restaurants to cocktail parties to campfire talk, always touched on the bear.

"I thought about it a lot," he said, "and it's like the boogie woogie man, or the big bad wolf—some kind of mythic holdover, a fear of the beast in the forest. Everyone talks about what kind of rifle or shotgun you should carry, the shot you should use, and the timing—how close you should let the bear get and when you should pull the trigger. The only thing people seem to talk more about up there are car accidents and everyone seems to know one person who was maimed or killed."

In the Amazon, it is the same, only you are told to carry guns because of the panthers and jaguars that stand on rocks and leap on people in passing boats. Glück was adamant about not taking weapons, saying they would get you into much more trouble than they would keep you out of, which was fine by me. Still, everyone said we were loco for not carrying guns.

It was settling to see the cat prints. I had been out of the States for only a week, but I still was not in the Amazon. Things had not slowed down enough. I was more aware of myself and my reactions and less of engaging things, none of which was helped by riding between that big river and sky. That wasn't new for me. In places where I had lived before, it always took a while for me to order things, to move them from the distant and strange and rearrange them into the familiar. Part of it seemed to be focus.

The year before I went to the Amazon, I worked for a newspaper in the San Joaquin Valley in central California. My only contact with the Valley prior to that had been driving on its edge on the interstate. When I first came into town, I remembered thinking how everything seemed blurred. I took things in, but they would not hold. Maybe it has something to do with going places in a car where speed tends to make colors and shapes run together. I had the sense of a freeway off-ramp, a strip of fast-food restaurants, a tower above an old movie theater, splotches of green, and then a maze of boxes around a swimming pool that made up something called a garden apartment complex. I passed those things for months as I and they both changed shapes. I seemed to grow larger and more expansive, while buildings got smaller and closer. Still, I always remembered how wide the streets felt that first day and how huge a supermarket was and how blank were the walls in my bedroom.

The way I figured, it took me awhile to adjust to a light myself and the outside world shared. Things were illuminated by a combination of sources, no doubt the strongest of which was me. The trick always had been to keep the me side of light to a minimum and at the same time continue to see.

When we stopped to swim and I saw the cat print in the sand, I felt the river and the jungle fill their forms. The print was soft and the sand moist, and I wondered if the cat had watched us pull to the shore and was watching us now. We were nude. Tano and I rarely wore clothes and Glück was almost as ready to shed his, although he usually kept a pair of shorts and shirt on when we were in the boat.

I walked in the water, along the edge of the sandbar, my feet sliding along the bottom, a walking technique I had picked up from one of Glück's Shtoopidity Lessons. He had warned us that stingrays were "much danger" and aside from wearing high boots, the only defense was to push your feet along the bottom of the river, rather than lifting and walking. If you stepped on a stingray, it would slap its tail in defense and send you into two weeks of delirium. Glück had stepped on a ray a few years back, and Indians he was with quickly stuck his foot in a fire and fried the poison.

"That was lucky," he said. "Instead of fifteen days fever, I had five."

I had my first run-in with a stingray just after I saw the cat print, but I had been dragging my feet and spotted the ray at the end of a slide of my foot, which pushed sand against him and he scooted into deeper water.

The rest of the afternoon we looked for Ilha Saudage, the Isle of Homesickness Glück called it, at the mouth of the Rio Padauiri. We planned to take the Padauiri north to the mountains and the pyramids.

It might seem impossible to miss the mouth of a major river, but being on the Rio Negro was like walking along a string under a microscope, with thousands of hairs scattering in either direction. Rains and drought changed the shape of junctions, lifting islands up and down out of the water and fragmenting forks into deltas and backwaters. We rarely turned and went directly up anything, but rather prodded possibilities, checking the strength of the current, color of water, and width of channels to match the way the river or tributary or stream had looked five years earlier during the dry season when our aerial pictures were shot. If nothing else, the Amazon was a lesson in flux.

We camped in a hut on a bluff on the south shore of Saudage. Glück prepared a special dinner, "joongle pancakes," light crepes made from flour, milk, and eggs, and cooked in lots of oil. They were *vunderbar*. Tano and I gobbled the three or four Glück served us, but Tano still was hungry, which left Glück amazed.

"Four should be enough" Glück said. "I don't need more than that."

I didn't pay attention to the remark, and only remember it because Tano repeated it as we took an after-supper swim.

"Shit, man, I was hungry," he said.

"Well, if he can last on three or four of those things, I can," I said, which was a stupid thing to say.

"Come on, I'm not here for no endurance test," Tano said, which wasn't a bad way to respond to a stupid thing.

We swam out and climbed up the bluff and sat on a makeshift wooden bench. The bench had its back facing the river and sunset, I don't know why, so Tano and I took the back off and sat in what we thought was a proper direction. Below us, four avenues of water spilled into the main river, and on the horizon, clouds burned the color of apricots in three different places, as if there were a trinity of setting suns.

Glück came up and while Tano and I argued about where the real sunset was, Glück tried to figure the map.

"It's crazy," Glück said. "I cannot understand. On the map, it's so big, the river, but we have to find it, no? ... Ah, so, the sky ... all colors. But now I want to see the shtars."

Dragonflies danced along the bank and a hawk perched in a tree near the bench. Birds with lilting staccato voices and long hoots that skipped octaves sang so loud it was difficult to hear each other talk, but as the sky darkened and the first stars granted Glück's wish, the birds quieted and then the insects and frogs and monkeys took over and peeped and croaked and screeched and said whatever they had to say.

I smoked a cigar to celebrate the night and Glück said he used to smoke a pipe from six in the morning until midnight, but then a doctor told him his throat looked like the inside of a chimney, so he gave it up.

"So, now you whistle," I said. "That's good. Your whistling is like we have a radio."

We talked until the moon rose and Glück said the next day we would pass the equator, "then we will have a baptism."

An hour after we broke camp, we found the mouth of the Rio Padauiri, which Glück called the Painted River. We turned right and headed north and a few miles after its junction with the Negro, it forked, with the Padauiri to the right and the Rio Praeto to the left. We stopped and took a swim and Glück tried fishing. He tied a lure to his line, took it in his right hand, and whirled it as if it were a lasso, letting the line run out until it swept a 12-foot circle. Sea swallows flew up and chased the lure, then Glück let loose. He was nude and when he let go, his body stopped and tilted a moment, an old man against the clouds, caught in the frieze of a discus thrower. The birds scattered and the line hit the water in a splash the current quickly erased. Glück wound it in on a piece of board, but the fish apparently were uninterested in friezes.

Dolphins circled each other at the fork of the rivers and tossed as if they were fighting, but Glück guessed that because it was spring and the time of the full moon, they probably were mating, though to me, it looked more like a rumpus.

Glück interrupted my musings. "There is a man who they call King of the Padauiri," he said. "His name is Lacerda. He lives above Allianca"—where we were heading. "The Eendyun work for him. They collect piacaba, the fine fibers from palm trees. It is used to make ball bearings. It is big business here. When I went up to the pyramids with the Austrian, we stayed with Lacerda and he cooked a wild pig. Maybe we will meet him."

After Glück gave up fishing, we headed north. The Padauiri is brown like the Solimões, the main artery of the Amazon, but

109

sometimes the color verged on yellow, which Glück called "jel-luf." Glück kept as much of an eye on the colors of the painted river as he did on his watch, but if he missed noticing a change, Tano would say, "Hey, Kurt, the river is jelluf again," and Glück would answer, "Ah, so."

The Padauiri also was comfortably narrower than the Rio Negro. Where on the Negro it was at times miles to shore, and the jungle looked like green ribbons, on the Rio Padauiri, it was only fifty yards wide near its mouth and the green ribbons grew to green walls. It made you feel more closed in, but more in contact. The only thing I worried about was that with brown water, I expected more mosquitoes. On the brown Rio Solimões, mosquitoes are much worse than on the black water Rio Negro. The continuous explanation I got for that was that black water was a mystery, though scientists speculated it was caused by different vegetation decaying in the Rio Negro basin.

Glück whistled "The Daring Young Man on the Flying Trapeze," and I thought how he would say mosquitoes "make nuhzing" so I forgot about them and followed the map and the bends in the river until at one o'clock we figured we had crossed the equator.

"We should take a dip and come into the Northern Hemisphere clean," Glück said, "but we'll save the baptism until later."

There were sun showers in the afternoon and we saw a sandbank covered with thousands of green and yellow butterflies that took flight when we passed, looking as if the wind had lifted cuttings of spring grass.

"What is the Portuguese word for butterflies?" I asked.

"Borboleta," Glück said. "What is the French word?"

"Papillon," Tano said.

"You know this book called *Papillon?"* Glück asked. "When it first came out, a German publishing company sent me a copy. They wanted my comment. 'It must be booshit,' I said. I lived in Venezuela when Papillon supposed to live there with the Eendyuns. He said the Eendyuns gave him a horse, but there are no horses there." He paused. "Oh, yes, and then if they kept money in their asshole for each escape, the French authorities would have found it. They must be shtoopid. Fifty percent of the book must be lies.

110

"All books about the Amazon must have Eendyuns attacking from the shore, wild jaguars leaping, and poison snakes. It's booshit. The only real danger is shtoopidity."

So, we expected the worst.

Tano asked about a book I had been reading, Peter Matthiessen's *The Snow Leopard.*

"It's about a trek," I said, "like the one we're taking, only it's in the Himalayas and it has a lot of stuff about zen and Buddha."

"Shit," he said. "Always has to have god or something for that literary gloss. Can't just write a book about riding up the river, looking at the trees. It won't sell."

The skies cleared and the sun hammered us and I didn't notice the trees. The river snaked back and forth, changing colors from brown to yellow to green but mostly staying jelluf.

Near evening, we found an empty hut and set up camp. I strung my hammock and immediately tumbled in, dizzy from the sun.

For dinner, Glück put canned Vienna sausages, which he called "sawcheechez," in pancakes, and Tano and I tried to explain the expression "pigs in a blanket" to him. He didn't seem to understand, but said, "Ah, so, yes."

As the moon rose, the current rippled the water into sparkling channels, like wobbly tusks of ivory. Tano and I hunched beside a candle by the sand, and I smoked a cigar for crossing the equator and we set up a jungle altar, with iodine, salt tabs, and vitamin B's to commemorate the event. The iodine was for drinking. As long as we were sure people were upstream, we put iodine in our water, and that night I used it to slug down my equatorial communion of four B tablets.

I had a good night's sleep and woke to a bright and cloudless morning that prompted Glück and Tano to develop a litany.

"When angels make trip, the sky is smiling," Glück said. "Even when it rains on us, that's because the sky smiles so hard it makes tears."

"No, the angels are pissing on us," Tano said.

A pause.

"I can't understand why we can't see monkeys," Glück shouted over the engine noise. "There were so many monkeys before along this river."

"We are the only monkeys," Tano said.

111

Glück accelerated the engine.

There was a strong wind and I had to keep my hat tied tight to my head, but at least because of the sun, Tano and I sang Nat King Cole's song about summer, and Glück perked up again, slowed the engine and talked about his time during World War II, how he played tennis to hustle extra money and on weekends listened to his radio for opera from Carnegie Hall.

"Forty days out for us and who knows what will happen," he said. "Maybe Russia and the United States will blow themselves off the map. The next war, they should put all the leaders in the Sahara and have them fight among themselves."

Tano and I became friends in a shadow of a war, but that was a shadow in a line of shadows. For me, the Cuban missile crisis brought the first and biggest shadow home.

I remember my parents watching Kennedy's televised broadcast to announce the sighting of missiles in Cuba. I remember better the days that followed.

It seemed immediately the highway that ran through town and on down the length of Florida became a major troop transportation route. Even to get to town, we had to wait at the railroad tracks for what seemed hours, as trains loaded with soldiers and weapons and what I thought were missile launchers rumbled toward Miami.

The blockade trouble reached a head for me the night I was coming home with my father from town, and we heard over the radio that Soviet ships, destined for Cuba, were expected soon to meet American warships. My father said, "Tonight, we'll know what's going to happen."

In bed, I imagined the Soviet ships getting closer and closer, and a finger reaching for the trigger and I didn't want to fall asleep, because I wasn't sure I would wake up.

Things passed, but the fear never completely left, pumped by air raid drills at school and neighbors digging shelters. That worried me most because I didn't think I could stand being underground in the dark for months.

For a while, at the sound of sirens, I cringed and looked quickly to make sure it was twelve o'clock or a fire engine was on its way down the street.

XVI

MAYBE because of Glück talking about war and maybe because it was May 1, Tano and I talked about another May Day, nine years earlier.

Tano had called me a few days before. When I picked up the phone, he didn't identify himself, but immediately asked, "Well, are you going?" I had not heard from him in the six weeks since the Florida trip, and though we hadn't talked about the Washington demonstrations then because we didn't know about them, by the time he called, I knew what he was talking about and almost as immediately said, "Yeah, you?"

"Leaving tomorrow."

May Day would be on Saturday and since I had less distance to travel, I told him I would meet him sometime on the weekend. Our plans never got more definite than, "We'll just find each other."

The week before, I worked with an antiwar group in New York. I don't remember much about it, other than spending a lot of time in a loft in lower Manhattan, sorting through posters and news fliers and then handing them out on the street in the Village. One of the posters was reversible. On one side, there was a picture of a hippie couple at a campsite I assumed was supposed to be a park lawn in Washington, D.C. The couple wore scout uniforms, with the girl in short pants and knee socks. She held a North Vietnamese flag in her left hand and she was saluting whoever happened to be looking at her in the picture. Her pal held a boy scout pennant that said BE PREPARED and he clenched his fist in the air. They had their camping accoutrements displayed around them, the way outdoor gear would be advertised in a Sears catalog. They had a stand-up tent with a weathervane, and on the side, another flag, the Olympic flag, except the four circles beneath the flame were the biological male and female symbols. Beside the tent, they had parked their Volkswagen, which had a box on the hood that said PEOPLE'S PEACE TREATIES, and provisions, like sacks of corn, rice, potatoes, and almonds, leaning up against the car, along with a guitar case with a flower on it, and a stolen road sign that said DETOUR AHEAD. Assorted barricades and more flags and placards decorated the site, including a United Farm Worker sign, a placard that read IF THE GOVERNMENT WON'T STOP THE WAR, THE PEOPLE WILL STOP THE GOVERNMENT, and barely visible, a sign that said RIGHT LANE CLOSED AHEAD. Below the picture, the poster read, "May 1-7, Be Prepared!" while above the scouts, still in the frame of the photo, a rainbow had been painted across the sky, and written in large letters across it, DAWN ON THE POTOMAC. I don't think the Movement got enough credit for its sense of humor.

Maybe to balance that though, on the other side there was a picture of an Indian with a feather at the back of his head, just below the words "May Day." He had a scar on his right cheek and looked something like a photograph I remember of Geronimo. Beside him, written vertically along the length of the page, and written like a poem, was the statement:

> If our people
> fight
> one tribe
> at a time,
> all will be
> killed.
> they can

114

> cut off our fingers
> one by one
> but if
> we join together
> we will make a powerful fist

Then, below it, "Come to Washington, D.C. May 1–7." When I got there, that side of the poster seemed to be the theme.

I left for Washington on Friday night. I had watched Walter Cronkite's news earlier in the evening and at the end of his show, commentator Eric Sevareid came on to lambaste the upcoming May Day demonstrations as the work of misfits, hard-core revolutionaries, and anarchists who could not present any viable alternative to the American system. He might have slipped and said "vile" alternative, but I don't remember. At the time, his spiel bothered me. I thought he had miscategorized what I still saw as a peace movement in a way meant to frighten. He saw it as a lunatic fringe, a fringe that included me. I disliked his labels, but since then I have thought fondly of Mr. Sevareid's commentary and in a way I metamorphized through his labels.

After the news, I went to work at the campus snack bar, where I stayed until almost midnight. A friend, who was even taller, thinner, and had longer arms and legs than me, and who went by the name of Spider, came to visit. Spider asked me if I knew if anything was happening, a question I remember him asking whenever I saw him back then. For once, I altered the usual reply and said, "Yeah, a lot," and told him I was heading for D.C.

I wiped off tables and emptied ashtrays while Spider sat in a booth and thought about things for a while. When I was almost finished and heading toward the grill and dishes, Spider asked if it was OK if he went with me. Although I was going to see Tano, which I knew could mean anything could happen, I also felt messianic and I said sure.

Hitching to the Turnpike, we got a ride with a guy in his early twenties, close to six feet tall, with short, red hair and the arms of a gorilla. I immediately recognized him. Tino was a senior in high school when I was a freshman and he was a bit of a thug. He would not have remembered me, but everyone in my class, at least the males, remembered Tino. What is probably best

115

remembered about Tino is a trip he and his buddy Jack took to Florida in spring 1968.

They left around Easter break, but they also skipped a few days of school, which at the time I thought was ballsy in itself, but even more ballsy was taking off in their car on a thousand-mile trip south, which seemed like a great adventure when you're hearing about it as a fifteen-year-old.

When they came back, tales of their deeds spread, most about booze and fireworks and girls and high-speed chases with cops. They all could have been written off as unbelievable, but the one I had to believe, because it was unbelievable, was the story about the monkey.

Tino and Jack bought a monkey in Florida, one of the kind with the long tails, the ones that went with an organ grinder. Tino and Jack brought the monkey back with them, but at a motel in the Carolinas, they got in trouble. Somehow the hotel manager knew they were harboring a monkey in their room. The manager expected worse, so he called the police. Tino and Jack were under age for some of the things in their car, so to prove their innocence quickly and avoid notice of their gunpowder and liquor and whatever cargo, they took the monkey into the bathroom and flushed him down the toilet. The monkey wouldn't go all the way down at first, and stuck his head out and came back up in the wake of the flush, so the story went, so Tino or Jack yelled, "We're coming," to the cops, then one of them rolled up his sleeves and with the next flush, jammed the head of the monkey down and into the bowels of the Atlantic coast sewage system. And got away with it.

Sitting in the car on the way to the New Jersey Turnpike and Washington, D.C., I couldn't help but stare at Tino's hands, and think about the monkey sticking his head out of the toilet and Tino or Jack jamming him back down.

"Oh, I'm just going to school," I said when Tino asked me what I did. "And you?"

"Boxing," he said, so I looked again at his hands.

Later, I had heard Tino made a reputation for himself in Golden Gloves, but I never heard how far he went. Jack, I had heard, moved out of town, got married, and got a job.

I wanted to tell Tino I remembered him and ask him about

116

the monkey story and whether it was true, but for a while, he talked about going into the city and boxing and some kind of job he was holding down, so he sounded like he was working on the future and I thought it might be cruel to bring up the past.

He left me and Spider near the entrance to the Garden State Parkway that led to the Turnpike. I was happy for the ride and a little relieved to be out of the car, which he drove fast, and because I arrived safely, I was glad I didn't ask Tino about Jack or the monkey story, though now I kind of wish I had.

The rest of the night went almost as quickly. After a short wait and one or two brief rides, we got a ride with some hippies from Boston who were going to D.C. for the same reason. They drove a station wagon and smoked a lot of dope and played Lead Zeppelin on a cassette player that kept me only briefly awake. I slept most of the way, curled up around sleeping bags behind the backseat. Then, just like the poster said, dawn and the rest of us arrived over the Potomac.

The guys from Boston let us off near the Washington Monument, by the main demonstration campground, then went off to find a place to park, while Spider and I walked toward grass, in the same direction as throngs of other people.

It was great entertainment to be in a place with crowds of hippies. I guess a lot of people realized that, as later the generic name most often used in self-description by people with long hair changed to freaks, a name I thought was more appropriate. That was the way the multitudes pouring into Washington looked. Males wore anything from earrings, American Revolutionary uniforms, strings of tin cans, war paint, buckskins, boy scout uniforms, capes, high-topped sneakers, low-topped sneakers, no sneakers, knee-length army boots, rags, and, of course jeans. Females tended to be less flamboyant, mostly sticking to peasant dresses, bibbed overalls, short pants, some Indian suits, nothing—or variations on that theme—and, of course, jeans.

Although females rarely wore anything more than a band around their hair, males often had something more elaborate. If you wore something far out enough on your head, you didn't have to bother with much else, as that did the job in setting you on the counterculture side of the fence. Male headgear ranged from feathers to World War II helmets, Viking helmets with

117

horns, khaki fishing and baseball caps (I never saw football helmets), beanies with propellers, scarves, red and white bandannas tied pirate-style (a big favorite, particularly for those who thought themselves cool), bowlers (for those who thought themselves funny), berets (for those who thought themselves smart or un-American), or nothing (for those who thought themselves handsome).

I spotted Tano easily because of his cowboy hat, usually worn by those who thought themselves tough and wild, though with Tano the hat came first. Tano got his hat when he was a boy, inheriting it from an uncle who had died. It was a classic cowboy hat, though slightly smaller than most worn now, grayish-tan wool felt, rounded at the back, with a point at the front of the crown and a brim that wasn't too big or too small, but just right. By the time I knew Tano, the hat already had withstood a good ten year's battering, and almost a decade later, he still had it on the Amazon, though that turned out to be its last trip. Tano always had a small feather or two coming out of the band, vulture and eagle are two I remember, and he had a buffalo nickel (with the Indian side up) in a metal frame sewn near the brim. He almost always had the hat on, either on the top of his head or dangling from a chin strap over his shoulders, except when it came off during extreme expressions, such as when he was awfully happy and slapped it against his thigh, which happened when he quit college for good, or when he was mad, like a time years later in Paris when he and his French-Algerian girl–friend–soon–to–be–wife were walking past a line at a cinema and another American in the crowd mockingly said, "Advertising?"

The only other position the hat had, aside from on, dangling from his back, or in his hand, was over his face. That was the way I found him and his hat in the park in Washington.

"I smelled you before I saw you," I said to the hat, which moved and I knew the face underneath was smiling.

"Well, that's a coincidence, because to tell you the truth," the hat said, "that's why I'm down here covered up, because I smelled something coming."

"Spider, met Tano."

He had been there for two days. The day before, he took part in a demonstration at the Justice Department and was anxious for the coming Monday, though he said something did not seem quite right, although that may be me and my memory now, knowing that as the day and night passed, things definitely were not going to feel right.

It began on the way into the park, when I saw something that up until then I had never seen before. As we crossed a bridge, I saw a guy without a shirt, waving a book in the air. He was twenty yards in front of us and because of the nature of events in the capital, I thought the book he was waving might be *Mao's Little Red Book*. The fellow had long, red hair and a beard, both hanging a good eighteen inches off his head, and he looked like any other hippie with those basic features, like he could be playing bass for the Grateful Dead, or operating the People's Bus in Haight-Ashbury, only he was different. He was screaming things like "Jesus saved me. He can save you. Accept him. Praise him. You don't need drugs with Jesus" (he said drugs in a deep, elongated baritone, "druuuuuuugs," the way the Righteous Brothers might sing it), then he would thump the book he was holding, the Bible, and say, "It's right heeeeeere" (saying "here" the way Mel Allen might stretch the word if it was one of those screaming line drives).

When I reached him, I stopped, and he called me "Brother," and I stood there looking for a while, not seeing the blood resemblance. Then I walked away thinking I still had a lot to learn.

"Jesus freaks," Tano said. "I've seen a few of them around. Assholes."

There was much more to see, most of which I had seen before, but some of which I was surprised showed. One thing I had seen before, and I knew would be there again, were the leaders. They were everywhere. Demonstrations were field days for leaders, and by the time I arrived, they already had the park divided, like states, into "organizational groups." When I found Tano he was in one, though I didn't think he knew it, as they had formed around where he had fallen asleep during the night. That also accounted for why his hat was on his face.

The leader talking above Tano's head had short brown hair, a pinstripe shirt with the sleeves rolled to his elbows, jeans, and desert boots. He was a typical-looking leader. He was almost clean shaven, with just a bit of a stubble, a slightly puffy face, like

119

even if he missed meals, he made up for them, dark eyes, the kind that are supposed to penetrate, the kind that helped him see through issues, and a cigarette, which always seemed to be between leaders' fingers and not in their mouths, because they were open and doing the talking. While everyone else had long hair, as that was supposed to be a statement, many leaders never grew their hair long. That was supposed to be their way of saying they did not pay much attention to the more transient, visual realities of the world because they were too concerned and caught up with the issues they were penetrating. I also suspected it was part of a bail-out mechanism. Even though leaders espoused radical chic, the short hair, semi-Ivy look made them look legit, which came in handy when they needed the folks to help them, financially or otherwise, get into law or business school or open a health food/bookstore when everything was finished. Anyway, leaders often looked like they were fed up with leading, which rarely happened, or if things simply disintegrated around them, which often did happen, they could say, "Well, I'm through with the Movement," in an offhand but cynical way, and then because they looked the way they did, they could walk out and apply for a job.

One other quality most leaders had, at least the ones who survived, was a sense of timing. For many leaders, timing was a brilliantly subtle way of exercising crowd control. Since the Movement thrived on self-righteous or purified notions of democracy, equality, free speech, and distaste for rules and regulations, organizational meetings, such as the one Tano and Spider and I were standing and listening to, often degenerated into shouting matches. Actually, maybe they didn't become or degenerate into shouting matches, they started that way. Things like whether Mao's communism was OK, especially in light of the Cultural Revolution, often caused disagreements to escalate into verbal battles, and all of that was futile anyway, as virtually no one had been to China and arguments became unresolvable. Mostly, it was ideas that got batted around, an amalgam of ideas, many distorted from the applicable pantheon of heavyweights—thinkers like Plato, Aristotle, Rousseau, Thoreau, Marx and Engels, Arendt, Gandhi, Trotsky, with sprinklings of Danny the Red, Martin Luther King, Bobby Seale, Eldridge Cleaver, Malcolm X,

120

Ginsberg, Camus, Hesse, Bernadette Devlin (she could've been Joan of Arc at May Day), Rubin and Hoffman (the latter, more for his sense of humor), Rennie Davis, Dellinger, Leary, Kesey, Heinlein (not the choking maneuver, the guy who coined Grok), Jesus Christ, McLuhan, the Kennedy Brothers, the Smith Brothers (cough drops), the Berringer Brothers, the Smothers Brothers, Our Black Brothers (always an argument stopper), Our Sisters (at first, ignored), Dylan, (the one from Minnesota. My favorite of his, "Don't follow leaders/Watch your parking meters"), Spock (not the guy with the ears, the doctor), the Beatles, the Rolling Stones and Jefferson Airplane, Chavez, Muhammad Ali (a tremendous contribution with, "I got no quarrel with them Viet Cong"), anything any Indian who died fighting the American cavalry said (including, "This is a good day to die"), and Porky Pig's sign-off, a standard for adjournments.

Of course, there were more, but often something distorted from someone above would find its way into a meeting. Mr. Sevareid was right, a consensus was never reached on an alternative, viable, vile or otherwise, which was less of a stumbling block than it might seem. More immediate things were important, like stopping the war, and for the more aggressive, or more wise, stopping the system. The Perfect World was the final goal and it could be achived only after the present one was taken apart. So, meetings, more often than not, centered on tactics, many of which were formed from the threads of the thinkers, and many of which caused arguments, which was happening at the meeting where we were listening.

The argument in Washington took the shape of Gandhi–Martin Luther King type passive resistance, versus Western-style "Kick 'em in the ass. If they fuck with us, we'll fuck with them." The forces behind the latter position, being tougher in nature to begin with, had the upper hand. The passive group, many veterans of previous D.C. peace-ins, could be shrill if called upon, but they were better at being impassioned and visibly torn apart by sudden or violent turns of events. If necessary, they also could cry. I tended to side with the passive group, though I didn't like any groups, but that didn't matter.

Between all split points of view, that was where the leaders did their thing. Usually, they were in front and sat (leaders rarely

121

wanted to stand or appear they were towering) and listened to all sides, occasionally interjecting an idea and trying to keep some order, a tricky thing to do when no one was supposed to be doing that. Still, it was in a leader's best interest to keep things ordered, because in a semicontrolled discussion, a leader could stay near the top, or at least, get in the last word. That was where timing became one of the leader's most important skills. If he had a course of action, and usually he did, he had to know when to slip in appropriate remarks that could turn the crowd. Leaders tended to ride herd. If they knew what they were doing, they let the herd run itself out before it turned on them, and if they didn't know what they were doing, the herd trampled them.

Leaders were in a ratio of something like one-to-six during the May Day buildup. I listened to the one talking above Tano for a while. He described a particular street intersection his organizational group was supposed to occupy Monday morning, and he left it open for discussion whether if it came to push and shove on the part of police, what the group should do. For me, the Movement's attraction had always been peace and the Gandhian, flower-children elements, which I thought were as revolutionary a pairing as I could imagine. Events in Washington were taking a different shape though, and most people in the group I was standing in could have just as easily been yelling, "Give us Barabbas." They wanted blood.

The leader in our group shut up for a while and let people argue the merits of violence. I suspected he knew what he was doing, though I didn't care to stay around and watch the end, as by then I was getting fed up with leaders and their business and the talk about busting heads, so I poked Tano on the shoulder and waved for him to come on, which he seemed glad to do.

We passed by other groups with leaders and I picked up bits and pieces of similar arguments, and by midmorning I was getting the feeling that come Monday Washington was going to be an ugly place.

It was sunny and hot that day, and we spent most of the afternoon at a bandshell area where rock groups I had never heard of played music that explained why. We camped nearby, at least camp was what we called the tree where we unrolled our sleeping bags and, for the most part, avoided the strategy meetings taking place in an open meadow near the chow lines.

I wandered around, took my shirt off, but kept my shoes on in case I had to wade to the porto-potties. Most of the day I felt like I was on the set of a bad remake of the movie *Woodstock,* an event not yet two years' history, but actually was the closing chapter of a book I thought I still was reading. I had not been to Woodstock, and neither had a lot of people in Washington in 1971, but I think most had seen the movie and they approached May Day as if they were starring in an updated version. The fair-er-skinned people, particularly those with a lot of body hair and excess flesh, took off their clothes, but like me, kept something on their feet. Some danced to the bad music, which must have changed slightly when passing through their inner ears as they often danced to a different beat, while others sunbathed or threw Frisbees or made love, if that was what you called it under those open circumstances.

Clothed people were not any less expressive, particularly those who were advertising homosexuality or dash as a transves-tite. There was something particularly pathetic about the trans-vestites, who, like the Jesus freaks, were a group I did not expect in Washington. Drag queens toned down their act, no doubt in deference to the times, and dressed as drag Indian princesses or drag peasant women. They were funny and animated and since they truly seemed different, they always had an audience, even if it was one that only watched from the corner of their eyes. In the chow line Saturday night, I stood in front of two Indian prin-cesses, one who spoke in standard faggot lisp, but the other with a throaty Hollywood starlet voice that sounded like it had years of practice. It could have been funnier except the princesses had old faces, burnt from the sun that day and broken into lines and triangles. One had a cheekbone that looked like it had been pushed into his eye.

I stood with a piece of cardboard in front of them. When I made it to the front of the line, a fat guy plopped a spoon of what looked like potatoes in gravy on my cardboard and, when I looked up, said, "That's it."

I had not eaten since the night before at the snack bar, and was hungry and could have used some more, but I was glad for

123

what I got. I had not heeded the poster's advice to be prepared. I never did then, as it seemed a sin against wanderlust, so instead, most times I felt righteous or pure, and hungry. If there was a hobo heaven, I was accumulating grace. That afternoon, professional hawkers with pretzels and hot dogs had worked the crowd at the bandshell, but Tano and I had almost no money and, out of respect for the event, weren't buying. The hawkers charged something ridiculous, like fifty cents for a pretzel and much worse for a hot dog, and more than once I heard people, including us, say "Let's liberate the pretzel man," but I didn't see it happen. The pretzel and dog men were in their thirties and forties and looked like they worked the stadiums and the bus crowds of out-of-towners in front of the Smithsonian or Lincoln Memorial. They had carpenter's pouches full of change, which jingled when they put their hands in it, and they looked out of place. Still, they did a brisk business and what they sold smelled good, but as I said, through the afternoon, all we did was smell.

By evening, as far as I could see, the lawns had filled with pup tents and tepees and sleeping bags, until, from above, the place must have looked like quilted wreaths around campfires. During the day, government men in helicopters kept watch, and by nightfall, I still heard them beating the air.

"I wonder what we look like from up there?" Tano said.

" 'The Late Show'," I said.

"What?"

"You know, the opening scene before 'The Late Show' on television. There's a picture of the skyline, with all the buildings black, then the music goes, *da dun dun dun dunn dun da daaaa* ... and there's a clock ticking like hickory-dickory-dock, and with each tick a light in a building goes on, until the whole city's lit up. Maybe that's what we look like."

"Or maybe an army," he said.

Smoke from campfires mingled with marijuana smoke, which mingled with incense, which mingled with other unidentifiable kinds of smoke, until around nine or ten the lawns were blanketed with fog. Throughout much of the night, bands playing music sounding like explosions and feedback, shuffled on and off stage, interrupted only by an occasional announcement about

124

bad acid that was being passed around and where you could take people who were flipping out.

People who did not appear to be flipped out, but in reality may have been the only flipped-out ones, stayed around the bandshell for hours, anchored by rumors, the most often repeated one that the Jefferson Airplane were coming down late that night from New York, just to sing "Volunteers."

When you asked someone who was playing at the bandshell, the answer most often was, "I doan know, man, but maaan, the Airplane's gonna be here later and this place is gonna blow."

The musicians, more than any other group, were the mystic overlords of the Movement. They had powers far beyond the leaders, but except for the isolated seances of the concert and occasional peaceful afternoon demonstrations, their powers were seldom used. Their music could be wild and anarchic and tribal and poignant and disliked by those who should dislike it and loved by those who looked like they should love it and most of all, in the distilled expression of the day, felt. When it was felt, it was like strapping everyone into the same nervous system, but instead, by Saturday night, there were mostly disconnected nerve endings, and near midnight, when none of the messiahs had shown, there was a feeling of being let down. Monday was going to be something like Custer in reverse, with a lot of Indian chiefs versus the revenge of the Seventh Cavalry. The new tribes had come to Washington all right, but there was a sense of futility and by Saturday night, perhaps even the first suspicion of being trapped. Fifty thousand people camped in the parks around the Washington Monument, surrounded by mountains of the Justice Department, the White House, Capitol Hill, the Treasury, and in the distance, the Pentagon, all of which were supposed to be closed down by the people's guerrillas entangling traffic Monday morning. Fat chance. Whatever was going to happen would be swift, and chances were, with the bust-heads attitude of many of the encamped, Monday would end with people bloodied and jailed.

Washington was looking like more of the "Meet the new boss, same as the old boss" vision of things. "If you can't beat 'em, whup 'em."

"Man, I don't like what's going on here," I said to Tano, though I don't remember what he said, or even if he heard me; the music was deafening.

We smoked hashish and climbed the trees for old times' sake, but soon came down.

"I don't know about you, but I'm starving," Tano said. I was, too, and the hashish only made it worse by giving us the munchies, but there wasn't anything to do about it, so we sat down and smoked more hash.

It was then we heard something coming through the trees, like a pine cone tumbling though branches. Whatever it was fell into the dust about five feet in front of us.

"Do you see what I see?" Tano said.

Then more sounds like pine cones and suddenly the ground was spitting dust as if it were raining pint-sized drops, only the drops were pretzels.

"I don't believe it," Tano said, but that was about all he said as the three of us ran and scooped up the pretzels, wiping them on our shirts and eating them, then looking at each other and spending as much time chewing as we did laughing.

I laughed until I hurt, and said something stupid like "manna from heaven," and got an appropriate no reply. We each gathered enough to fill our stomachs and pockets and what Tano couldn't fit after that, he kept in his mouth for a while. Then we sat down and watched and thought and talked about the miraculous possibilities of our food supply never mentioning the probable because nothing in the world seems probable when you are high but cynical and happy and the sky is raining pretzels.

The government moved just after dawn. I woke with a helicopter directly above our trees. Over the roar of the blades a voice on a megaphone said everyone had to clear the park.

"Pigs ready to move in" swept through the grounds in seconds and quickly the park was a whirl of dust and smoke from doused campfires and people rolling up sleeping bags and taking down tents, only occasionally stopping to flash the finger at the helicopter.

We walked down one of the main boulevards, I don't re-

126

member which, although I do remember a limousine driving slowly through us with a man in a suit and a still camera looking out the back window, clicking photos and getting us all down. People talked about going to one of the universities, there was talk about free food at the American University, but many people did like Tano and Spider and me and walked to the highway on-ramps. For me, it was all over.

It was long into the night before we got back to New Jersey. Hundreds of people lined the on-ramps in Washington and Tano and I got separated from Spider, who made it back on his own. We got a ride out of D.C., jammed into the back of a flatbed truck, then squeezed in one car after another as the highways north were filled with jitneys of hippies. In Delaware, state troopers blocked the entrance to gas stations and rest areas and waved on any cars with people who looked under thirty.

When we reached southern New Jersey, we were left off at the Turnpike. Since we hadn't stopped at any rest rooms, we started to walk back off the road and into the woods when we heard a siren and then a state trooper yelling, "Freeze," which with Kent State in mind, I knew enough to do. After we walked back to the road, the trooper told us it was illegal to be on the highway and said he was going to be back in five minutes and we had better not be there. We watched him zoom away, then stuck out our thumbs. The nearest on-ramp was a mile away, and we knew when we got there we would be last in line.

"What d'ya think we should do when he comes back?" I said.

"Run."

"Are you crazy? Did you hear that freeze shit? He'll blow us away."

We argued awhile, until I thought I had him convinced, when we saw the trooper pass in the opposite direction, all of which was looking too much like Georgia.

"Well, we either run for it now, or hope we get a ride in a minute," I said.

The run would be a long one, back across a quarter mile of field before we reached the woods, and even if we made it, we thought the trooper might try and track us down and charge us with resisting arrest.

"Let's try for the ride," Tano said. That was the right move as, in less than a minute, it came, and we rolled on north.

More than twelve thousand people were arrested during the following week in Washington and less than four years later, after a class-action suit, many were awarded $10,000 in damages for being illegally arrested.

"We should've stayed and got busted," Tano said when we were on the river.

"Yeah, I suppose."

As to Spider, I'm not sure it was because of Washington or Tano or me or pretzels or a combination of things, but soon after, he became a Jehovah's Witness.

XVII

WE stayed in New Jersey for a few days, then left for the Midwest, where we hoped to see friends before the end of the spring semester. The trip out was fast and uneventful, except for a ride with a trucker in Iowa. He stopped for us midafternoon, after we had been waiting an hour on I-80. As soon as I climbed in his cab, I wanted to climb out, but as a point of honor, I never turned down a ride.

I was in the middle and Tano was beside the door. The trucker looked like a bad guy character in "Dick Tracy." His nose and chin were on opposite sides of the center line down through his face, and his skin was red-brown and creased and looked like it had been taken off, crumpled, stepped on, and stretched back over his skull.

"Where you goin'?" he said.

"Des Moines," I said.

"That's where I'm goin'," he said, which if it had been said by anyone else, I would have been elated.

"I'm goin' to cut up the governor," he said matter-of-factly while staring at the highway.

Tano and I found it difficult to respond to that; also our eyes

129

caught a shining piece of three-foot steel across the front dashboard.

"I'm gonna do it with that machete," the trucker said. In
case that wasn't enough, he also had a shotgun behind the seat.

For a while, he talked about the governor and why he was
going to meet his doom, which had something to do with a recent tax, which I seem to remember was upping fees at the
scales, but I might be wrong. We went along and called the governor a "shithead," too, but whenever we could, tried to change
the subject to baseball or truck engines. That only distracted him
for a minute or two before he was back on the governor. I saw
Tano had his left hand in his pocket, so he was holding his knife,
and his right hand on the door, so he would be ready to eject us
cheap James Bond style, but it never came to that and the trucker
did as he said and in about two hours, drove us to the outskirts
of Des Moines.

"Good luck," I said as I hopped down, and immediately realized that had been the wrong thing to say, so I corrected it and
said, "Take it easy with the governor." That was about as wrong
and did not bring a smile to his face, so I closed the door and
started walking fast down the road, holding my breath until I
heard the clutch ease out and the engine lurch into low gear.

I read the papers next morning and the next morning and
the next morning until I assumed the governor survived.

I don't remember anything else from the next few days, because it was all overshadowed by my first drug trip, which, as it
turned out, was also my first bad trip. In Des Moines, Tano and I
got a ride from two guys in a van, who happened to be from Florida and also happened to be dealing mild acid. Tano and I took
a quarter tab, and I popped mine in my mouth like an aspirin. In
retrospect that was a strange thing to do as I had never dropped
before, even though I knew the potential problems. Quite a few
times before, I had played Florence Nightingale to people who
were on bum trips, staying up all night to convince them there
were no evil spirits, something I really was not convinced of myself. Still, I guess I was soothing enough as everyone eventually
came down all right, and in some circles, I got a reputation for
being the Chris Kraft for psychedelic astronauts.

130

"Get Zalis. He'll bring him down," which was a funny notoriety, but I usually did.

Part of my taking acid at the time might have had something to do with May Day, or maybe it was simply shame. Up until then, it was like I had become a coach without ever playing the game. Then, another part simply was curiosity. I had been curious before, but not that much, and then, maybe too, I was scared, as in the previous year or so, I believed this life stuff easily got to be psychedelic and sometimes it was difficult to stay balanced. Anyway, when we were offered the acid, I felt like doing it, though surprisingly, I gave it little thought.

An hour or so later, it hit me. We were talking with friends in a room, and a stereo was playing in the background. The Crosby, Stills, Nash and Young song "Marrakesh Express" came on, with the high-pitched voices and tinselly-steel guitar strings and lyrics about Africa, when suddenly I realized I was very, very gone. There were five people in the room and voices and faces were being shuffled and mismatched, like a male voice was coming out of a girl's mouth, then heads began to bounce a bit and the room looked like a picture on a television screen where the horizontal had gone out of whack. The scene began to float up and around, until finally I turned to Tano and said, "Man, I gotta get out of here."

Outside, things weren't much better. The brick hallway dilated like a contracting artery, and when I walked to the doorway, it seemed to get farther and farther away.

"I'm on a bummer," I said to Tano, who had followed me out.

"Just hang in there, man. You'll come down in a while."

I braced myself for a long night. For a moment, I felt panicky. What if I never came down and things stayed that way, a standard freak-out reaction about never-ending hallways and voices and exaggerated expressions on faces. Then I got scared. I wanted to run, but at least had enough sense to know that wouldn't do any good, and then heard an inner voice come out of the sludge of catechisms and tell me to pray. I laughed, at least that was what I thought I heard myself do. That made me feel a lot better. The next thought was to try and see if I could get someone to take me to a hospital and see if I could pump the madness out of my system, but I let that one go as fast as the one about praying, as I assumed it would mean getting busted. So, then I sat on the floor and said to myself, if I die, I die, a fate, at the time, I preferred to getting arrested. Anyone who's had a bad trip immediately thinks about other drug overdoses and dying, as if Janis Joplin or Jimi Hendrix were waiting to let you in to wherever they went.

Resigning myself to dying and dismissing thought about praying calmed me. Still, the night seemed to take days to pass, with me perceiving myself floating dispossessed over the landscape, until two or three o'clock in the morning when I began to bounce down, which came as a bit of a thud at first. Tano and I had wandered into a television room where we sat down in front of a set, flipped it on and watched the static, something we had done together many times the previous semester. "Watching the fuzz," as we described it, was more entertaining than it may sound as it involved waiting for a mystery man who occasionally would get control of the station in the middle of the night and create galaxies of geometric designs on the screen.

It must have been a while, maybe a half hour, that we sat in front of the television without seeing the mystery man, when a flashlight cut through the darkness and a shadow with a police hat walked through the door.

"What are you fellas doing here?"

"We just turned on the television to see if anything was on," I said, not believing I was sounding coherent, and not believing he was hearing me sound coherent.

"You students?"

"Yeah."

"See your ID's?"

"Sure," I said and pulled out the card I knew I still had in my wallet. "This is a friend of mine. He's just visiting me."

The more I talked, the more I was amazed I seemed to be pulling it off.

"What dorm you in?"

I repeated the dorm and room I had the fall semester.

"Well"—he handed me back my card—"just checking. We've been having trouble lately with outsiders on campus."

132

"That's OK," I said.

"Get some sleep," he said as he walked out.

"Right," I said and sat back down and pretended to fool with the dials on the television.

"I don't believe you just did that," Tano said. "I couldn't talk."

"I don't believe I did either," I said. "I didn't think I could think."

The rest of the way down was a snap.

XVIII

THINGS still were coming down more than a month later. My birthday happened to occur on a Saturday night that year, which also happened to be the final public performance at Fillmore East, so I made sure I happened to be there. I was turning nineteen and wanted to begin the end of my teens right.

The Fillmores, East and West, were rock music Meccas and their closing was a bad sign. I was trying to catch up on a decade I had mostly missed, and whatever was left of that time was passing fast. As soon as Woodstock was over, it immediately was declared the high-water mark, and everything after would go downhill. History would not even be consulted. Maybe that was just another element of the era.

If Woodstock was the official end of the sixties, the death knell was echoing down unexpected corridors the next couple of years. The Hells Angels beat a guy to death at the Stones concert in Altamont; Jimi Hendrix, Janis Joplin, Jim Morrison, Tim Buckley, and how many more died drugged deaths; the National Guard opened fire at Kent State and Jackson State; the Yippies either went underground or to Wall Street; the Beatles quit; everyone started to grow their hair long and go to concerts (even our high-school football coach, who a few years earlier had seen hippies as Communist faggots, was spotted at a rock concert. That was a sure sign things were on the way out); instead of uppers and psychedelics, drug preference changed to downers and booze, hitching became impossible, Haight-Ashbury closed, Europe got expensive and India overrun, fewer people bought used Volkswagens, Stevie Wonder and Peter Frampton and Cher got famous, the Lennon sisters made a comeback, cops started growing mustaches, football got super, no one dropped out of college anymore—they either flunked out or were kicked out—"Then Came Bronson" and "The Smothers Brothers" went off the air, Charles Bronson went on, Muhammad Ali lost, student standby airfares were discontinued, rock concerts became acts, McGovern got clobbered, Tom Hayden ran for office, David Crosby stayed on a yacht. Charles Manson surfaced, and women started wearing dresses, makeup, and bras again. Later, Phil Ochs hanged himself, Dylan and Eldridge Cleaver found Jesus, Henry Kissinger won the Nobel Prize, to camp you had to make reservations through Ticketron, cigarettes got elongated, mentholated, charcoal filtrated and weaker, everything got expensive, and for another five years, the Vietnam war continued. As far as I knew, only Allen Ginsberg didn't change.

Those signs were spottable as indicating a turn for the worse, as was the end of the Fillmore.

I didn't have a ticket, and although the concert, which was to include Albert King, J. Geils, and the Allman Brothers Band, was sold out, I went hoping to get in, which I did, though it took some time.

I spent the early evening barricaded behind police lines, with crowds of other, mostly bearded, long-haired people yelling "Spare tickets?" to other mostly bearded, long-haired people who ignored them. I didn't yell "Tickets?" because everyone else was yelling "Tickets?" and no one else got any. An hour after the show began, Bill Graham, the operator of the Fillmores and the man everyone called a "rock impresario" came out. Graham had black hair almost to his collar, sunken eyes, and looked like he had been in a four-day card game. The ticket shouters immediately pounced on him.

"Capitalist Pig," "Oinker," "Rip-off," they shouted. "Why don't you have a free concert?"

135

That last statement made Graham spin around and say something like, "Ask the band members."

Concert ticket prices had been going up, and not surprisingly, it was people like Graham who were taking flak from people like me, waiting empty-handed outside concert halls, although then, I wasn't giving him any.

He came out a few times, always to the same reception, until finally he pointed to a few people in the crowd to duck under the barricade and come into the lobby. I was one of them, though I'm not sure why. During most of the anti-Graham volleys, I stayed propped against the side of the Fillmore, reading a book, and as I said, I looked like everyone else, with long hair, flannel shirt, baggy dungarees, and work boots, but also I may have looked like I felt sorry for Graham, which for reasons I am not sure of, other than sympathy, I did. Maybe that was why, or maybe he just noticed I hadn't yelled at him. Whatever the reason, I got in, though I did have to cough up five bucks for a ticket, but it got me a seat center section, about ten rows from the stage.

Although I was straight, the rest of the evening passed as a cross between a drunken wake and an opium dream psychedelic blast-out. I am not sure what that means, but it fits. The men's room was fogged in from smoke from incense to hashish and even the lobby, where Fillmore posters and memorabilia were being sold, was misty. Inside, the theater was nightmare black, except for stage lights and strobes that made the place feel like a black-light washing machine stuck on the spin cycle. During one of the spins, I got hit by a drumstick thrown by the J. Geils Band drummer, and when I went to pick it up, I was tackled by something I assumed in the darkness was human, but by then I had learned something about being tough, so I ended up with the drumstick. It was a wonderful night.

Sometime around 2 A.M., Duane Allman, one of the leaders of the Allman Brothers Band (he would die in a motorcycle accident the next year), said, "This is the most exciting thing we've ever done. We're gonna play all night," which they did, until around 6:30 A.M., when the curtain calls ended and I stumbled into the blinding Sunday morning light of New York.

136

XIX

SCREECHING orioles with black wings and yellow stripes arced like arrows across the river. We passed dozens of empty rubber worker huts and Glück said, "They've all gone back to Manaus. They want no more out here."

For two days, we had not seen another boat. As we moved farther north, we used up gasoline and food, our skin got browner, and there was a sense of us moving out of one world and into another, all of which added up to a sense of stripping down that Tano described as "getting closer to the bone."

The river was higher than when Glück had come in September, and a house he had stayed at was surrounded by water, when before it had been well above land, and he kept saying he did not understand where the monkeys had gone. Finally, he explained it all away as, "All things are crazy."

Time, too, was crazy. Our next landmark on the aerial maps was Allianca, a ring of rapids and waterfalls around a small settlement upriver and the last village at the edge of the frontier. We stopped at three cabocolos' huts and each time we asked how far we had to go to Allianca, the cabocolos said either thirty minutes or a half hour. I figured there must have been a government pamphlet telling natives that if they are asked by gringos where something is, answer a half hour, but Glück said it had something to do with the sun.

"To some Eendyuns, there are two hours in a day," he said. "The first is from dawn to when the sun reaches its highest point. The second hour is from then until sunset."

That day the sun never seemed to get much higher than right on top of our heads, and felt like it hung from a wire that dogged us. For hours it pounded, with only an occasional angel to block. I kept my hat on, but it only did half the job, as going upriver was like being on a magnifying glass. Light struck from all directions. I got red under my chin and could have used a wimple, the winged headgear the Flying Nun wore.

The hotter and longer the day became, the more incoherent I became. I lost my thoughts easily, and talking to Tano, the end of a sentence would escape and my mouth would have to stumble on and finish what my mind lost.

Midafternoon, a fish jumped six feet out of the water, over the back of the boat and Glück's head. We took it as a sign to start thinking about dinner and finding a place to camp, but the closer we got to the end of the Indian's second hour, the fewer accessible spots we saw to camp. The river bank was steep and along much of it we would have needed grappling hooks to climb to shore. The few huts we passed had people, who no doubt would have told us to keep going another half hour. The sun faded and a thatch of shadows fell on the water. Glück said that at the next house we should ask if we could stay.

The next house was a teacher's. He lived in a small hut with his wife and two children, but he said he was glad to have company and offered us another, larger hut, the schoolhouse. It was empty, except for some wooden benches, but it had strong rafters and a solid roof and walls, a three-star combination. We tied the skiff to a piling and climbed a ladder up a steep bank. I was dizzy and blank from the sun, and I waddled, a short-stepped waddle, to keep from falling.

We had rice and Spam for dinner, and after, as we were down at the river washing, I told Tano I was still hungry.

"Man, that's been a sore spot with me," he said. "It's ridicu-

138

lous, the amount of food we've been getting. Coffee for breakfast, crackers with a little honey for lunch. Now some rice." He said he had kept it to himself since Glück complained he only needed two pancakes, but now that it was bothering me, too, he said we should both speak up. To hear Tano complain about food was like having a camel talk and say it needed more water. Tano can eat like a horse, but when he has to, he can survive on birdseed. One winter, when he was broke and stayed in a cabin in Minnesota, he lived on rice and potatoes until he got sores from malnutrition. It was something he had to do then.

"But we shouldn't have to be doing this," he said. "This ain't no survival expedition."

I agreed and we decided that the next day we would use behavioral modification, the positive reinforcement approach. That was my idea, though I didn't say it that way. I said something about encouraging Glück to feed us more, but since he was not feeding us much to begin with, it was a difficult thing to reinforce, unless we hovered over him while he opened a can and poured it in the pan. Then we could say something reinforcingly subtle, like, "More."

I didn't like talking behind Glück's back. I felt conspiratorial, but then again, more than that, I felt hungry, so I didn't let it bother me.

Our brains were steamed from the sun, so we drank a lot of cinnamon tea, and with an evening breeze, my thoughts cooled to simmer and I thought about a story Glück had told us in the morning, about a man catching a plane. According to the story, a man wanted to fly from Manaus to Lima, but when he arrived at the airport in the morning, a woman at the ticket counter told him his plane had changed schedule and left at 4 A.M. He complained and told her to look at his ticket, which said 10 A.M., but she said, "So many planes falls down. Maybe you are lucky."

I knew I was still woozy to laugh again at the story, but it felt good and I thought again about the woman's answer and I laughed again and knew the heat was passing out of my brain.

The teacher came in to talk with us, but for a long time, he mostly listened, to Glück. Occasionally Glück would ask him questions and the teacher would tell him something and Glück

139

would translate to us, like that the teacher was thirty-six and made $40 a month. His wife looked like she could be his mother, but I guess they didn't talk about her.

Glück showed the teacher pictures of some of his trips, and then the teacher started talking and Glück stopped.

"What's he saying?" I asked.

"He says that in November, Tatunka made speech in Allianca and said two thousand Indians above the waterfalls are armed with rifles and preparing to attack people on the river."

Glück turned to him and asked him more questions, and the teacher talked fast and waved at the river.

"He says that throughout November, day and night, through the whole night, people are coming down in canoes, in boats, in anything that floats. Teacher says now there is only one man left above the waterfalls. This is good, maybe we can see the jaguars."

The teacher talked some more and Glück translated.

"Tatunka said he got the message about the Indians from his sister, via telepathy. I know his sister. She is married to one of the Indians and lives with them in the jungle.

"The people coming down the river told the teacher that the Indians came to them and gave them eight days to leave. Now, there is only one man left above Allianca."

Later that night, while we laid in our hammocks, Glück said, "I wonder about this one man alone. Much courage, no?"

No one answered.

"So, now we have a story, excitement," he said. "Maybe people will say we cannot go past Allianca."

"But we'll go anyway?" I half-asked, half-stated.

"Yes," he said. "We go anyway."

We asked Glück what he thought about the Tatunka story and he speculated, "Maybe there is a man up there who has hired the Eendyuns to scare everyone away so he could claim the land and become the piacaba king."

Glück told us a story about a Lufthansa pilot who paid for a sixty-day trip, but after three weeks, he heard rumors about Indian troubles ahead, and he told Glück to return. The pilot wanted part of his money back, but Glück told him Mrs. Glück had spent it.

140

I wasn't sure if the story was just a loose connection or Glück was trying to tell us something.

I asked Glück if he ever had trouble with Indians, and he said, "Never.

"As long as we don't make trouble, trouble won't come after us," he said. Then, in an afterthought, "I don't know why the Eendyuns with blowguns never shot me."

XX

WE had cold cereal in warm powdered milk for breakfast, and because I still felt addled from the sun, I wasn't ready to start Glück on B. F. Skinner's rat maze. Besides, he made more than I could eat, which had less to do with how much he made than how I cannot eat much in the morning. Tano was more aggressive. He told me I should "anticipate" how hungry I would be at supper (an expression that would become a standard for the rest of the trip), but all I could anticipate was not wanting anything for a while, so I gave Tano what I couldn't finish.

It started to rain as we packed the boat, and when we were ready to leave, it poured. We stayed an hour, until the rain let up, then said good-bye. The teacher said we had twelve hours to Allianca, which, depending on the time system he used, meant anything from a day and a half to two weeks.

In a half hour we reached a hacienda Glück had been asking about the day before and everyone had told us that it, along with Allianca, was a half hour away. Glück tied on to the dock and a man came down a hill to greet us. Behind him, there was an open shed with spools of rubber and bushels of piacaba and, in the

142

fields behind the shed, a herd of cattle near a colonial-style house. Glück said the time he had visited the hacienda with the Austrian, he had got fruit, but the caretaker told us he had just arrived, after being away for months, and there was nothing on the trees.

Glück and the caretaker talked and I wandered up the hill into the grass. In a few minutes, Tano followed and asked if I had seen the caretaker's ear.

"Go up and have a look," he said.

I pretended I was going to look at a spool of rubber and walked by the old man. His ear was purple and swollen, like it was a cross between a turnip and a cauliflower.

I walked back and Tano told me he had shaken the caretaker's hand.

In a few minutes, we left and waved at the man as we slid into the middle of the river.

"What was wrong with the man's ear?" I asked Glück.

"Maybe leprosy," Glück said.

I saw Tano dip his hand in the river, and I laughed. He turned and wiped his hand on my thigh and I swung at him. Then we both laughed.

"It's difficult to pass on," Glück said. "In Manaus, maybe four thousand people have leprosy. There are twelve hundred in a hospital run by German nuns. I went there with a Norwegian who made a film about it."

It began raining hard again.

"You know the leper colony outside Manaus?" Glück said. "The one with the cross." I remembered from the first night on the *Emerson.*

Just then we turned a bend and a rainbow split the sky and anchored into the river. We all said it was a good omen.

When the rainbow faded, Glück picked up his story about the leper colony.

"It was horrible," he said. "Many of the lepers cannot move. They lie on boards without mattresses, just on the springs, with pus from their sores spilling to the floor. It left a terrible stench. ["T-e-r-r-y-y-y-b-l-u-h" was the way he put it.] The Norwegian got sick and I had to do the filming. A Dutch priest came to say mass there. They were to film part of the mass, but I told the priest to

143

hurry and finish or I would get sick. He should have put strychnine in the hosts. That is no life."

Clouds covered the sun most of the morning and I thought how the angels were flying to protect us, but then the rains came again and stayed all afternoon and I thought about what Tano said of the angels. Whatever it was, because it had done such a good job of hammering me the day before, I was glad for the break from the sun.

Under the tarp, I read Tano excerpts from a book on the Amazon.

"It says here, one out of every two people in the Amazon gets worms."

"Come on, man, don't read me that stuff."

The rains came down hard and I closed the book and we made a tent in the boat, while Glück whistled in the back "The Daring Young Man."

"The rain is good," his voice came through the plastic. "It will make it easier to pass over the waterfalls and get through the rocks above."

We passed a house with a big family and waved, but no one waved back. An old man looked down and the family looked at him, then he waved and everyone followed.

"The oldest man must wave first," Glück said. "Then the next oldest and on down. Women are not supposed to wave."

Dolphins spouted near us and Glück said it was cabocolo lore that dolphins mated with their women, so maybe that had something to do with the waving business.

We began looking for a house at 2:30, but it was an hour more before we found one with a roof that was not badly damaged. It had tattered walls and so-so-rafters, so it got a single star. Glück made joongle pancakes with sawcheechez again, and said he wished he could take vitamins instead of eat meals. We positively reinforced his cooking and said we loved his pancakes.

"The Eendyuns, they just eat farinha. It swells in their stomach and makes them feel full." South American farinha comes from the manioc root and, after a complicated cooking and straining process, is dried out. It tastes like mealy grain, but it is the staple of the Amazon. It is put on everything, rice, meat, beans, or soaked in water by itself and cooked into a warm gruel.

144

We told Glück we liked farinha. He shrugged.

After supper, it was still raining and we swung in our hammocks, and for three hours, Glück told more stories about the years he had spent in South America. They were a quiltwork of adventures and mishaps, told out of chronological order, and maybe because it was dark, Glück told them as if he was talking to himself. We had a candle between us, which gave off some light, but lying in a hammock, everyone naturally faced the ceiling and Glück spoke like he was explaining things in a confessional. Midway through the stories, the candle went out, but no one said anything and Glück kept on.

When the war ended, the fatherland called wayward Germans home. Glück said Standard Oil wanted him to return, but I was not sure if the edict was echoed by the Venezuelan government. Glück's answer was, "I want not to go back. Germany is broken." But the police had Glück's passport, "So, I go rooning away.

"What was I to do? I cannot go to the police and say, 'Give me my passport.' So, I go rooning away."

Rooning is a word Glück used whenever he expressed movement. "So, then I go rooning into the joongle," he would say in many stories, rolling his *r*'s and stretching the vowel as if he could capture all the ups and downs of whatever jaunt he was describing.

For seven years after the war, he went rooning in South America, winding his way down the west coast until he reached Peru, and then because of trouble with a colonel there, embarking for the Amazon. He supported himself by fixing typewriters and playing tennis, the latter, I understood, as a combination of giving lessons and hustling. He moved without a passport and had to sneak through frontiers. He was caught as he tried to leave Colombia, but avoided jail by bribing the soldier who nabbed him.

"I lived two years in the mountains of Ecuador, and I finally decided to go down into the joongle in the east and then into Peru. I wanted to go down into the real joongle. This was the time I was not married.

"I stopped at a Jesuit missionary and they told me not to go. There was a tribe near there that made the shrunken heads, and

145

another tribe that had been killing many people. All that shit, what they tell.

" 'Yes, yes, I know,' I said, but I tell them I want to see real Eendyuns and I want to go. I have time and it takes nuhzing. They told me—they were at the Mission Macas—'We are the last mission here and inside there is nobody more. It is all finished inside.'

"I went anyway. I walked. I was still in the mountains and it would be impossible to go by boat. So, I go walking. I'm walking, walking, for about ten days, going down. Then, I find a street, in the joongle, a road, like in Germany, with canals on each side for water drainage. Well made. I could not believe it. Impossible. I had a map, not a good one, but it had none of that. And the missionaries, they said nuhzing. So, I go along the street and in a half hour I come to an orange plantation, many orange trees, in lines. I ate some oranges. B-e-e-e-y-o-u-t-e-e-f-u-l. Then, I go farther on the street, and I come to a lake with fifteen houses, round ones, like the ones the Jivaros, the headhunter Eendyuns make. Then I come to a man on an old broken bicycle. 'You are German?' he said. And I said, 'Yes, like you, Bavarian, too.' I recognized his accent. 'You play chess?' he asked, 'I play chess.' 'Oh, please, come in,' he said, 'and have something to eat.'

"He had a nice house and on his veranda, we played chess. For fifteen days, we played chess. Not one time did I win. He would beat me in less than eight moves. He was fantastic. He told me he had been there since 1911, and when I came there in 1949, he said I was the first white man he had seen in all those years. He did not know about the last war, and he did not even know about the war of 1914. I wanted to tell him about those things, but he looked at me and said he was not interested. 'C'mon, we just play chess,' he said.

"I saw many men and women there with blond hair and blue eyes and I said, 'Who are they?'

" 'They are all my children,' he said.

"He had come from Germany and made a Jesuit mission there. He was young and strong then, and he still was strong when I saw him. All the missionaries, then, they would take an Eendyun girl to sleep with. Naturally, in the jungle, with good

146

food and all that time, they would get crazy if they did not have anyone. They need a woman. But, he doesn't take one woman, he takes five or six and makes a harem, like the Arabs. But then the main mission gets against him and they want to put him out. He was a strong man though, and he said, 'No, I stay here. I like this.'

"Back then, when you were a missionary from Germany, you did not come out like a beach boy. You had to know something, about things, like medicine and carpentry and agriculture, many things. They trained them in Germany, so he could help the Eendyuns in the joongle. For that, they sent him out and he liked it. Then the head of the Jesuits, they gave him and his mission up. They declared the mission was finished. They gave it up.

"I asked him, 'How come the priests from the other mission never spoke of you?' He said they made him die by silence. They call him *'tauchwagen.'* Nobody speaks about him. He is dead. They even excommunicated him from the Church. The Jesuits wrote and told his family that he was excommunicated, which for the family was worse than he was dead. He was finished. If he had died, that was OK, but since he was excommunicated, his family never wanted to hear from him. So, from 1911, he was absolutely out of the world, but he liked the life with the Eendyun. It was fantastic, he said.

"One time I went into his room where he slept. He had a bed made of animal skins, and above it, I found a Catholic Bible. It was big, bound in leather. So, I opened the Bible, but there was nothing in it. I asked him, 'What's going on with the Bible?' He said, 'All my life, I like to smoke cigarettes. We have tobacco here, but we have no paper. So, I went through Matthew, Mark, Luke, and John and I rolled them into cigarettes. Other times, I roll cigarettes from the inside of corn husks.'

"In the fifteen days I was there, he took all my letters, from my mother, and sisters and friends in Germany, all those letters written on fine airmail paper, and he rolled them into cigarettes. When we played chess, I could read my letters in his mouth.

"Then, after fifteen days, I said, 'Now, I go.' He said, 'Oh, stay here. We can always play chess and I will have someone to speak to.' For fifteen days, all I had done was lose, and if I stayed there,

I would get crazy. I said, 'No, I want no more. I go.' He wanted to give me many things, a house and girls, but I said, 'No, it's not important. I'm too young. I go.' "

Glück had two accidents in Ecuador. In one, he was riding a public bus, returning on a Sunday from a mountain market. The bus lost its brakes and crashed against the side of the mountain. Many people were killed and Glück was thrown out and knocked unconscious. He suffered internal bleeding and had to spend three weeks in a hospital.

Later that year, he went hunting for deer in the mountains. He said he had gone for a friend who had wanted a pair of antlers for his house. Glück tracked a herd up a saddle between two tall mountains, but late in the afternoon, he got lost. The mountains were volcanic and steep and, trying to descend, at one point he had to jam his rifle into a crevice and hang and try to drop down to a lower ledge. He pushed his rifle into a hole and tried to slide down, but the barrel snapped and he fell. He said he didn't know how far.

"At two o'clock in the morning, I woke up. My watch was still running. My head was on my rucksack and I was in a puddle of ice water. If it wasn't for the rucksack, I would have went face in and drowned."

He said he tried to stand, but could not. The moon was out and it was cold, but he had warm clothing, "that was lucky."

He crawled down, on hands and knees, and by the afternoon of the next day, he got off the mountains and reached the Pan American Highway.

"I tried to stop cars, but they would not. It was a trick the bandits used, lying beside the road and then jumping someone who stops. I thought I was dead. Many cars drove by and finally one stopped. It was the doctor who treated me for the bleeding from the bus accident. He had been in Iquitos and was on his way back to Riobamba."

Glück had damaged a vertebra, but not seriously, and after another stay in the hospital, he was out again. This time, he decided to pack up and go to Peru, where, as he had told us before, he met his wife. What he hadn't told us before was why he left Peru four years later, in 1952.

"I had trouble with a colonel," he said.

148

On Christmas night, 1952, he went to the movies with his wife. There was a long line at the theater, and he and his wife had to wait.

"At that time in Peru, there was a military dictatorship, and only the military people were big men. The other people were mud."

A colonel arrived at the theater and pushed people away as he walked to the front of the line, until Glück stopped him.

"I said, 'No, sir. You go on to the back and wait until it's your turn. Then you can get your ticket.'

"He had his uniform, and all his military shtuff. He said, 'Who are you?' I said, 'I am the man that pays for that uniform you wear.' (I had to pay tax in Peru, stranger tax. I could not do any of the short pant shtuff there). 'Then you do nothing.'

"It was dark and people in the shadows shouted, 'Bravo, bravo.' He got angry, but then he went in.

"Next day, the general in Iquitos came to talk to me. He knew me. My wife's father, who had died, had been the mayor of Iquitos and the mayor knew our family.

" 'What you have done yesterday was a shtoopid thing,' the general said. 'I tell you what. You take your canoe and leave the country. Go out. Today, the colonel plans to take some soldiers and come and they will break you, bone by bone. I tell you this now, but if it happens, nobody can help you.'

"So, I bought some food and said good-bye to my wife, who went home to her mother, and I took my canoe and I go rooning down here to Brazil."

He planned to go to Manaus, but when he reached Tefe, in the western Amazon, he met Dutch missionaries who convinced him to stay. They told him Manaus was a dying city and he should stay in Tefe, where they needed a man who could do mechanical work. They gave him a two-hundred-meter plot on the river, about two hours outside of Tefe, and there Glück built a fence and a house, planted bananas, oranges, beans, and sugarcane, and worked for the priests. Sometimes he would go with them on trips into the jungle and other times he would make money repairing things, like rifles and alarm clocks people brought him from Tefe. Then, he wrote his wife and she caught a Peruvian tanker and moved to Tefe. They stayed for six years, until 1959, when his children became old enough to attend school, so they decided to move to Manaus.

"It was wonderful for me in Manaus," he said. He was one of the few mechanics in the city and quickly got a contract working for the national bank, repairing typewriters. On weekends, he began making excursions by himself into the jungle.

He met a man from London, then, who asked if Glück would take him for a week-long trip. Glück said he would like to, but could not afford losing the time from work.

" 'No, I will pay you for the time you lose,' " the man told Glück.

"Oh, that was nice, no?" Glück said. The man enjoyed the trip and told his friends, and soon the business snowballed and by 1962, Glück became a full-time guide.

As he'd told us before, he said there were people from all over the world who had taken trips with him, and "there is even a club in New York called the Kurt Glück Club. It has all the people there who have taken trips with me."

Glück's stories kept coming long after the candle burned out. The more he talked and remembered, the more excited he sounded, and though I could not see him, I heard him lying down, then sitting up and lying down and sitting up again as if memories were working him like a puppeteer. He talked steadily, but his voice was erratic. To get through background information, his voice sped along consonant sounds and compressed words, then when he wanted to emphasize something, like the way the Iquitos general warned him he must leave or "noooooo one will be able to help you," he stretched the words on air that sounded squeezed.

We asked him how far in advance he had booked trips, and he said he had one planned with a German professor and his daughter for the year 2000.

"That will be my last trip."

XXI

RAIN returned at dawn. Glück had been up since five making pancakes, so maybe we were having an effect, but breakfast slowed us and we didn't leave until eight, enough time for the rain to work itself into a solid storm. We made a tent out of the tarp and slumped into the bottom of the boat. In ten minutes, we were moist. I told Tano about an Australian I had met in Crete. The Aussie recently had been in Southeast Asia, and was impressed most by the way Orientals (whom in a few moments, I realized, Tano saw as Buddhist monks) could compact their bodies, squeezing into buses or riverboats, or third-class trains, like "itto bawxes" was the way the Australian put it.

For an hour, I tried to make a box and sat with my knees pressed to my face, my arms around my legs, and my ass on the wood panel above the floor. Tano and I sang the Doggie National Anthem three times because we were particularly miserable. It was cold and the moist was turning to wet and soon I was sure we would be soaked. Glück was not singing, so I assumed everyone felt the same.

For a while, I didn't move and no one talked. All we heard was the drone of the motor and the drumroll of rain on the tarp.

I stuck my head below my arms, felt water dripping off my face, and looked at Tano, who was under his hat, motionless.

"Hey, you asleep?" I said.

"No."

Another ten minutes passed. I spent the time counting water drops as they dripped off my nose. I looked under my armpit again and Tano struck his head out of his hat and said, "Them Buddhist monks ain't got nothin' on a doggie."

Midmorning, the rain eased and we poked our heads out of the tarp and saw our first toucan.

"In Germany, they say toucans fly as if they chase their noses," Glück said.

It looked like they did, beating their wings, then diving as if they were after something falling just in front of their beaks.

We stopped at a sandbank and I saw something slip into the water. Without thinking, I yelled, *"Jakaré"* [the Portuguese word for alligator I picked up from Tano's brand of cigarettes.] It was a small alligator, maybe three feet, and was the first one we saw. When it moved, I yelled, *"Jakaré, jakaré,"* again, then it dived into the river.

We started again with the rain still falling, so Tano and I went back under our tent. We were cold and wet, but every time we looked at each other, we laughed. I fell asleep in a puddle on the floor and woke soaked, so I didn't have to worry anymore about relative wetness.

Noon, it was still raining heavily when we passed a cluster of huts with two men standing outside. They waved to Glück and asked him to pull over. Tano and I were sitting in the bottom of the boat. We had made the tarps into a giant cape and watched from beneath our hats. We may have been mistaken for children.

Glück asked how far it was to Allianca. One man rolled his pant legs up, waded into the river, and grabbed the boat. An older man with gray hair came down from the huts. He said something to Glück in Portuguese and Glück answered, *"Não comprende."* The old man waded into the water and asked for *"cinco cigarros."* The two younger men wore tattered clothes, their hair was matted from the rain, and even from almost ten feet, we could smell *cachaça.*

Glück said he must go, but the old man shouted, *"Não."*

"Porque?" Glück asked.

I looked at Tano in a "You know what we've got to do" look and he looked at me in the same, and then I said what didn't need to be said, "It's time to get up."

We threw off the tarp and stood in the center of the boat and tried to look as ornery as we could, hat brims down, scowling, the way Clint Eastwood might have done it.

For a moment, we all stared at each other and only the rain broke the stillness. Then they backed off.

Glück told them we were his sons and the old man let go of the boat.

After that, we did not go back under the tarp, and when we ran into other people, we always sat up straight.

The river closed in, getting narrower and rockier and, in some sections, only a few feet deep. Glück said it was lower now than it was in the fall 1979. It was supposed to be higher. "All things are crazy."

The pattering of rain drowned under a roar of water as we rounded a bend and the river opened into a wide ring of rapids.

"Allianca," Glück said.

The waterfalls, as Glück had called them, were a series of sharply descending rapids that wound a quarter mile around a settlement of four or five huts. Though it was not the vertical drop we expected, the river was fast and violent. Some of the rocks were as big as hippopotamuses while others were jagged and stuck out like sailfish fins. A boat trying to go through would have been shredded.

"We stop here and see how to pass," Glück said.

Glück maneuvered the boat between rocks before Tano and I jumped out and pulled us to shore. Glück went up to one of the huts to see about staying. On the way, he stopped to talk to a white man who was walking down. The man was broad-shouldered and his skin was tan. He wore a straw hat that looked Chinese, with a wide brim and rounded crown, a checkered shirt and long pants. He said little to Glück and passed a few feet from Tano and me without looking at us. His face was square, as if it was cut from a block, and he had a big mustache, a stubbly beard, and small, dark eyes. He pushed a canoe into the water and climbed in. On the seat in front of him, a rifle gleamed in the rain.

153

He paddled deep, easy strokes and slipped into the ripple of current and silently wound, like a leaf, downriver until the mist that had begun to settle on the Padauiri swallowed him.

Something about the way the man with the gun and the canoe did not look at us, as if we didn't exist, stopped and separated things. When he slipped into the river and the river and the jungle took him, it was as if they breathed together. Tano and I still were on the outside, but that wasn't so bad. It made things separate. I watched something, felt something, and thought about something, which all had to do with the same thing, but were all a little different.

The guy in the canoe was as tough a looking guy as I had seen. He looked like he could be a killer, like the way Sonny Liston, the heavyweight champion, did, like he could put you down with indifference. That made me anxious, in part because of what had happened with the three men in the morning, and in part because you cannot pass a guy as rough looking as the man in the canoe without thinking about tangling. All of that made me think about other things, about what you had to do to survive, and about how we were crossing into a place where morality would not make much difference.

When the man disappeared into the mist on the river, it felt like Tano and I reappeared, just as five men appeared beside the hut where Glück had gone. Because of the last few minutes and because of the morning, Tano and I stood up, tipped our hat brims down, paced beside the boat, and, again, tried to look tough.

Two things we figured we had going for us. With our gear under tarps, it might look as if we had guns hidden in the boat, and if not, we were bigger, at least in terms of height, than anyone we had seen. We flashed our size the way street toughs flash switchblades, a message intended to read, "If you guys want to fuck with us, we're going to take some of you with us."

Anyway, it sounded good in theory.

Mike Stefanic, a friend of mine, who is almost exactly my size, only more muscular, told me once he figured the only guy who ever would come after him either already would know he was tough enough to handle someone that size, or crazy.

154

"Either way, you lose," Mike said. "So, I just run."

Glück came back down with the head honcho from Allianca, a man with a big, purple nose, a bulbous head, a palm tree shirt, and striped, bozo, bell-bottom pants. Lacerda, the real king of the jungle there, was away, Glück said, and the man with the purple nose was running things in the meantime. He told us we could sleep in an open-walled hut where they stored piacaba. Glück sold him three of our tin gas cans for thirty cruzeiros, and later purple nose sold them to the cabocolos for seventy-five. We never saw the money as we exchanged it for coffee and powdered milk. Allianca was a company town.

It took a while to unload, and six men came down to watch. They were dark-skinned and barefoot, some in shorts and others with long pants and buttoned shirts that were open, disco-style. No one spoke, they just inspected everything we carried to the hut. Maybe it was because no one talked, but the faces looked rougher than they probably were, except for two Indian boys, about fifteen years old, who had their arms around each other and watched us with wide eyes.

Tano stayed on shore and guarded our gear in the boat, while Glück and I carried things to the hut. Then we rotated.

I didn't like being around people. Even the night at the teacher's, I was uncomfortable, and at Allianca, I couldn't wait to get over the rapids.

The trip had settled into three segments, the Manaus–Rio Negro leg, the Padauiri, and the next, into the place where we were told we would see Indians, jaguars, mountains, the people from the stars and pyramids. I was anxious for the last leg.

In the piacaba hut, we hung our hammocks beside bushels of palm fibers and rearranged our gear. An old man, a younger piacaba worker, and one of the Indian boys followed us up from the boat. The worker's name was Chico and he said fifty men lived at Allianca, but in November, before Tatunka had come and made his speech, there were three hundred.

Chico asked us if we were going to the mountains. I said yes, and immediately realized I had made a mistake, as saying we were going to the sierras branded us as *oro* men.

Glück offered the three cigarettes. Tano and I refused, but

Glück said, "Smoke the cigarette of peace," which we did. I felt light-headed. I had not smoked in a long time, but I liked the peace pipe idea.

While Glück set up for dinner, Tano and I hung wet clothing on rafters and checked our pockets for our knives. Glück made small talk with Chico, while the Indian boy stared at Tano and me. The Indian had a big jaw that dropped his face lower on his skull, and his eyebrows always seemed arched. His eyes followed motion. When I reached into my pack, I felt his gaze run down my arm, and when I pulled something out and looked up, he followed back up and stared at me, not in a blank way, but since my body had stopped and now my brain might be working, it was as if he was trying to look inside.

Glück found pictures in his gear, pictures he had taken when he was at Allianca with the Austrian. One of the shots was of Chico. Glück gave it to him, and Chico ran out to show his wife. That was enough to get everyone moving and the other guy and the Indian boy followed.

Glück made hot soup, but we still were hungry after the cup he ladled, so we got blunt and asked him to make a real supper, which he did, of rice and eggs and canned meat. After, we went down and pulled the boat out of the water and as we walked back, Tano and I sang, "Another Saturday Night."

156

XXII

TANO askd one of the piacaba workers if purple nose sold razors, but no luck. I never thought I would see the day he would be concerned about finding something to cut his hair, even if it was for his face, which always had some clear space on it. He was like Samson the way he protected whatever he grew on his head. He usually wore a mustache, drooping, the way an outlaw would have had it, and since I had known him, he had cut his hair only once, and that was after I prodded him. We were making our first trip to South America and I was sure we would have trouble at every border we crossed, so I convinced him we should look like GI's, or as close as possible.

I had taken a train from New York to Illinois to meet him, and we spent a few days setting strategy. The trip began for me on the train out, the Broadway Limited. I sat beside a fortyish journalism professor from Moscow, who, if he wasn't asking me questions about the United States ("What does zip-lock mean?"), was reading a Thomas Pynchon novel on which he didn't comment.

He also played chess with me, and I appreciated how he appeared to study his moves and carry the games farther than I thought they would go, so he made me feel I did well to hold out that long. I liked him. We had supper together in the dining car, with black "Yessuh" waiters, and after dessert, my Russian friend asked, "Now, do we leave extra money?"

It was the end of January when I took the Broadway Limited, and that year the winter had been severe and the tracks were in bad shape. The conductor said we could not go more than forty miles per hour, so we arrived in Chicago eight hours late. I missed my connection south, but just getting off and wandering around Union Station in the cold was a relief. I had ridden the train in a T-shirt because the heaters were frozen on high.

The next train out would not be until the next day, but AM-TRAK accommodated me with a room at a downtown hotel, and the next morning, I was on my way south.

I was apprehensive about visiting Tano. I had not seen him in five years, but suddenly we were putting together another trip. He had called me in October. He had recently seen an Ali fight and the night he called, saw *Butch Cassidy and the Sundance Kid* for the second or third time, and the two events were too much for him, and the next thing, I got a phone call in the middle of the night.

I was living in Trenton, teaching at a school for emotionally disturbed kids, which meant mostly ghetto kids who had been in touble, and at night, to avoid thinking about them and their troubles and whatever trouble I might have been having getting through to them, I spent a lot of time reading. Television or booze would have been more doping, but I didn't have a television and saved booze for weekends. It was midweek when I was reading something about the destruction of the earth's atmosphere, or maybe it was Paul Theroux's book about the train ride through Asia, when the phone rang and I picked it up and heard this voice with a Midwestern twang, say, "Frank?"

"Jesus Christ, where the hell are you?"

He had to be in trouble. I remember thinking what I had in the bank and figuring I probably could go one way, anywhere in the world.

I was addressed as Frank because it was a nickname I had picked up when we were in college and referred to as the James

Brothers. Somehow I got stuck with the less romantic name. Tano explained that meant I was the smarter of the pair, although I didn't buy that, but I let him get away with it. The fact he used "Frank" to start the conversation also immediately figured with my suspicions he was in trouble and the phone might be tapped.

"You wanna take off somewhere?" he asked. That completely changed everything I thought the second before, and I felt relieved and laughed.

"Actually, I'm about ready," I said, which ended the crazy side of the conversation and commenced the sensible. "You goddamn son-of-a-bitch. Where the hell are you? What are you up to?"

He said he was back in the States. The last I heard, he was in France or Greece, and by then, I thought he had permanently expatriated himself.

He said he had got himself married to help a Frenchwoman into the States, but she was in California, or back in France, I forget which, and he wanted to take a trip.

"I got some jack stashed and I'm thinking about Southeast Asia," he said.

That was getting ahead of me, as I still was stunned by the marriage part.

"Oh, that was nothin', man," he said. "I spent the wedding night with my head over a toilet I was so drunk and sick," which sounded like a contradiction, but if he wanted to, he could explain it, and if not, I figured he knew what he was doing. Anyway, he said his wife was now living in California, and for the time being at least, he was free.

We talked for a while, not too much, just enough to lay a skeleton down for a trip, and said we would fill in plans and the empty spaces from the past five years when we met again, a few months later, at the end of my train ride.

Riding from Chicago to Bloomington, where he said he would meet me, I drank coffee and tried to remember details about the last time I saw him. I couldn't put it together then, and I can't now, but when we referred to the last time we saw each other, we had called it the Night of the Living Dead.

It had been Thanksgiving and I had returned to Des Moines

159

to see old friends. Two or three of them shared a house together and that was where Tano and I would stay.

I had hooked up with Tano in Illinois, after hitching out from the east coast. It snowed heavily when I wound my way down through Illinois to meet him, and most of one night I stood beside a road outside Decatur, tamping myself a spot in a snowbank. I had my heavy fire-proof army trench coat and lace-up GI boots that went midway to my knees, but by two or three in the morning, after I had spent the day on the road and most of the night in the same spot at Decatur, I felt my fingers and toes getting numb and I worried about frostbite. Tano had got caught in a snowstorm once while hitching, and got his thumb frostbit, but I wasn't anxious to match him.

By the time I reached Decatur, eight inches had fallen. The wind blew hard and most of the time I kept my back against it, and kept jumping up and down. I was in the proverbial middle of nowhere with cars passing at half-hour intervals, and there weren't even any cops out to bust me.

Every once in a while, I caught myself thinking about being dug out by a plow in the spring, but I cut those thoughts off fast and kept jumping and then, to keep my mind occupied, I sang. I was in the part of the country where song usually meant country western and country western meant lament, which would have been appropriate enough, but I didn't know any country western songs then and instead sang some Jefferson Airplane song about how you have to roll with things. I did my best, and I guess it worked, as my blood kept circulating and finally a trucker pulled over and when I climbed into his cab, he said the obvious, "You must be crazy."

It was out of his way, but he took me all the way to Peoria, where, after an hour or two of having watched slow windshield wipers and having exhausted all the information I could muster about that year's basketball season, both college and professional, I thanked him, profusely, got out, and climbed a cliff above the Illinois River where I vaguely remembered Tano lived. My senses were working OK, and I found him and tapped on his window, and we had a hell of a quick-drunk reunion.

I didn't get much time to thaw. Next night we were off, hitching west for what we hoped would be a Thanksgiving reunion with friends whom we'd banded into something called the Magnificent Seven.

We got good rides across Iowa, but it took us most of the night, and near dawn we rolled into Des Moines. The next few days passed in a haze, not because of any induced alteration of consciousness, but because I probably just don't want to remember. I do remember Tano spent most of the days and nights with a girl friend locked in a room with a waterbed. The room was attached to a living room and occasionally I would see him come out and walk to the bathroom; otherwise, I just heard a lot of sloshing.

For the most part, I was bored, and the place and stories and faces seemed stale, which might have something to do with my not being able to stand stopping. That might also have accounted for the way things began on the Night of the Living Dead.

Tano spent too much time with his woman, I thought, and I didn't have a woman, and everyone else seemed leaden, so to liven things up after supper one night, instead of helping wash dishes, I started throwing them. Tano appreciated that and joined in and we threw them at each other and then at walls, which, justifiably, upset everyone else. Circumstances drove one person to tears and the next thing I knew, there was a lot of shouting and crying with demands for explanations and apologies. We heard all of that coming from the living room, as Tano and I stayed by ourselves, screaming and laughing and throwing dishes in the kitchen, which by then was pretty much turned upside down.

Occasionally, an emissary from the living room would come in and try to talk with us, using words like responsibility and crazy and clean up and pay up, but all paths were crossing without meeting. No one was getting the point, or lack of it, I was trying to make, and I certainly was missing theirs.

Later, when things cooled down, Tano and I and one of the emissaries from the living room went out for pie and coffee at an all-night café where we knew better than to throw dishes. Tano and the emissary, whom I always had liked, talked amongst themselves in a way I did not understand, almost as if it was in code. Even now, trying to piece it together, I have no idea what they were talking about, other than somehow I was getting a message

161

that they and their world out there had a much different vision of things than me and my world, wherever that was.

Next morning, before anyone woke, I hitched out.

On the trip to Bloomington, after I had come from New York on the Broadway Limited, all I could remember about the last time I saw Tano was the Night of the Living Dead, and how at the time, I didn't care if I ever saw any of those people again, including Tano.

The conductor shouted "Bloomington," and I picked up my pack and stood between cars. As we rolled through the outskirts of town, the conductor leaned out and waved at a house.

"My mother-in-law's," he said as explanation to me. "She used to come out every day and wave, but last week, my father-in-law accidentally drove the car over her leg. Now, she waves from the window."

It was good to be back in the Midwest where everything had an explanation.

When I stepped off the train, I didn't see him at first, but, in a second, heard my name and turned and saw a long jacket billowing and above it a smiling face and hair longer than my arms. I had a parka shell, World War II Marine Corps pants, lug-soled boots, and an oversize pack, and hugging each other, we must have looked like soldiers embracing after a war.

The next few days, we hovered over maps with whiskey bottles for grips. Both of us had as much money as we had ever had in our lives. I had spent the year before teaching, and he had done work in a railroad yard, and as my grandfather would have said, we were nigger rich.

"There's no place in the world we can't go," I said, liking the sound of the double negative, which somehow strengthened the statement.

Tano leaned toward Asia and I was pushing for the South American mountains. I had spent time in Iran a year and a half earlier and, because of heart strings, had blown a chance to go to the Himalayas. I thought it was the right decision then, and still do now, sort of, but in any case, I somehow associated missing

162

going to India and then on to Nepal as a bit of a capitulation, as if I might have made a mistake.

Tano wasn't eager for mountains, he had his sights set on Burma, though when we considered that half of the world, I suggested Australia. South America was my first choice, though, particularly the Cordillera Blancas, the spine of mountains along the west coast. Tano didn't yearn for snowy peaks, but we agreed we could split up after Panama and he could keep to the coast and I could go inland and upward. The arguments I tried to use for the trip to South America were cost and time. We would go overland. Instead of plunking down a grand for airfare to Asia, we could use that cash for living time in South America. I let that idea carry most of the weight of my argument, as to me, the primary concern was how much time I could spend outside the States. If anything, sediment from my hippie days had hardened into stone. I was fed up with living in the States as ever, and after a year of Bicentennial blues, I figured so was Tano.

It would be a hell of an adventure to go to Asia, I agreed, but if we went to South America, I argued, we could stay out of the States longer.

No decision was reached, but within a few days, we had narrowed the world to Asia and South America. Tano worked on air fares west and I worked on trains south.

There was a problem with trains, the Panama Limited or the City of New Orleans, I forget which, so I also checked flying directly to the Mexican border, where we could catch a train to Mexico City.

Wherever we went, I hoped we wouldn't have to hitchhike. I figured if we started doing that together again, we were bound to run into trouble. We were something like dancers coming out of retirement, and at least in the beginning, I wanted things to go smoothly.

They started OK. The day after we sliced the world in less than half, I decided I needed a haircut, and the cheaper, the better. Tano had heard of the Peoria House of Beauty, where future hairdressers of America learned their skills and let you be guinea pig for $2 a head. Tano thought it was a joke, but I took it seriously and he dropped me off there.

Peoria House of Beauty was what you would expect, a beauty parlor set up like a stockyard. I had to wait in line to get in and then got shuffled five rows and twenty yards into the pen. Heads turned and there was some giggling and pointing. None of it bothered me, as it reminded me of earlier years when my hair made it to my shoulders.

I was introduced to my coiffeuse, to whom I said, "short, real short, otherwise, it's up to you." She took to that and after I told her I was from New York, we quickly became friends. Her name was something like Tammy and somehow she tied my coming from the east as one of her first connections with the Great White Way.

She told me that all her life she had wanted to be a country western singer, "awl mah lahfe," and then go to New York. The two things seemed a contradiction, but were one and the same to her.

"This thing here," she said, waving her scissors too close to my eyes, "it's just in case, just in case getting to New York takes time."

It was the same kind of conversation you might have with a stranger in a bar, the same kind of conversation you could have on the road.

A lot of hair dropped on my shoulders as she talked and when she would spin me around, I would try to catch my face in the mirror and when I did, I thought I might have been rash in my first instructions to her, but she kept clipping and kept talking. She talked about her high school and a boyfriend who really did not want her to be a country western singer and go to New York, and would just as soon have her stay a beautician, but she said, "I'll change his mind." Soon, she only was snipping at errant threads around my ears and I knew she was finished and just taking her time to keep talking, when I heard a voice boom across the stockyard.

"Moo's sister's dying, man, so Moo's going toward St. Louis. We got ourselves a ride. Australia is out. Too much jack. We got a flight to Laredo, then we can catch the train to Mexico. Gotta go fast, though. Mexico, man. Mexico."

All of that made sense to me. Tano yelled his message over

164

the bulbs of hair dryers and flew at me so fast his coat spread out like wings.

I put two bucks on the counter, told Tammy I was sorry I had to leave early, waved good-bye, and chased Tano back across the aisle, then in an afterthought, I turned and yelled back at Tammy, "Good luck in New York," which was a good thing to say as she put on a big smile.

Next night, Tano was propped on a standing ashtray in St. Louis airport, his shirt wrapped tight around his neck, ready to get the Peoria House of Beauty treatment. A friend of his had given us a ride across the Mississippi. To help pass the night in the airport, we bought a bottle of wine, opened it in the lounge, and I began telling them stories about trouble I heard long-hairs had undergone trying to cross borders in Latin America. I don't remember my sources, but the stories included beatings and passport thefts and bribes, and they sounded bad enough to get me worried.

Although I didn't plead with Tano to get his hair cut, I pre-vailed on him with reason.

"If you don't, we'll just get fucked with," I said.

It worked. Tano's friend had a pair of scissors in his van, and in twenty minutes, we had Tano trimmed. We didn't know anything about how to layer or shape or whatever you're sup-posed to do with hair, so we just cut it bowl-style without the bowl. We cut a line from the base of his neck up along either side, then cut a straight line across his forehead. The total effect was something like a cross between Gainsborough's "Blue Boy" and early Beatles.

It was just about midnight when we finished, and when the big hand reached twelve, the date on the lounge clock switched to February 14, and I told Tano his valentine should see him now. He looked in a mirror and said a few things to me, not worth repeating, but I told him it was for his own good, so he shut up.

So I laughed at him when he searched for a razor in Allianca and reminded him of the airport in St. Louis.

"Don't worry, you'll never do that again," he said. We both caught hell on the way down and after we split up in Colombia,

165

Tano caught hell on the way back, and afterward said he never would cut his hair again, because "Man, it wouldn't matter a god-damn bit."

By Allianca, I was beginning to nurture a beard, which I hoped to let go for the full forty days, if the itching did not drive me crazy, and Tano asked me why I didn't grow a mustache.

"You'd look good," he said, and I answered I just would look like every other cop in the States. That shut him up.

XXIII

A rooster crowing woke me. My first perception was that the rain had stopped. I stayed in my hammock since we had nowhere to go immediately, while I heard Glück's joongle pancakes sizzling. Pancakes always came after Glück was able to find eggs, which he did easily in Allianca, swapping them for a couple of packs of cigarettes.

Tano shook himself awake. I saw his hammock swaying, before he announced, "Maybe, with the lighter sky, there's hope," meaning it would make it easier to cross the rapids.

"There is always hope," Glück said, "except for the people, the Jewish, in the concentration camps, when they passed through the last door, then there was no hope."

Glück said something about a Jewish man from Tel Aviv, whom he took on a recent trip.

"In World War II, they say six million Jews were killed, but this is impossible. There are only about fourteen million now, mostly in New York. They would have needed an atomic bomb to kill that many."

"Now, wait a minute, Kurt," Tano said. "What difference does it make if they killed six million or three million or three? What they did was still horrible."

167

Glück immediately got defensive, "Yes, yes, if one Jew is killed it is wrong."

The conversation left a pall over the morning. Once, Tano whispered and asked if I had seen films of the concentration camps and I just said I had.

We had our pancakes and an Indian woman with a child came and asked if we could take her picture. Glück told her we were going to the United States soon and it might be years before we returned, but we took her picture anyway. Tano said that with a boat and a Polaroid and film, we could live forever on the river, an idea that did not make me jump.

Glück told stories about misadventures in Manaus, including a retelling of the hail-that-comes-because-God-is-Brazilian story. The jokes lightened the air from the other talk and we broke camp.

Glück found Chico and asked him if he knew an easy way through the rapids.

"Go through the forest," he said.

He wasn't kidding. We agreed to give him one of our tin cans for his help, and in a few minutes, he rounded up six cabo-colos and the two Indian boys to help us. Chico's plan was to take us through a quarter-mile path that would avoid the rapids.

Eight of us lifted the boat out of the water and carried it down a path that was meant for a single man carrying a pack of piacaba on his back. Going through, we widened the path to three lanes. The men on the port and starboard side of the skiff were torn from thorns and needles on palm trees. I was on the stern, because everyone said I was big and could handle the weight.

We stopped a few times and sometimes pulled along an old man who was supposed to be helping me with the stern. He was drunk, and most of the way we dragged him. When we dropped down into a stream that had a log as a footbridge, Chico, who handled the bow, stayed on the bridge. As the rest of us waded and floated the skiff above our heads, the old drunk pretended to lift the boat above his head, but it was too high for him, so he walked, like a prisoner, with his hands empty but up in the air.

None of the men wore shoes, and I saw one man step on a needled palm branch and not utter a sound.

168

The forest opened and we rejoined the river, which spread wide like a lake above the rapids. We paid the men with a half carton of black tobacco cigarettes and after the cabocolos left, we called the two Indian boys aside and gave them each a pack of cigarettes as they had been left out of the divvying.

By midmorning, we were set to leave, and Glück said, "Now begins the adventure."

In response, the sky opened and the sun came out and the gray melted into the horizons.

We only went about two hours, past where the river had backed up behind the rapids, up to where it was again narrow and winding, when we found a pair of empty huts, and already developing traditions, we stopped to give Sunday its due.

We tied the boat up, hung our hammocks, went for a swim, then did our laundry—three naked men in a boat rubbing clothes and soap together—but the piums were soon on us, so it was less of a laundry and more of a quick rinse. The piums are the no-seeums of the upper Amazon. They seemed to prefer white flesh, the whiter the better, and left my ass, my feet, my lower back covered with welts topped by dots of blood that looked like tiny pomegranate seeds. Whenever we got bit badly, Glück would tell us not to scratch, scratching only made it worse, then he would tell us about the time he went with the television men to find the craters in the jungle and what it was like being attacked for thirty-five days by flies, "the moment we got up, until the sun went down."

When he told us that, it did what it was supposed to do, and I felt lucky, but I had more trouble trying not to scratch.

Our huts were across from a bend in the river where we could see the Padauiri come from the north, curl toward us around an elbow of jungle across from our hut, then turn and flow south. Wherever you stand on a river you always see it come and go, but the way the Padauiri came directly at us and then immediately swept back and away, gave the river a flourish, as if it curtsied.

In the elbow of the jungle, feather palms, like giraffes with sombreros, stretched above the roof of the forest. The wind caught them easily and they had the sun first, and looking at the palms, I always felt lighter.

169

To the north, a rainbow formed. We all said it had something to do with smiling angels, then clouds that could have been
the hems on the angels' robes dragged across the sky and Tano
told me about an Indian tribe who tried to build a tower so they
could ride the clouds.

While we talked, a leaf shaped like an elephant's ear tumbled through vines, touched the river, slid toward us, then
dipped and curled under a branch, rose to the surface, caught another branch, pirouetted, then drifted into the bend and away
with the current.

The day was like the day I saw the cat print on the shore of
the Rio Negro, only more so. There was a feeling of slowing
things down, but also one of stillness, or maybe it was just peace-
fulness. Then, there was something else, something off and un-
stable.

Sometimes, with me, if I stop thinking, things outside me
can vibrate, as if suddenly there is not air buffering me and a
chair in a room and a square of light from a paned window, and
the fact I have collided with those things in a spot in time seems
extraordinary, and even dangerous. Things can get too raw and
feel just a notch away from crazy or dead.

"I don't know," I said to Tano. "Sometimes I get the feeling
there's something else going on besides us going up a river."

I don't remember what he said, so what I said, by itself,
sounds half-baked, but I had the feeling we were getting caught
up in something.

Near sunset, another rainbow split the clouds and then a
warm breeze carried us to evening. The breeze built into a wind
as ripples in the river curled into swirls and small waves.

That night, Glück straightened out the Tatunka–space people–pyramid story. We had got bits and pieces earlier, but maybe
because we were being superstitious, we didn't talk much about
it. Once over Allianca, it seemed OK to talk. We would soon be
there.

We set a candle in the middle of the dirt floor. Tano and I
sat on crates and Glück swung in his hammock and began the
story.

Tatunka Nada No Se was the key.

In 1979, four expeditions were mounted to find the pyra-

170

mids, and two included Tatunka. On the first two, Ferdinand Schmidt, a Swiss man and the secretary of Erich Von Däniken (author of *Chariots of the Gods*), went with Tatunka, along with a Brazilian military officer and an archaeologist. Glück said the Brazilians went along on the government's insistence.

"They want a Brazilian to discover the pyramids," Glück said.

Von Däniken would have gone, but he wanted to skip the canoes and use helicopters to find the pyramids.

"But Tatunka tell him the helicopters will make the Eendy-uns crazy, so Von Däniken didn't come," Glück said.

The expedition was short-lived. On the way up, one of the Brazilians accidentally shot himself in the arm and had to be taken back to Manaus.

Schmidt went back to Switzerland, but a few months later he flew back to Manaus and talked to Glück.

"I tell him, 'Shut up your mouth, and go to the pyramids alone. It is not necessary to take these Brazilians.' "

Schmidt went, and after a month, returned, saying he had found the pyramids and contacted the underground people from the stars. He also said he found Phoenician pottery and ancient bows and arrows, but on his way down the Rio Padauiri, his boat overturned in the rapids at Allianca and he lost everything, including film he supposedly had taken that documented his discoveries. Glück did not believe it. He said the pottery had a French inscription on the base, and a woman saw Schmidt buying the bows and arrows from Melnick.

"It's all booshit," Glück said.

Next, Glück and the Austrian went up in September 1979.

"The Austrian tells me he has thirty-four days to make a trip," Glück said. "I tell him about this pyramid shtuff, and say, 'You want to go there?' 'Oh, yes,' he says. He wants to go. So, we go."

They went, but only made it to the mountains above the pyramid valley. On the way back, Glück and the Austrian ran into another Brazilian expidition that included six soldiers and a Manaus journalist named Perret.

"We met them in Allianca, and they told me it was *verboten* for me to be on the Rio Padauiri. I told them, 'How do I know it is *verboten*? There must be a sign saying 'Rio Padauiri *Verboten* for Strangers to Go Up' the way it is on parts of the Rhine in Germany.' They not like me."

The Brazilian expedition was the one Tano and I read about in the Manaus newspaper. The Brazilians, too, claimed to have discovered the pyramids, along with shards of ancient pottery, and, like Glück, they took a blurred picture of a valley with triangular nubs.

"All these crazy stories," Glück said.

"If we go up and find out these pyramids are bullshit," Tano said, "then when we go back, we're gonna make a lot of noise in Manaus. But, if we go up and just by chance they really are pyramids, then there's gonna be just as much noise. 'Kurt Glück goes up with two Americans and discovers pyramids.'"

"It'll be a terrybluh thing," Glück said.

As he finished his story, lightning flashed near the hut.

"That's the people from the stars telling us to go home," I said.

Glück stopped and said, "Oh, look, here comes the wind."

It came suddenly. At first the air in the hut stirred slightly and the bugs clustered around the candle. Then for a moment everything was still, and Glück said, "I hope not comes the rain," and then immediately comes the rain. Wind roared through the sides of the hut and shook the walls, and the rain pounded the roof. We made a rush to keep things from blowing away or getting soaked, but Tano and I were so completely overwhelmed by the suddenness and power of the storm, we stopped and laughed until there were tears in our eyes, which was our way of telling the skies we gave up. The skies ignored us. The wind felt like it was from a hurricane and the rain fell so hard it seemed to stamp the air to the ground. The storm belonged more to the ocean, it was so sudden and severe, but it was a great equalizer. The three of us were as consequential as ants, and that was a good joke that was true.

For a half hour the storm swept through us in a knot of wind and rain and lightning and thunder. We stood in the center of the hut where it was the driest, and still had to shout to talk. We thought the stars might be commenting on our pyramid stories, but then, figured it had to be the fates.

Then, almost as suddenly as it arrived, the wind drove past, leaving only a slight drizzle that would continue through the night.

It was a rough night. I lay in my sleeping bag while bugs made expeditions across my body. Every time I almost fell asleep, something tickled me awake. My skin was a thin wall between me and the jungle and for the past few days it had been under siege, with bites, scratches, bumps the size of small hamburger buns, welts and blood where it had been broken.

The night followed me into my dreams, where I had long hair again, hitched across the States and had run-ins with the police, while Richard Nixon made a comeback. The hair dream must have had something to do with a conversation Glück had with Tano during the day. Glück asked him why he wore his hair long and Tano said, "I just like it that way." The question must have irritated Tano, as later in the day he told Glück, "I'm not a hippie who just hangs out all day. I work hard for a living," to which Glück responded with a rambling story about his son growing his hair long, then getting in trouble with drugs, with Glück's apparent position being that one leads to the other.

So, between the bugs, long hair, and Richard Nixon, I got little sleep. For a while, I watched the river in the moonlight, or actually I watched a river of fog above the river in the moonlight.

In the morning, a dugout with seven piacaba workers glided into an inlet beside our hut. Glück offered them coffee and the oldest man said two of his men, his sons, had malaria and he asked if we had any medicine. I gave them four quinine pills, knowing they would do little good, but it was something.

When the men left, Glück said, "It's nice to be with people sometimes, but I like it much better when we are alone." That was true and a good thing to say, so we did not mind it so much when we packed the boat in a downpour. The river had risen almost two feet during the night, maybe more, and it had turned color, that time to jelluf-brown.

Allianca had been a boundary, and once we crossed over, we stepped back into the world as it was. The piacaba workers only had been a brief interruption, and though we didn't know it then, we would not see anyone again for weeks.

Glück did not whistle that day. He said that during the night

173

he went to bail out the boat and slipped and fell on his chest. I had heard him coughing during the night, but I thought it was because he was cold and wet. When we asked him how he felt, he said, "Makes nuhzing," but he winced when he moved.

Once before he had told us how he fell from a tree and broke a rib. A couple he was with made a cast for him and for a week he laid in the sand during the day, while his clients went exploring.

"But it was beautiful," Glück said. "I would lie in the sand—I could not move—and then the animals would come along beside me and drink from the river."

The river narrowed and the jungle creeped up on us and sometimes I thought about blowguns. Glück had brought bags of hard candy to defend ourselves against Indians.

"Eendyuns are like children," he had said. "If you offer them food, they will eat everything you have.

"For bonbons, they will give us their oysters, grub worms from the tree. And, too, the Eendyun always has beer, but I don't like. Eendyun woman piss and spit in the beer to make the ferment go fast."

He didn't let us chew much on that one.

"Near the end of the river, there will be a fork," he said. "To the left are the Janooari Eendyuns and an American mission, and to the right, where we go, are the ghost mountains and the wild Eendyuns."

Strings of butterflies snaked above the river like dragons in Chinese New Year's parades, and Glück told us a story about a butterfly collector.

"He used nigger shit to attract butterflies and he wanted me to go and help him collect the shit in Manaus, but I said, 'No, sir.'"

Midafternoon, Glück called out, "Who is the Heeltone? Who is the Heeltone? We need a fine Heeltone with an icebox and a television and ice cream," but the sky answered by darkening and we saw no Hilton.

"I don't know," Tano said. "I feel like an ax is hanging over our head."

"What do you mean?"

174

"Things have been going too well. Something is waiting for us up there. Maybe somebody will get hurt bad, or we'll lose something important, or we'll run into two thousand Indians armed with military weapons."

"Man, you're casting out bad vibes."

Late in the afternoon, we found a Hilton, high on a hill on the west shore. Maybe it was because the weather was turning sour again, but we didn't talk much while we unloaded. Later, we ate dinner in silence, which was unusual for Glück. Tano and I worried about how badly he might have hurt himself.

After cleaning dishes, Glück went to fill the gas tanks, came back with his machete, and stuck it in the ground beside his hammock.

"So," he said. "Now comes the nice moment to jump in the hammock," which also was one of those pin-prick moments that tell you things are different on that spot on the earth, an old man mumbling about dreams and beside him, a three-foot blade.

Tano rigged a string to a rafter so he could rock himself to sleep, and we all climbed into hammocks and, for a while, swung quietly.

From the northeast, lightning came at us, short bolts that looked like javelins. No one said anything, but I knew Tano still was awake as the hut swayed and creaked as he rocked. I watched the lightning from below the eave of the hut, then heard a loud crack in the jungle, like a rifle, and then a ka..ka.. kaaaaboooom, as a tree crashed to the ground, ignorant of wonderings at who heard it, though it did get conversation going.

"M-a-a-a-a-n," Tano said.

Whatever light was left in the sky faded, then came the rain.

Twice during the night, Glück got up to bail out the boat, and again slipped in the mud. The night left him sour and, over a "Quaker breakfast," he complained about Brazilians who, he said, were ruining Manaus.

"They break one of the most wonderful places in the world with shtoopidity." He said their main problem was they stayed in hammocks too long, and for the "joongle, they have plans to settle two hundred million people and fill the Amazon with roads. Why can't they build canals? The river is the best way to travel."

When we left, fog clung to the river, then in an hour, it lifted.

175

"When it rises in the morning, that means rain," Glück said. "When it presses down, that means the sun is pressing on it and there will be a sunny day."

The day stayed gray.

Tano drew pictures of trees and sections of the shoreline in his journal and I told him I used to draw a lot, but I hadn't done anything in ten years.

I took art courses in high school and when I was a senior, majored in art with the thought of maybe going to an art school, but it is an education gone fallow.

When I was a freshman in college, instead of a journal, I kept a sketchbook, which I gave my girl friend in California, hoping it would serve as some kind of an explanation. Years later, I saw her briefly in Maine, and she tried to return the sketchbook. The pictures were terrible and I insisted she keep it, and she did.

I only remember one picture, a young man walking along a highway, kicking a can. I never did anything since. I don't exactly know why, it wasn't a conscious decision, I just stopped drawing. It was like everything got cold and leaves withered and it was a different season.

XXIV

AFTER Tano got his hair cut in the St. Louis Airport on Valentine's Day, we flew to Laredo, Texas, took a bus into town, bought a jar of peanut butter, and asked an old Mexican woman to show us to the border. Then we crossed the bridge over the Rio Grande. There is still doubt whether that was a good move.

In customs, two middle-aged federales with mustaches, blue shirts, and tan caps stopped us.

"Donde vas?"

We looked at each other and in chorus, said, "Mexico."

"Fie dollah," they said.

We looked at each other again, and I said, "No dollah por Mexico," which thankfully was not taken as the insult it was not intended to be. We pointed at other gringos who walked by, and asked, *"Por qué?"* which with our almost-no-Spanish, was supposed to mean why were we being singled out?

"Fie dollah," they said again.

"Man, I can't believe this," I said to Tano. "We walk into the country and it's already baksheesh time." I still had to learn the word *mordida*.

I was carrying a pack and Tano had a sleeping bag tied on a leather strap and a duffel across his shoulders.

"Let's just keep going," I said, which could have been a pretty stupid thing to say, though I guess it was not, because it worked. We walked out of customs in Nuevo Laredo and they didn't even yell "fie dollah."

I got overconfident. At the train station, children selling "cheekletz" and shoeshines clung to us like flies, and as I walked away from them a police officer motioned for me. I expected another "fie dollah," so I waved at him, "No," like I was swatting air, and tried walking down the train platform fast to get away from the "cheekletz." The policeman started yelling at me, but I shook my head without turning around, and the next thing, he ran up and grabbed my arm and started yelling some more, none of which I understood, except the word *"pasaporte."* By then, I realized I had made a mistake.

I handed him my passport and threw my entire semi-Spanish repertoire at him, *"lo siento, no entiendo,* and *pardone me,"* repeated over and over, as he continued to yell the same things at me, over and over, and flip through my passport.

After I said, *"Lo siento, no entiendo,"* enough times, the policeman said, *"Loco,"* shook his head, handed me my passport, and walked back down the platform, which I was sane enough to understand as a merciful thing to do.

Tano had been sitting on a bench, watching, and when the officer left, slid up to me.

"Are you crazy?" he said.

"That's what he said."

"Shit, we crossed the border an hour ago and we've already had two good chances to get busted. Man, we've got to be cool."

Because of that, we decided to isolate ourselves on the train. Maybe it was also because it was the first time we had left the country together, but we decided to toss away, at least temporarily, our third-class days, and get a Pullman to Mexico City.

If being together and on a train in Mexico was a luxury, riding in a cool room, stretched out over linen sheets, with the Sonoran Desert, where Pancho Villa and Geronimo had ridden, passing outside your window, and your buddy in the bunk below, and all of a continent and seemingly most of the time you would need to do it, ahead of you, well, that was just damn wonderful. *Kathunkah, kathunkah, kathunkah,* the rails sung us to sleep that night in a lullaby that took the wheels off my brain, tucked me in, and promised the sweetest of dreams. I could think of few things better in life than to fall asleep in a bed and keep moving.

It cost $15 and took twenty-four hours to get to Mexico City, twenty-four hours we split three ways—in our room, standing on the platform between cars, and in the dining car, where I drank beers and coffee and, for fear of the water, wiped my silverware on the napkins (which made me feel hoity-toity, so I only did it once). An Australian and a Canadian girl had a room a few cars down from us. They lent us a book called *People's Guide to Mexico,* written in early 1970s hippie, and it was good and helpful.

Our plans were to catch a train south the next day, so after we arrived in the Mexico City train station, Tano suggested we spread our things across a bench and sleep in the station.

"It's not worth getting a hotel now. It'll take us most of the night to find a cheap one," he said.

I agreed, though the local police did not.

"No dormir aquí," one of two with holstered guns yelled when we walked toward a bench.

"Shit, man, we haven't even rolled out our stuff," Tano said.

"No dormir. No dormir," they yelled as they walked up and put their hands on their holsters. We responded, *"Sí, sí"* (we were getting better with Spanish), and lifted our packs and walked toward a door. As we left, an old woman on a stairway above the station restaurant waved to us. I had noticed her before, watching us. She had black skin, red hair, and a wide Mexican-looking face, but with a sharp nose. She was barefoot and had a patchwork dress that stretched to the floor. Across her shoulders, she had a blanket, and beneath it, she was knitting something with an orange ball of thread. Her eyes were brown and dilated. She was the kind of woman I would have imagined knew voodoo.

When I walked up to her, I don't know what I expected, but it wasn't what I heard.

"Looking for a place to sleep?" she asked in perfect down-

179

home American. In a weak connection, her question reminded me of the girl on the beach in Daytona.

"Go downstairs," she said. "You can sleep on the floor there."

We thanked her and with her hands still working the thread under her shawl, she slid past and down a hall, her shoulders teetering as she moved, as if she was humming a tune to herself or standing on an invisible boat that carried her just above the ground.

Tano lifted his eyebrows. "Wheew."

Walking into the basement was like walking into a Marxist mural. Across the floor, hundreds of peasants were stretched over boxes and crates and burlap sacks, with machetes and handles from picks and hoes stuck in the air as if everyone had collapsed around a forest of tools. Chickens clucked and babies cried and in a corner a group of men were arguing over a card game. Broken fluorescent lights buzzed from a high ceiling and made everyone look slightly gray, like worms.

"This is going to be a long night," Tano said.

We found a space in a corner, near a bench, but lying down was like curling into a slot in a jigsaw puzzle in which you did not quite fit.

Tano had his gondora, a black Algerian cape he wrapped around himself, and I laid on a pad and covered myself with a wool shirt. Tano smoked a cigarette and in a few minutes, the voodoo lady came down and sat in a space against a bench where two bundles wrapped in rags had kept her spot in the jigsaw. She was about ten feet away, but she didn't look at us. Instead, she unraveled one of her bundles, stuck her arm down inside, and pulled out bottles of a dark liquid she poured into a cup and drank. While pretending to sleep, I watched her, and I guess Tano did, too.

"Druggy," he whispered. I said, " 'Spose," then rolled over and slept through much of the night, except when I heard a thud and saw a baby on Tano's back, as if someone had just thrown it. We gave Moses to a woman on a bench, but she didn't move a muscle and looked through us, so who knows?

Tano crawled back under his cape and said, "M-a-a-a-a-n," then a few seconds later, I heard muffled giggling, and I giggled, then went chasing after my dream.

180

We spent the next day hopscotching through officialdom, trying to get visas at the Panamanian, Costa Rican, Colombian, Nicaraguan, Honduran, and Guatemalan consulates, all of whom told us we would have to get them at their borders. By evening, we were back at the train station and found that the night train to Veracruz was full, but we also found a blond Mexican kid who sold us his tickets on a Pullman he was supposed to take, but could not. They cost $5 each and were for a bed, washroom, and a night of movement. I was even more shocked when the conductor accepted them.

After the train left the station and before we went to sleep, I wandered down the corridor, out of the sleepers, through the brightly lit first-class section and into second class, which immediately was apparent because it was dark and smelled like urine and vomit and sweat and you had to step across bodies on the floor, like at the basement of the station. It was not until the second to last car that I found what I was looking for, a woman with a kerosene lantern and a white bucket sitting against a wall and occasionally singing, *"Encheelaahdas, taaahcos."* They were wrapped in newspaper and after Tano and I finished three each, we wiped our hands and mouth on the paper, then laughed, because as nouveau-uptown hoboes, we forgot we had a sink with running water, which we used. Then, like very uptown hoboes, we lay down, with full stomachs, and again on clean sheets and bunk beds, listened to the ticking of the rails.

"Laaaaaaafe is good," Tano said.

An hour or so after dawn, we were sitting with old, bereted Spanish men with cigars and newspapers, in an outdoor cafe on the main plaza in Veracruz, drinking *café con leche* and waiting for waiters with white jackets and bow ties to serve us *huevos rancheros*.

After they came, and in between bites, Tano said, "Man, we can't keep this style of living up."

"Right," I said, while wiping my mouth and asking for more *café*.

We spent Mardi Gras in Veracruz and managed to get out of town without Tano's getting busted for causing a ruckus near the plaza, though it was close.

On the train trip south, there was little difference between first and second class, except first class didn't have seats facing each other and the banho had a door, so for the extra couple of dollars, we opted for the door. We were heading for Tonalá, a town near Mexico's Pacific coast, in the southwest corner of the country, where we heard the water was warm and there were wide open beaches. The trip would take eighteen hours and most of it was a delight. We made stops at every dot of a town on the map and at each, vendors, mostly children and women, boarded and ran up and down aisles, singing, *"Caaaafé neeegrrro, caaaa-faaay con lehcheeee ... taahcos, boooooreeetoze, encheeeeela-das, cheekletz, tomallays, horechada."*

I sampled it all, along with pieces of chicken, corn, pop-sicles, and pineapples tossed at our window by an old woman in a white dress running beside the train.

At one stop, an old blind man with a guitar boarded. He had a round face that was only slightly longer than it was wide, and his skin was the color of varnished pine. He wore a straw hat, a tan work shirt, loose cotton trousers with a rope for a belt, and scuffed black tie shoes. He stood in the front of the car until the train began to move, then he picked up his guitar, and over the clanging of the rails and the *huff, huff, huff, huff,* of the engine, he sang in a high, beautiful voice about love and a girl, which was all I could understand, although that was enough, because if I knew more I would have had tears in my eyes at the end when he dropped his head and his hand slid across the strings making the guitar sound like a harp. For a moment, the dozen people in our car were silent. All I heard was the creaking rattle of the train and the belch of the engine. Even outside, fields of palmettos, golden in the noon sun, seemed to hold still until I remember feeling a breeze and someone started to clap and then we all did, and the old blind man waddled down the aisles, his eyes pointed at the ceiling as we dropped money in his hat.

"South America," Tano said.

We stumbled off the train two hours before dawn, which was not too soon. By then, first class had become sludge class. Despite the doors, banhos at either end had erupted and the overflow spread to the fourth or fifth row. That left the car filled with more flies than passengers.

When we got off, we walked ten feet to a bench, dropped

our bags, and went to sleep. With the sun, we were up again, and had breakfast in town at a restaurant outside of which a truck with a loudspeaker had parked, so we ate deafened by a man making a political speech.

"Whatever language it's in, it sucks," Tano said. I didn't answer because my mouth was full of water as when we first sat down, I mistook a bowl of salsa for tomato soup.

We waited two hours near the marketplace for a bus to take us to Puerto Arista, about fifteen miles away on the coast. The wait seemed longer than it was.

"Do you believe in flashbacks?" I asked Tano.

He looked down the street.

"Not if we're both seeing the same thing."

It was near noon, the temperature was in the nineties, a sandy road shimmered in the sun, and a hundred yards away, the lines of stone houses wobbled. But, as they walked toward us, the silhouettes of four elephants were straight and dark.

A man in a black hat led them as they thudded past, followed by a dozen small boys. With one eye, each of the elephants glanced our way as they passed, then dropped pancakes which kicked up puffs of dust.

"Must be a circus in town," I said.

"Must be."

The bus, an old schoolbus painted blue, left us a mile from Puerto Arista, a distance and walk that was just about enough to get ourselves straightened out from squeezing between vegetable crates and old women in the backseat. It also was a distance we thought about retracing when we arrived. Puerto Arista was much bigger than we expected, with dozens of thatched huts on the beach, a dirt road with about twenty houses behind the beach, and loads of gringos.

"Not what I thought," I said.

"Nope."

Still, a beach was a beach, and we walked onto it, dropped out bags, stripped down to underwear, and dived in the surf. It was rough and warm, but because it was February, it was also special.

The waves dumped us twice before we were out and running at a man we had seen crawling from behind a sand dune toward our gear. He turned and ran when he saw us coming.

"How long did that take?" Tano said. "A minute?"

That was about all that went wrong there, and we ended up glad we didn't walk back that mile.

We carried our gear to the south end of the beach and found a *palapa* with no sides, but a solid roof. We had stopped at a hut a hundred feet closer, where a Mexican couple were charging ten gringos, mostly Canadian, $1 a night, but they said it was OK to sleep in the last hut; that was free because it didn't have walls and the roof was rotten and bug-infested.

Our first night, we went to the main café in town. The café was a concrete carport with four Formica tables, folding chairs, a propane stove and icebox, and a record player with one record, Bob Dylan's "Blonde on Blonde." The proprietor was a heavy, middle-aged woman named Maria, who as California hippies in the palapa next to us would say, made "outrageous" omelettes for fifteen pesos. Our first night, we went for *pescado frito* and *cerveza,* but soon got on to bigger things.

Maybe it was the *cerveza,* or maybe it was "Blonde on Blonde," or maybe it was just that we still had not filled in a lot of the empty five years and it was time to have the conversation. I only remember the jist of it, except for some things Tano said, which began with, "Man, life is a gift."

I had been in Tehran, Iran, teaching, two years earlier. It was at the height of the Shah's power and the city and country were undergoing convulsions of growth and westernization that eventually would fuel revolution. Tehran was mad with modernization. For some outsiders, like me, evidence of sickness was blamed on development that was more cancer than growth. I thought a story I had heard about the Tehran dogs was part of that, though later, when I was talking to Tano in Puerto Arista, I didn't connect the dogs with development. The dogs were about something else.

Other people had told me the story of the dogs, and even though I saw the dogs myself, I never saw them die.

South of Tehran, at the entrance to the city, there is an archway, built during the Shah's regime to symbolize Iran's passing through the gate to the modern world. There is a grassy park around the arch, the same park many people would see on television a few years later, as it was the site of demonstrations against the Shah. When I was there, sometimes I would see people in the park, Iranian construction workers or occasionally couples, but most often, I saw the dogs.

When I passed the arch, I was always in a car or a bus, so I never saw anything for more than a few seconds, but that was enough to see that the dogs lying on the grass were tired and sickly. I had passed the archway only a couple of times when an Iranian told me the dogs went there to die.

"They lie there and wait in the grass for a while and watch cars and trucks pass," I was told. "Then, when it is time, they get out and lie in the road. It is quick."

I never had heard of animals committing suicide and I believed the story though maybe I shouldn't have.

At dinner, I told Tano the story, using it as evidence that existence was not always in and of itself worthwhile, and when things become overbearingly miserable, even animals call it quits.

He didn't say anything for a bit, just took a puff or two from his cigarette, while I stared back and sipped my beer. Then he talked.

"Man, life is a gift," he said. "What you say about it being meaningless, what difference does that make?" He leaned against the table, his hands on the edge. "I don't know where I came from, and you're right, when I'm dead, I'm probably gone, but now I'm here and breathing air that's come off the sea, and there are stars out and I'm going to sleep under them tonight and I'm going to hear the ocean. I'm sitting with you and we're drinking beers and smoking cigarettes and I'm alive and I don't care what those people say in the books you've read, I'm here now and this is life. No matter what it does to me, it's precious."

I didn't argue with him then, but I didn't agree with him either. Life seemed much more indifferent and what it dished out was not always precious, and I knew Tano knew I was thinking that, but we let things be.

"You and your dog story shit," he later laughed as we stumbled half drunk toward the beach.

It was good to have someone like Tano, someone you could pass your dog stories on to. There were only a few other people I could do that with, including two guys I had known since high school, Bill Saupe, whom I went to Iran with, and Chris Kronberg, a fishing guide in Montana. I was smart enough to know that to have people like that was lucky. As it is with every generation, when I grew up, truths were a hard thing to come by and it was good to have a reference point. Things would happen so fast then, it was difficult to find something solid, which often was someone, someone you trusted to swap stories with and share the exploration. Unlike the way I first thought it might be, life did not line up. It was more like a jigsaw puzzle and sometimes pieces were shared.

When Tano and I were in Puerto Arista though, neither of us was trying to put anything together and that made a week pass in a blissful succession of sunrises and sunsets. We had stepped off the other world. I would wake up on the beach and when the sun got high enough, drift back to our palapa, then down a glaring white sand road to the café for breakfast, then take a swim, go back to the hut, and loll in a hammock and read or scribble in a journal or nap or go back out for another swim, until the sun was ready to slide behind the ocean and we would go out and watch it and then head to Maria's for dinner, all of which gave weight to Tano's argument about life.

Two Italian women showed the next day. Angelina was twenty-nine and Merina, thirty-one. They had been living with the Huichol Indians in the state of Nayarit. The Huichol were probably the most primitive tribe extant in Mexico and were best known for their ability to run endless distances.

"They run down deer," Angelina told us.

Angelina and Merina had lived with them for two years. I wish I could remember how and why the women first went there, but I do remember they came to Puerto Arista to recover from hepatitis they had contracted from drinking bad water at a Huichol well. Most of the day they said they had to stay in the palapa and rest, a state of being that suited us, so we quickly became friends.

We had met them at the café and Tano immediately coaxed them to the beach, where he said he could point out different constellations in the sky. He told them he knew only a few, and I looked at him with a "You bullshit artist" look, because I thought he hardly knew any, but he had told the truth. He knew Orion and the Big Dipper and a few more, but it was OK, because the girls were giggling and we kept trying to find the Southern Cross, a futile effort because we still were too far north. When we failed at that, we tried saddling clusters of stars with contemporary names, which across the barriers of Italian, Spanish, and English, proved great entertainment, and demanded unified effort, so Angelina and I and then Tano and Merina got paired in the sand. Nothing came of it though ("I wonder if we could get hepatitis from them?" I asked Tano later), as nothing was attempted, though Tano thought he might have got the short end of the deal.

"I had the idea about the stars. How'd you end up with Angelina?" Tano said. Angelina was pretty, with shining brown hair and eyes, a bright smile and cheeks that looked like they could be as soft as her breasts, but that was only an assumption. She looked like if she was made up, she could have passed as one of those pouty European models who wore bright red lipstick and puckered their mouths.

Merina looked more like a tired schoolteacher who always helped out her brothers with work around the farm. She had a craggy face, the remnants of acne, a wide jaw, and straggly black hair. Whereas Angelina was shapely, Merina was stout, with thick ankles and broad shoulders, but what Merina lacked in looks, she made up with personality.

"I have a question, with no intentions," she would say to us every time she had a question, no matter what the intention, a preface that Tano and I never understood, but it was a preface always followed by a delightful question.

"In America," she would say, "where you find these hotcha doggies?"

For days, Angelina and Merina told us about their life with the Huichol and their lives in Italy, while we answered questions without intentions, shared pineapples and tortillas, and tried to make ourselves seem as un-American as possible. The women tired easily and every afternoon they would take a nap, which we did too, or else watch a young Canadian woman in the hut beside us, who spent the day between her hammock and the beach where she flashed a deep brown tan, only slightly interrupted by a black tonga.

It may have been restlessness that finally pushed us on, although I think it was just a sense we had better get going. Angelina and Merina were planning to leave for Guatemala City to sell

Indian blankets the following week, and Tano and I debated about asking them to leave early and come with us, but then decided against it, figuring things were better left as is.

The evening we left, the people in the Canadian hut invited us to a bon voyage shrimp dinner. We accepted, as did Merina and Angelina. The tonga-clad Canadian was there, too. She said she was from Montreal and spoke French, which we spoke with her, although it was a brief conversation with us telling her where we were going and where we were from, and she seeming to be less than interested, which Tano and I blamed on our short hair.

After dinner, Merina and Angelina came and sat with us while we packed. Merina wrote a poem in my journal.

The solitary bird's characteristics are five.
The first that he flies toward the highest point.
The second that he doesn't need companions, not even
    similar ones.
The third that he aims at the sky with his beak.
The fourth that he hasn't a definite color.
The fifth that he sings with much sweetness.

Beside the poem, she pressed a violet flower that she said was a palenque. Then they both gave us tiny pouches with something magical inside and I felt my throat knotting, so we quickly hugged and kissed them and walked away.

It was almost nine o'clock and we had bargained/arranged for a taxi driver who lived on the road beside the café to take us to the train station. He drove an old Ford Fairlane with a trunk without a hood, where we put our gear. The driver didn't talk, but turned on a radio station that played loud music that sometimes faded, so we would listen to the buzzing of insects outside. The radio was the only light on the dashboard, while at the front of the car ony the right light worked, so in the darkness, the driver seemed like he was taking us somewhere by flashlight. He drove fast, but the ride to town seemed like it went on forever.

"You know we've left paradise," I said.

"I know it."

188

XXV

THE river wound back and forth, fifty yards in one direction before it would reverse itself. Left to right, right to left, left to right, right to left. It was like we followed a stairway north up the skin of the earth.

Most of the way above Allianca, the current was marked by suds that Glück said were minerals the rains had scraped off the rocks in the mountains. The river narrowed to forty feet and the green walls closed off much of the sky. We looked for mountains between breaks in trees, but the clouds or the angels, or whoever they were, blocked the horizon.

We motored north until the river forked, with a small, fast running branch to the left, and a larger, slower-moving arm to the right. We went left.

In twenty minutes, the river contracted to twenty feet. Tano and I got on either end of the bow and used machetes to hack through fallen trees, slashing into the water to break off limbs that might jam the propeller.

Mountains seemed farther away than ever, while the jungle closed in. At some points, trees arched over the river, and the

Padauiri, if that was what we still were on, looked like a drain clogging.

When I am asked what the jungle was like, those are the places I first remember, not the openness on the lower river or the big skies of the Rio Negro. I have tried to think of a word or a sentence to pass off as a quick explanation, but the Amazon cannot be distilled, though many try, including me.

The more I thought about it, the more I sensed the Amazon was like the tree that fell the night before and the noise it made. Maybe even the absurdity the philosophers argued about had meaning. The Amazon, and every other point in the universe, was an immense interaction, a composite of everyone's stories, and everyone who had stepped foot in it added to its form, even if, as Glück had suggested, a good part was lies. The Amazon is a tangle of life fighting for a piece of the sky, a pressure of green that forces you to react. It is a place that with its bugs and its heat and sun and animals and size and diseases is always at you. It never lets up until it draws you out, and when you become part of the tangle, then for you, that is the Amazon.

XXVI

THE jungle got thicker, the river narrower, and the sky grayer. We could not see the mountains yet, but Glück expected to see Lacerda's settlement that day. He also said we should have passed a couple of huts he remembered from the trip with the Austrian, but as yet, we hadn't seen any. Maybe we were lost, but Glück said he thought the river looked familiar.

Late in the afternoon, we stopped. The trees were as dense as any place we had seen during the day, but an indentation in the shore gave us a sandy spot to beach the boat. It took more than an hour to hack out a campsite and tie our hammocks to trees. I wrapped my pod tightly, but when the rain came, I knew it would ignore the effort.

"I don't have this down to a science yet," I said to Tano.

"Yeah, but neither does the man," he said.

Glück fussed over his hammock in an extension of his kitchen routine, mumbling to himself over victories, "Ah, so," and defeats, "Ah, *sheiss*."

After a dinner of rice and what Glück called "coronet beef," we tried to shape plans for the next day. In between, Glück made tea and asked me, the way he would ask me every time we had

191

tea or coffee or oatmeal, if I wanted sugar. I said no, the way I always did, and Glück said, "*Zucker* is good with that. I like a little *zucker* with it," the way he always did. Every time he would serve us something to which sugar could be added, he would ask us if we wanted any. Every time we would decline, he once again would counter with, "*zucker* is good with that. I like a little *zucker* with it."

The tea was hot, but not much hotter than the night, which settled down like a warm sponge.

"Even if this is the wrong river." Glück said, for the first time conceding the possibility, "we should go on. Maybe we will find Indians."

"I don't know, Kurt," Tano said. "I think we should go one more day, and if we still think this is the wrong river, then turn back. This whole trip has been directed toward the pyramids."

When Tano set things to a point like that, his voice drawled and sounded more Midwestern, like the words got fat from all the thinking the statement had consumed. His voice came from a place where the land was flat, the rows of corn straight, the rivers smooth-flowing, and when someone said it felt like rain, chances were it would rain.

Glück's voice sounded more like opera and science. There was adventure and romance in it, but then there was a drive for conclusions, a push for conquering frontiers, even unexpected ones.

I just sounded desperate. "We've got to find the pyramids."

The big problem would be gas. We had started with three hundred liters in Manaus, but by the time we reached Allianca, we had one hundred fifty, and now we only had forty. We could go another day upriver, then if nothing, we could turn around, drift downstream, and try the other fork. So, the gas made our decision.

We sat by the shore and listened to a macaw squawk from the opposite bank. The river ran by fast and brown. Flies and small bees droned around my ears and we watched the sky through a window of trees. I didn't look forward to the night. I expected rain. It did, throughout the night.

I told myself to ignore the rain. It was a discomfort that was

192

relative, a weak argument that at least for one night held. Instead, I dreamt how our provisions were swept downstream.

"Hello," Glück called in the morning. "I dream last night that all our shtuff gets washed down the river." Tano didn't say what he dreamt, and I didn't want to ask.

Progress slowed even more as the river seemed to lose its edge over the forest and the two became more embattled. We had to guide the boat through sunken logs, vines, and sandbanks, and then as Glück announced, "Ten and ten minutes," the trouble began. A tree, four feet in diameter, had fallen across the river and closed it off.

We pulled to shore and walked around the tree, but decided the easiest way around would be over the top. At the tree's lowest point in the river, we swung the ax. The three of us worked in shifts, slamming into the trunk until we cut a wide but shallow notch. We took our supplies, the gas tanks, and the engine out of the boat, lined them on the trunk, then jumped in the water and heave-hoed the boat over the top. It took exactly an hour, and when we reloaded the boat and got set to take off, Glück announced our success with, "So."

"So," was premature. The current drove us back into the tree before Glück could yank the starter cord, so Tano and I had to use oars to hold our stern from the tree. Glück yanked again and got the engine started, then threw it into full throttle, which was something like hot-rodding and popping the clutch.

We stopped to eat crackers with iodine water on a sandbank, and a butterfly with a half-foot wingspan floated overhead. It was so brilliant blue, even against the clear sky, that when its wings flapped open and shut, they looked like flashing neon. I have read that a naturalist, Frank Chapman, described them, the electric-blue morpho butterflies, as the bluest things in the world.

"*Vunderbar,*" I said to Glück, who answered, "Naturally."

We were excited after humping the tree, but Glück said he would like to lie in his hammock and take a nap. He had worked hard and deserved it, but I was flush with overcoming the log and said something stupid like, "to the mountains."

At the next curve in the river, in fifty yards, we were

blocked by another tree. Its trunk was tan with dark spots and Glück said he might have gone over it with the Austrian, but he was not sure. Near the west bank, it hung above the water, so instead of axing our way over, we decided to hack our way under and through, which we did, quickly.

For the next hour, we sheared a half dozen propeller pins, then stopped when we were cut off by another tree. Again, we passed by pulling the boat under at a point near the shore.

Through the afternoon, Tano and I rode at the bow of the boat. We kept our machetes with us and pointed Glück the way he should maneuver as the river was low and thick with logs, and in some places, rocks. Sitting on the bow also helped balance the boat and lift the engine closer to the surface, which seemed to make Glück happy.

"Excelente," he would say as we eased over a bed of rocks.

It seemed every two or three turns in the river, logs and trees stopped us. One was nine feet in diameter and as hard as ironwood. When we rounded a bend and saw it, Glück slowed the engine and no one spoke. It was one of the biggest trees I ever saw. For a few moments, we just sat there and looked. When we reached the other trees, the boat had to stop, but at least our thoughts kept going. The big one stopped everything.

"Come on, now," Glück said, and we went. We unloaded and carried the engine and gas tanks and supplies to shore. We tied a rope to the bow and Tano and I walked across the tree, which was as wide as a single lane bridge, and at a dip in the trunk where the river was only four feet below, we hauled over the skiff.

Ten minutes farther upriver, another log. That time, we kept everything in the boat, got into the water, which was to our waists, and with Glück leading our efforts with heave-hos, teetered, then tottered, the skiff over the top.

On the other side, Tano and I held the stern from the log. Glück started the motor. We climbed on the log, leaped over him and into the boat, then he gunned us away.

By 3:30, there were no signs of mountains, rocks, or anything Glück could remember from his trip with the Austrian. Once, we saw a golden eagle staring at us from a branch of a tree. Tano said it was a good sign, because golden eagles usually live

194

near the mountains. When the eagle saw us, he turned and flew upriver, but when we followed around a few bends, there were still no signs of the sierras.

The river was becoming less of a medium and more of an adversary and we looked for anything that might give us an edge, even if it was golden eagles. Back and forth we zigzagged, with each turn in the river feeling like we had opened a door, and behind every door, we expected another log. Sometimes it would be too shallow to motor through, and we would get out and pull the boat until it got deep again. Other times, when the river narrowed to fifteen feet and a small tree would block us, Glück would give the engine full throttle and we would roar forward until just before we hit the log, when Gluck would lift the propeller out of the water and we would shoot over the log as if the tree were a ski jump. Then, again, sometimes that didn't work and we would get hung up and have to get out and do the old "heave-ho." Tano and I kept our machetes and paddles at our side. We couldn't go thirty feet without hitting a log, sand, vines, or rocks, and anything we touched would have ants, stinging caterpillars, or thorns. We lost count of how many trees we had to beat and by the end of the afternoon, we were low on gas, hungry and exhausted. We found a spot on the west shore where the forest was thin, although there wasn't a place to pull up the boat. Tano grabbed a tree and then jumped out of the boat to pull us in when a crocodile leaped off the shore and shot past his leg.

Tano jumped, then laughed. "Man, it don't let up."

Glück went to sleep after dinner, while Tano and I sat out beside a candle. Tano's face was red-brown, his teeth shone in the light, and he wore a red bandanna around his head.

"You look like some BC creature," I said.

"Man, you look like you got your skin off a pair of old chaps," he answered.

We both laughed and talked about what had happened since we left Allianca, how we should have seen the mountains by then, should have been close to the pyramids, should have seen piacaba huts, and should have been able to figure what river we were on, but there was nothing on the aerial maps that resembled whatever we were navigating.

"We're lost," Tano said.

195

"Well, lost really doesn't have much meaning here," I said, which was my way of making up for earlier saying, "To the mountains."

Tano rolled me a cigarette from moist tobacco and soggy papers.

"Well, if nothing else, maybe we've discovered a river," I said.

That got Tano thinking, which he did silently for a while, then said, "Yeah, well people always have to go and name a river, so instead of naming this one, let's just call it our river."

That was OK by me, but in a minute, everything still felt as bad as it had two minutes before. We had hacked our way upriver for two days and kept hacking because of the commitment of gas and time and effort, but now the possibility of not reaching the pyramids began to gnaw at us.

"One thing, for me, anyways," Tano said, "if we don't get to the pyramids, it's going to be a big disappointment. This is a beautiful, great river, but the whole time I've been writing in my journal, 'We're going to the pyramids, the magical trip to the pyramids.' If we don't make it ... God, it'll be a bummer. Tomorrow will be our day of reckoning."

With only nine hours of gasoline left, there seemed to be little choice, yet the suddenness of how quickly the trip had reached a boom or bust point took us both by surprise. It hadn't given us time to think how rough it was going to be to go back down the river, crossing those logs in reverse.

"Well, with nine hours of gasoline left, maybe we'll use the extra hour or two the next day to keep going farther, and then maybe we'll start dragging the boat by a rope," Tano said, laughing at how ridiculous that sounded, though it was a prophecy that would be fulfilled.

"The river can't last must longer," I said.

Bats swooped through the air, and through a break in the ceiling of trees, we saw Orion's belt. Tano took a deep drag from his cigarette, flicked the butt into the river, and blew out a cloud of smoke. "I just hope the pyramids are up there."

It was good to be back in the water in the morning, but around the first bend, another fallen tree. Tano and I, our hands

196

empty and dangling between our legs, turned and looked at each other.

The day would be a succession of downed trees. We were constantly moving in and out of the boat. Our clothes stayed off, but we kept our sneakers on, as three-inch needles transformed sunken palm trees into underwater barbed wire. We would unload the boat, then, "Hoooa," it over a log as Glück hollered, then leap into the skiff on the other side of the log. "Watch out," Glück would yell at the man on the point to duck down as we skimmed through webs of branches covered with things that either stung, scratched, tore, or bit. When the river cleared, the point man would use his paddle, dip it into the water, and measure depth until we hit a spot where he would yell, "Shallow," and we would get out and drag the boat. We hacked our way through bushes and trees and stumps of logs, until all of us had blistered hands and Tano sprained his wrist. When it got deep enough to use the motor again, we moved slowly until we hit something and Glück's *"Sheiss,"* would tell us we had broken another propeller pin.

Three hours into the day, we came to a small waterfall with black, rounded boulders and a fifty-yard maze of rapids. Glück said he did not remember the rapids, but, as with everything else, that could be due to a difference in seasons and river depth, though we really didn't believe that.

We carried everything from the boat up and around the rapids, then tied the boat with a rope and slowly dragged it through and over rocks. After we reloaded and rounded the next curve, we reached another downed tree.

Noon, we stopped on a sliver of a sandbank and had a lunch of sardines and crackers interrupted by a discussion of tapirs, as a pair of them, maybe two-hundred pounds apiece, slid across the river just above us. Other than that, none of us talked much as we were taking our place in the pecking order, the jungle edging the river and the river edging us.

As the day wore, so did we. No mountains, no Indians, no pyramids. I thought about being lost, but that drifted away fast, as there was not much time to think.

The river continued to wind and Glück often would say, "Who is north?" and then check his compass and say, "Yes, I sink we go in right general direction."

After about the sixth time he said that, Tano whispered, "I wonder if he's spacing out."

The night before, Tano and I had talked about how for the last two weeks we hadn't been more than twenty feet from one another, and it had gone well.

"We could be ready to kill each other," I said. "Even Glück, he could drive us crazy."

"Really."

That turned out to be another prophecy to be fulfilled.

Glück was tough that day, though. He took his blood pressure pill in the morning, hacked away with the ax and machete, and hooa-ed alongside of us, and when the day was finished, he went fishing, whipped dinner together, then washed his boat, with an explanation, "All dis shtuff gets dirty."

We saw more jakaris and large snapping turtles and toucans, and Tano found a tiny turtle the shape and color of a maple leaf.

"Beautiful, beautiful, and *vunderbar* to be on an unexplored river," Glück repeated, perhaps sensing the pyramid discontent on the seats in front of him.

When we asked him why not turn back and try to find the Padauiri, he said, "Datz booshit," which was supposed not only to mean our idea was bad, but also referred in general to the story he pieced together about the pyramids.

Late in the afternoon, the angels, or whoever, threw us the proverbial crumb. A small fished jumped in the boat and Glück smacked it over the head with a paddle, held it up, and smiled.

"Fish soup for dinner."

At 3:30, we sheared another propeller pin in a spot where we could pull the boat ashore, so we decided to camp. After setting up, we took a swim and I put on an old white shirt and my long jungle pants and felt pretty good.

For two days, it had not rained, but we were beginning to hope for it. The river was getting shallow. If no rain came, it could be a long walk back.

Rain did come for supper, but it only lasted a few minutes, just long enough so we had to eat our fish soup under tarps. After it stopped, we sat next to the boat and talked about where we had come from and where we were going.

"On our day of reckoning, we're wrecked," was the way Tano put it.

198

XXVII

AFTER Puerto Arista, things went from bad to worse to more worse and eventually got close to hitting worst. We slept in the railroad station in Tonalá and woke in the middle of the night when we heard the train whistle. I had been dreaming about leaving a woman, but it was one I didn't know.

It took us a combination of bus and train rides to make Guatemala City, along with a few conversations that essentially were a refrain on blown chances.

"Angelina, Angelina, mon amore," I sang to the tune of Nat King Cole's "Mona Lisa."

"Man, you got it bad, didn't you?" Tano said.

"Maybe we're doomed to make mistakes," I said.

"Sometimes I think so, too."

Guatemala City came on us like a bad dream. I was half awake when we arrived, around 10 PM, and my first impression was that we had entered a bombed city after a war. Buildings were mostly single-storied, the air was a gray-jaundiced color, and the city was divided into numbered zones that compounded the postwar effect. People in rags slept across pieces of stone that were supposed to be sidewalks, and in the bus station, families with four or five children huddled around bound cardboard

199

boxes I assumed held most of what they owned. Guat City, as Tano called it, was a place you would want to leave, and we were going in the wrong direction.

After a miserable night in a flophouse, we hitched south. At the border of Guatemala and El Salvador, we met a young black guy who looked like Jimi Hendrix, was barefoot, and had a pack made out of a white sheet tied to three tree limbs. He was heading back to the States, but had been stuck at the border for six hours because the Guatemalans said he didn't have enough money to get into their country. He had $10 and an "I'll just wait" attitude I am sure he needed. He was the second poorest traveler we had run across on South American hippie trails. In the Mexico City train station, down in the basement, we had met a crew-cut American teenager whose only possessions were his white boxer shorts and a wool blanket. Otherwise, he was shoeless, shirtless, moneyless, passportless, and, we assumed, homeless. He said he got by, by begging and hopping freight trains. Dragging his blanket around the station, he looked something like Linus grown up.

By nine o'clock, we were in La Libertad on El Salvador's Pacific coast. We ate dinner in an open café on a square, where I guess Tano overheard a man talking with a woman at another table, because Tano asked him, *"Vous êtes français?"*

"Oui, et vous?"

"Non, non ..." which though it may have disappointed the man, led to Tano's asking him and his lady friend to join us for coffee.

He told us his name was Bruce, which struck me as a funny name for a Frenchman, and his friend, who looked like Peter Pan, was Murielle. Later, Bruce told us his name actually was Gérard, but Americans never could pronounce it right. Instead, he used the name Bruce. At the time, I wasn't sure if that said something about the previous Americans he had met or Gérard, but for Gérard's sake, I assumed the latter.

Often, when I have met foreigners, particularly young French, the conversation sooner or later, usually sooner, gets to Americans and how rich they are. With Gérard and Murielle, it happened sooner.

"What's wrong with Americans?" Gérard asked. "They come

200

to places like this and spend a lot of money"—meaning that because Americans are willing to spend a lot of money, they ruin it for everyone who is not.

"And then," Murielle said, "if they're not spending money, they're selling stupid things. I don't think everyone in the world wants Coca-Cola."

Tano, who had lived in France for a while and married a Frenchwoman, whom he had temporarily split up with, at least geographically, was quick to ally himself with Gérard and Murielle. I didn't say anything, I agreed with them, although I was more neutral, as I thought if the French had the Coke patent, they would be just as quick to market it in East Jibbip.

Being American wasn't easy. Abroad, you always were assumed to have more money than you did and, tangentially, were responsible for Vietnam, Kissinger, bad movies, pollution, military dictatorships, repression, Wonder bread, Nestlé milk, imperialism, and whatever else might have hastened the demise of man. Thankfully, Germans began once more to vie with Americans for having big mouths and Japanese got the rap for cameras. All that was OK by me, as long as I didn't take part of the rap.

The other side was that often you ran into other Americans who liked to tell you that you came from the land of clean toilets, sanitary water, vegetables that were treated with chemicals instead of sewage, directions that were right, appointments and schedules that were met, hamburgers, cheap whiskey, ice cubes you could chew safely, telephones that worked, electric lights, well-fed pets, cheap gasoline, tender meat, straight news, brave men and gorgeous women. Of course, all of that was generalizations and oversimplifications, but the world seemed awash with that junk. The problem was how to escape it.

My plan was to get to Peru and hole up in the mountains. I had a pack, wool clothes, heavy boots, and enough traveler's checks in a waist pouch to keep me in food and a cheap house for months. Tano had the patched clothes on his back and a sleeping bag and enough $50 bills sewn between patches in his pants to keep him going for almost as much time, but as he had said in Illinois, he still was interested in the beach.

When questions of money arose between us, it often was me who opted for the extreme side of cheap.

"Man, the more money we save, the longer we can stay out," I said. It was an argument I had used in Illinois, an argument Tano answered then the same way he did every time I used it.

"That's fine and good, but I'm not going to torture myself to stay out of there. I want to enjoy myself"—an argument that almost always won.

The first night in La Libertad, we didn't argue about that though, as Gérard and Murielle offered us the floor of their room in a house on a cliff above the Sanzal beach. We slept on straw mats, and in the morning they took us to a nearby stream in a wood of aspens that looked like a New England postcard. We took off our clothes and washed them on the rocks and went in for a swim while they dried, as enjoyable a way to do laundry as I could imagine.

Sanzal was part jet set, part van set. There were some expensive hotels with cabanas and striped umbrellas in the sand, and a few miles in either direction, haciendas rented for a couple of hundred dollars a month. There was even a California Surfers Inn, complete with picnic tables and barbecue pits in a glade near the sea. The Inn attracted the people it was supposed to attract, including us in a vain attempt to get information about travel father south.

"Why go any farther?" a guy with a goatee and long black hair asked us. "This place is far fucking out."

I got Tano out of there after he said he was going to puke, and we spent the afternoon on the beach below Gérard and Murielle's.

The Sanzal coast was much like the rocky sections of California, with small stretches of sand in coves surrounded by tall bluffs. It was a peaceful place and in a way it was an apparition as El Salvador was on the verge of being ripped apart by violence that would continue for years.

That night, Tano and I and the French couple hiked to the La Libertad market, where I sampled a dish from every open food stall. The binge prompted Tano to suggest I write a book, *Eating My Way to South America.* Gérard and Murielle said nothing. I suppose that meant they were thinking it was lucky some Americans didn't have a lot of money.

Outside the market, we passed an empty church. The night

before, the church had been full and surrounded by soldiers with bayoneted rifles, and near the front steps, a tank. When we walked past, we heard singing. It was in Spanish and it took us a few bars before we recognized it as "Blowing in the Wind ."

We found out why they were singing that the next day.

After we passed the empty church we tried hitching, but no one was on the road, so we gave up and walked. An hour later and less than halfway back to the beach, an old man with a Panama hat pulled his Lincoln Continental to the side of the road and rolled down his window.

"Soldiers don't ask questions after eight P.M.," he said. "They shoot."

He told us there was a curfew because there had been trouble in the capital.

"If you stay out on the street, you're gonna get shot."

When we got in the car, he drove fast and told us the El Salvadoran defense minister got hot under the collar about an antigovernment rally and started shooting up the capital. Children were shot in the streets, and after a day of rioting and burning, three hundred people were dead. Martial law had been declared throughout the country and everyone had to be off the streets between 8 P.M. and 6 A.M.

"Like I said," the old man, a retired Texan, said, "if they see you, they ain't gonna ask any questions."

Tano and I slept on the beach, although it wasn't much of a sleep as I half expected to be woken by soldiers with lights and guns and no interest in questions.

Next morning, we blew out of the country. Murielle and Gérard stayed, hoping that after a few days the heat would pass. Gérard was shopping for a passport. He had left France to avoid the draft, and in the year since, his passport had expired. He hoped to make a connection in Sanzal.

It took a day and a half to get out of the country, most of which was accomplished with a ride in the back of a cement truck, followed the next morning by a ferry to Potosi, Nicaragua, a hot, dusty customs station beside a parking lot. From there it was another five hours by bus across washboard dirt roads and through volcanic lowlands dotted with thatched huts before we arrived in Managua. The bus stopped at dozens of towns along

203

the way, and at each stop, a small boy in the front seat would hang out the window and announce, "Managua, Managua, Managua," saying it in fast, rolling Spanish as if it was a tongue twister. At nine o'clock, the bus did what the kid said it would do, and got us into "Managua, Managua, Managua," but at the outskirts of town, where we were told by vendors selling dinners of grilled chicken cooked over a fire in a garbage can that there were no nearby hotels. For a while, we sat on a curb and gnawed at delicious garbagecued chicken, until one of us said, "Let's see what we can find."

After an hour of wandering through side streets of single-storied homes, what we found was a sandlot soccer field.

"Well, it's the best we're gonna do at this time of night."

"Fine by me."

We laid our bags down at center field, trying to move as little as possible, as the ground was more like the dumpings from a vacuum cleaner. Puffs of dust rose with the slightest stir.

In the middle of the night, the moon rose, and with it came the dogs. At first there were only two, forty yards away and howling. The barking attracted two more, until Tano got up and threw rocks at them and they retreated to behind the goal mouths, which was a safe distance.

"This is gonna be a long night," Tano said.

A half hour later, the dogs tripled their numbers and advanced upfield. It was my turn to get up and throw rocks, though the dogs pulled back only ten yards, once more out of range.

They maintained that distance most of the night, with only sporadic barking. I assumed, incorrectly, the dogs' vigil was one of curiosity, but actually, they were digging in and gathering strength. Just before dawn, the barking started again, in earnest, and when I lifted my head up, I quickly shook Tano awake.

"Man, we'd better get out of here."

"Oh, shit."

The two dogs who came with the moon had swelled their ranks to two dozen. They circled us in a pack, and they circled in decreasingly smaller rings. I rolled my sleeping bag, tied my shoes as fast as I ever have, and picked up and threw every rock I could get my hands on, but because the field was so dusty, it was more like throwing balls of talc. We waved our arms, yelled,

204

"Malos perros," something, of course, they knew, and back-stepped off the field to a side street. From above, we must have looked like a pair of bar magnets pulling clusters of iron fillings.

They followed us down side streets, but they knew enough to keep away from downtown Managua, Managua, Managua, which was like Guat City, only worse.

An earthquake had devastated the city Christmas Eve, 1972. Five years later, Managua, Managua, Managua still looked as if the bomb just had been dropped. Shells of buildings with only the foundation and maybe part of the first floor remained. Sidewalks were torn apart. Many sections had been razed, with piles of stone and weeds lying in a corner lot, like architectural bones.

Despite bright morning sun, rats skipped along steps and piles of rubble. Most of the streets were unmarked, and no one was out to ask directions of, but it was easy to figure how to go places, as with only a few buildings standing, you could see through sections of the city.

We wanted out, fast. Our plan was to hitch to Rama, a river town seventy-five miles from the coast, and then catch a boat down the Rio Escondido to Bluefields, a Caribbean port town where we hoped to board a ship, south.

It wasn't until evening that we got the ride we wanted with a trucker, a thin man in his early fortys, who wore a flyer's jacket and hunched slightly over the wheel, a position he held for the almost three hours it took to reach Rama. He said nothing, other than, *"Sí, gracias,"* whenever Tano offered him a cigarette.

Although he didn't talk, Tano and I felt obliged to stay awake and keep vigil. For the most part it was silent, except when one of us would say, "This is a great ride," and the other one would say, "Yeah." Then we would be quiet for twenty minutes or so, when the person who said "Yeah" last would open the next round by saying, "Sure is a great ride," and the other person would answer, "Shit, yeah."

The ride was more than two hundred kilometers over a bumpy but paved road that was elevated above swamps and long, slightly rolling stretches of jungle. Moonlight bathed everything silver and made the land look like it was webbed.

It was close to midnight when we reached Rama. By then, clouds covered the sky, and whatever there was of a town was dark. The truck's headlights swept across a furrowed dirt road and then against wooden buildings with slatted sidewalks that looked like the nineteenth-century American West.

"A ghost town," Tano said.

We stopped in front of a two-storied building that had a porch and a sign reading, "Hotel Lee." A shadow came out the front door and spoke to the driver in Spanish that was too fast for us to understand. When they stopped, the man from the hotel waved for the driver to come in, and the driver turned to us and said, *"Él tene aposento por usted."*

"Bueno, gracias," I said to him and then to Tano, "I don't believe how lucky we are."

Our beds were hard. A warm breeze lifted gauze curtains, and just after one of us said, "This is the life," I fell into a deep sleep.

In the morning, for $5 we caught a ride on a river cargo boat, the *El Cairo,* heading for Bluefields.

I rode on the roof of the pilot house, only climbing down to hang over the edge of the boat, soak my shirt in the river, and wrap it again around my head. The sun was blazing, but there was a strong breeze that rocked tall, broad-leafed palms along the shore. A few times, men in dugout canoes motored up beside us to sell bunches of bananas, then drifted back to thatched huts on the shore. Compared to the Amazon, the forests along the Rio Escondido had a crew-cut, with a matting of dense brush broken only by a scattering of palms and, sometimes, large, broad-trunked trees. The landscape looked African, or the way I imagined a central African river might look.

With us looking like sheikhs, our heads wrapped in wet shirts, I yelled above the drone of the engine. "This is the best ride we've ever caught."

Tano answered with the widest smile.

Just after the sun set behind our stern, the moon rose full above our bow. It came up small and distant, in a break in a mountain range of clouds. Before it was a quarter way into the sky, we docked in Bluefields, a rambling Caribbean town with whitewashed wooden buildings and roots. Many of the towns' inhabitants were black and spoke West Indian–accented English, but there were also Spanish-speaking Latins and some Chinese.

We ate dinner in a restaurant with tablecloths and paintings on the wall, meaning we splurged, although I don't remember for how much. To compensate, and because the only hotel room in town we could afford was something of a drunk tank, we went searching for a soccer field of sorts. We found it in the form of a cemetery behind a church and above the docks, with an expansive view of the bay. If I should have been superstitious about sleeping in a cemetery, I wasn't, although I thought about it, but only briefly. That night it was the Ritz.

The moon already was on the downswing when we spread out between graves, and a breeze came in off the bay and cleared the air of bugs.

"The life."

"The life."

Whatever nervousness about sleeping in a cemetery behind a church I didn't have at night, I acquired in the morning, half expecting the local pastor to nab us. I was up before dawn, and while Tano slept, went down to the docks in search of information about boats going south. On the way down, I met an old black man with a fishing cap and a short, gray-black beard. He told me a boat, the *Costa Azul,* was scheduled to leave from the bluffs, a harbor three miles across the bay from Bluefields, and the boat was bound for Colombia.

"I doe noa ee gib eoo pahsage, mon, but eoo ken triee. Ee leet sen 'clock. 'N wenney minetz."

I thanked him and ran and roused Tano. We rolled our things together, almost as fast as we did at the soccer field, ran back down to the wharf, and hired a boy in a skiff to race us across the bay, which he did, pounding us through the waves in a *thunkaaa ... thunkaa ... thunkaa* that shook up our insides and soaked us on the outside.

It was quarter after seven when we arrived, and as we had hoped, the *Costa Azul* was late and still being loaded on the docks, but not as we expected, although I should have known by the name, the *Costa Azul* was a schooner, the kind you would see docked in places like Costa Azul.

We found the skipper, just what you would expect, a man

207

in his fifties, with horn-rimmed glasses, a white cap, and white trousers. He spoke English, said he was from Colombia, and was heading for the Colombian coast.

Since neither Tano nor I had any connection with the sea-going community, we had no sense of its propriety or customs, so I don't know if we did it the right way, but we asked the captain to take us on. "We'll work, or pay you, whichever seems best." He said he would think about it.

For about two hours we bargained with him, and he took his time before he gave us each new installment of his "I'm not sure if I can do it" offer.

Finally, he agreed.

"OK, listen, I want to help you out. There is another dock, about a mile north of here. I could pick you up there and slip out of the harbor without anyone knowing. It is the dock the shrimp boats use. Go there, quickly. Don't stop and eat at the restaurant [which we had been talking about], and I'll be there in thirty minutes."

We ran to the docks and in the distance, saw the *Costa Azul* lift anchor, unravel her sails, and drift toward us.

"I can't believe we're this lucky," I said. "We've been making all the right connections, zipping out of El Salvador, the ferry to Nicaragua, the trucker across the jungle, then the *El Cairo*. Even last night and the cemetery worked out fine."

"I know it," Tano said through a smile of closed teeth.

The *Costa Azul* came up slowly, its sails flapping in a slight wind.

"Come on, baby," I said in a whisper.

She eased toward us and we waved and then when she was about forty yards offshore, she slid past us, with neither the crew, some of whom were standing by the rails, or the skipper, who was at the stern, turning to look at us. For a few moments we waved frantically and then, as the *Costa Azul* eased past, we dropped our arms and stared at her. I don't think I moved for a few minutes, and I watched until she turned to sea and all I could see was the white dot of the stern and the line of the sails.

"The fucker," Tano said.

The trip turned around after that.

208

XXVIII

AT the waterfalls, Glück finally had admitted the river we were on was not the Padauiri, "But who are we?" he asked, again mixing up the "who" for the "where," an appropriate enough mistake.

Glück said he did not know who we were, but he wanted to continue.

"This river is b-e-e-y-y-o-u-t-i-f-u-l," he said. "We have gone four days, and no signs of man."

That was true, as at many of the logs, we had looked to see if anyone else had tried to hack a way across, but there were no signs.

"I still think we should go back and shoot for the pyramids," Tano said that night while we sat out by the boat. "Everything we've done has been toward the pyramids. If we're wrecked, we're wrecked. We should put all our money on the highest stakes and shoot for the pyramids."

We still had two hours running time in gas and a reserve of twenty liters. I suggested to Glück we might paddle back down and try and find the Padauiri and give the pyramids another whack. He said he thought we could, but he would rather go forward. Still, he listened to us, saying that if we decided to go back, he would do it. That sounded gentlemanly, but in truth, I suppose he had no choice.

We decided that the next morning we would go until we used what remained in the gas tank, then if there still was no sign of mountains, we would turn back.

"OK," Glück said on the way to his hammock. Tano and I laid out the tarp by the boat, melted down, and tried to discuss all our options.

Tano said that whenever we gambled, we lost, something I didn't argue with, yet all bets in the situation we were in seemed to be bad ones. If we turned back, and could not find the Padauiri, then the extent of the trip had been to go half-assed up a shallow, log-jammed river with some tapirs and monkeys. If we followed the river out and could find no mountains or pyramids, we would lose too, except for extending our time on the log-jammed river with tapirs and monkeys. Of course, there was always the possibility we would come up with the royal flush, but we didn't talk about that, though I think we both half-believed it. We talked more in terms of the different ways we could fail, something more familiar.

I wondered where the angels were. In the afternoon, and perhaps because of our own position, we had talked about higher things in the universe, an ontological possibility in which none of us in the boat had any confidence. Glück said he had grown up Protestant in Bavaria and when he was seventeen he went to the government to renounce his religion. The next day a priest came to his house and slapped the seventeen-year-old across his face. Glück said he remembered his mother crying, but he refused to budge.

More than a half century later, he said he did not make any of his children have a religion.

"When they're twenty-one, they can choose," he said. "Then it's their own fault," which to me was a good way to end the story.

Tano took his machete and lifted a mosquito off his arm, taking a tissue of skin with it and lifting me out of my daydream in the process.

"Two days ago, we laughed about being at a similar camp

210

with the river staying the same," he said. He laughed again, and I did, too, as prophecies, even the little ones, were beginning to come true.

After two turns in the river next morning, another log stopped us. No one said anything right away, and Glück didn't even try to spur us with a "Come on."

I jumped in the river, it was at my thighs, took my clothes off, waded upstream, over the log, and around the next bend. The jungle opened. As far as I could see to the west, blue skies, and to the north and northeast, clouds, but a wide enough opening at the horizon to see there were no mountains. Tano and Glück came around the bend, took a look, then Tano climbed a bank where he got a farther view north, but "No sierras."

"So, we go back?" Glück asked.

"We go back," I said.

The trip back was something like being in a funeral procession for someone you liked, but only half knew. You remembered things you did together and things that were said, but the ache wasn't in the passing, it was in things that could have come. It was a sorrow we thought we could handle, but Tano and I still believed in resurrecting something.

To conserve gas, we paddled, so the ride was quiet and smooth.

Glück took the stern, though he was not particularly adept at steering. Earlier he had told us paddling would be difficult because Tano and I were greenhorns.

The boat had a tendency to sideswipe banks as the river wanted to drive us in straight lines while the jungle forced us into bends. We took a scourging from thorn branches and trees, but we gobbled up the river. Logs that were submerged just below the surface, logs that had forced us to heave-ho the day before, we now took with a fast paddle and then a thump. Paddling speed and current pushed us across. Although it had not rained for two days, the river level had not dropped as much as we expected. That bolstered the hope we might be given another whack at the Padauiri, wherever that was.

It took twenty minutes to squeeze the boat through a jam of logs that took an hour the day before, and by noon, after we had gone much farther than we had expected, we were ready to

211

take a break. Lunch was slim, four saltine crackers each, and whatever we could scrape out of an empty jar of honey.

"This is bullshit," Tano mumbled, but we were too tired to make a fuss. Instead, Tano said he was "starving." Glück countered by saying he never ate lunch, "only a good Quaker [oatmeal] breakfast and some dinner. I'm usually more thirsty than hungry."

"Well, maybe I'm still just a growing boy," Tano said.

Glück cast for fish, got nibbles, but not bites, while Tano tried to take a measurement from the shadow off a stick, hoping that when we returned we could figure out where we were.

For a while, we lay in the sand, until we were startled by the sound of castanettes in the forest.

"Oh, wild pigs," Glück said as humped shadows passed through a net of light between trees.

"The click, click, click," Glück said, "that is the pigs cracking nuts in their mouths."

In the afternoon, we cruised quickly downstream with everyone guessing when we would reach the waterfalls, where we planned to camp. About two o'clock, the current slowed as we hit a stretch of stagnant water. Tano said he remembered passing through still water above the waterfalls. Rounding a bend, we heard rushing water.

We unloaded and dropped the boat stern first down through the rapids and made camp just above a lump of rocks where Glück set up kitchen. I was exhausted, more from riding nude and having the sun suck the energy from me than actually paddling, so I jumped across rocks and sat in a shallow pool. Water cascaded around me as black rocks scattered the river into a delta. It was the kind of place you would expect in the Green or White Mountains in New England, where on a sunny day it would be mobbed with people, inflated tires, pickups, and radios, and farther upstream men with beards and white-skinned women would be sunbathing. Maybe for that reason, I didn't feel completely alone. It was as if I were hearing echoes. At dinner, Glück put things in a more Amazonian perspective.

"This is a beautiful life," he said. "Forty years in the jungle and I still like it. When I go back to Manaus, after five or six days, I get sick," a statement meant to be taken literally.

212

Actually, there had been little thinking on my part that day, but as evening came, my tiredness ached itself into thoughts about comfort. I had never been used to being comfortable. It made me feel that I might be giving in, or I had been doing something wrong, like getting soft. I usually get comfortable when I'm still, which had occurred for up to a year's stretch, the last time being just before the Amazon, in San Francisco. My thoughts headed there that evening on the river.

Like the Amazon, everyone has his own version of San Francisco, and mine happened to be seen through windows of an attic flat beside Golden Gate Park. There were a lot of nice things about that place, but one that I thought about that night by the rapids was watching the sun set over the western end of the city before sinking into the Pacific. The kitchen of my flat faced west, at the back end of the house. Sitting there with a cup of coffee, late in the afternoon, I got a sense of the world moving. Depending on the seasons, the sun hit the water at a different spot each night, though my seeing it depended upon there not being any fog. That was not something to depend on at all, but when I could see the sun, watching it was like watching a clock move. As the months and seasons passed, it was a good thing to watch the sun yo-yo up and down the coast, like it was doing what it was supposed to be doing, even if you were sloughing off.

We emptied a ketchup bottle at supper and as it got dark, bugs that looked like a cross between flies and bees buzzed into the jar. By the time I noticed them, there were hundreds in the bottle, which I picked up and capped.

"They're gorging themselves," I said, "and don't know that in an hour or so, they'll be dead." Then I tossed the bottle into the river and watched it get swept away. The heavens should have opened up.

"Playing God?" Tano said. I didn't answer and felt guilty and wanted him to say something else, something dumb or funny, but he didn't. He just watched the bottle float downstream. It was a stupid thing for me to do, though I had done it many times as a kid, with ants or bugs, when it was something like playing soldiers, but with the ketchup bottle, the abuse came home and I wished someone would forgive me.

213

There was more to the ketchup bottle business than that, though. Tossing a bottle full of insects to their death may seem silly, even to consider twice, but after I did it and Tano said what he did, I felt like I had transgressed something. The transgression also made me aware my expectations had been changing. A few weeks before, we had set out to find the pyramids, but I think in the back of my mind, I also was hoping to find another treasure, one that I could not define, just a vague feeling that the Amazon had secrets and if I proved worthy, some or even one of them might be shared. After my ketchup bottle mistake, I wasn't sure.

That night, the darkness seemed to fall with a thud. The waterfall drowned the whine of bugs, but the mosquitoes were out in clouds—maybe out for revenge—and I lacquered myself with the superstrength varnish. It worked, but I had it on so thick it melted the plastic on my pen as I wrote and left splotches on my journal, as if someone had fingerpainted the jacket with turpentine. I had used the gook before. I hadn't noticed any ill effects, but then I looked more closely at my fingertips and palms. They were beginning to peel.

Tano and I spread the tarp on the rocks and sat down. He unrolled his last pack of cigarettes, then rerolled them with cigarette paper, getting three hand-rolled butts for each one he unraveled. We smoked a cigarette, but didn't talk much, just watched the stars appear.

The jungle was bright, but quiet in the morning, as if it had curled up and decided to remain asleep. The river had dropped two feet since we had gone up, a drop that would force more heave-hoing, with the heave sometimes becoming a big heave. On one log, we developed a tip-the-scale technique. We got a little more than a third of the boat over a log, but the river had dropped so much we couldn't push the boat all the way over. Glück climbed in and sat at the bow. At first the boat slowly swayed, then the stern lifted and the skiff went crashing over the other side. Immediately, the current swept Glück and the boat down, and Tano and I had to pull ourselves over the log, dive in, and swim fast to catch him.

An hour later, we reached the Big Log, the nine-footer we crossed on the way up. This time though, the river had dropped

214

to our advantage. We found a break in the limbs of the tree where we were able to slide under and through.

The day passed swiftly with Glück's commands, "paddling, paddling," whenever we were about to smash into a log or a rock or the shore.

The paddling became hypnotic. I took long, deep strokes and felt my chest, arm and leg muscles fall into a rhythm. We talked little, I thought little, and that felt good. No troubles, only the gurgle of water, the swirl behind my paddle, and the contraction of my muscles.

Once we heard a bird that sounded like it was whistling while pecking at a tree.

"It's the rain bird," Glück said. "Go away."

Late in the afternoon, we passed big logs none of us remembered. I suggested maybe we had made a wrong turn on the way down, too.

"Who is the river?" Glück said.

The river was not a single channel, but a web of passageways, something like roads to beaches in Baja Mexico, where tracks in the sand seem to fork every hundred yards, and you follow the deepest, most traveled path.

Usually, on the river, the main channel was obvious. We went up against, or down with, the strongest current, but there always was the possibility that one of the tributaries was flowing stronger and somehow we had slipped off the river we were on and into a network of other rivers. That, too, was the only way we could have got off the Padauiri and Glück's aerial map.

"Where the hell are we?" began to come up in conversations even more frequently than Glück's announcements of the time, which at five o'clock brought us to a stop.

At a point where the river switched back, we set up camp. It was marshy, with tall grass, but the river had dropped fifteen feet, so there was a beach of white sand. It was like camping at the sea and it lifted Tano's and my spirits, but Glück complained that on the sand it would be difficult to sleep.

"If we had wood, we could make a fire," Glück said.

"Yeah, we should have thought of that earlier," Tano said.

"In the water, there is a lot of wood. We can take it out," Glück said, "but it's wet."

215

We were full of profound thoughts that night.

"We can use the bottom planks of your boat," I said.

"And we could start the fire with the pages of Zalis's journal," Tano said.

"And we could light it with what's left of the gasoline," I said.

"Ah, so," Glück said in a tone that left me unsure whether he thought all that was funny, a good idea, or he didn't understand. Then he said, "We can put alcohol to start it," referring to the alcohol we used for the stove, so I guessed he was going along with us.

"Oh, look," Glück said. "There is the firefly. Catch him. Catch him."

"Leave him be," Tano said. "I caught enough of those when I was a kid. I would stuff them in a jar and make lanterns."

"I used to run around and leave ketchup bottles open and when I caught a bunch of bees, I would throw them in rivers," I said.

"Perverted," Tano said with a smile.

The moon was waning, and as yet had not risen. Glück said an old moon meant there would be good weather in the jungle. We guessed at how long it might take us to get back to Allianca, then to Manaus, but that didn't take into account the possibility of our being seriously lost, nor if we would continue to get lost.

"This is the lost river," I said.

"It sure is," Tano said, laughing.

"Where the hell are we?" I said, laughing louder.

"Where the hell are we, Kurt?" Tano said, laughing even louder.

"What you do?" Glück said. "You unroll cigarettes and put in other one," which was a simple and direct way to avoid someone with a laughing question.

"Yeah, I can get about three or four hand-rolled cigarettes for every one in the regular pack."

"Economic," Glück said.

"Yup."

"In Hungary, they have good horsemen who could do things I could never understand," Glück said. "The horseman, he has one hand and his tobacco and paper in one pocket, and with the

216

other hand, he holds the reins of the horse. While he's riding, he rolls the cigarette and takes it out, and it's finished. With one hand."

"It's the same in America," Tano said. "I've seen cowboys do that. They roll a cigarette with one hand in their pocket while they're riding, then they take it out, and use their thumbnail to light a match, and they've got it. I've tried, but I can't do it."

We watched the stars fill the sky, and at one point, I thought I saw a plane or a satellite. Glück said I still thought I was in the boat and everything in the sky was moving.

"But, we have many shpootnicks in the sky here, too," he said.

I sang a verse from "Another Saturday Night," and Tano added, "I'm gonna miss somebody, when I'm gone."

"Kurt, do you miss your wife on these trips?" I asked.

"No," Glück said quickly and we all laughed. The "No" seemed to come out of the back of his mouth, like it was readied and had been used before.

"I know her so many years, thirty years," he said. "No. It makes nuhzing. If I've been out for two months or something, then when I come back, we have a honeymoon again. All time we have new honeymoons."

"Yeh, that's true," I said, and heard a pinch of longing slip into my voice.

"It's nothing new," Glück said. "Though when I've been out and I come home to Manaus, for the first few days, it's a new thing.

"You know, the cavalry men in Hungary? It is said the Milky Way comes from the dust when they attack through the streets in other stars."

To the south, we saw lightning, and Glück said, "I hope not comes the rain. That will be shit, I tell you, in this sand. If that happens, we will load everything in the boat and cover ourselves with plastic."

"Then you can tell stories," I said.

"What is your profession?" Glück asked Tano.

"Me?" Tano said, as startled by the question as I was. It was something Glück should have asked the first day or two we were together. I guess it slipped by Tano and me that he never asked,

217

but I think Tano, with his long hair and unrolling of cigarettes, intrigued Glück.

"Yes, you," Glück said.

"Oh, I'm just a laborer," Tano said.

"Laborer, you work in a library?"

"No, I've done a little of everything. I've worked for the railroad, done carpentry, plumbing..."

"And he's doing archaeology now," I said. The day before, Tano and I had talked about telling Glück that Tano was involved in archaeology and it was important we get to the pyramids. I was trying to get Tano to push the archaeology angle to dissuade Glück from rearranging the trip to one of discovering a new river.

"Well, yeah," Tano said. "Last year, I started doing some archaeology, in the desert in California, and I liked it and I hope I can do some more."

"You know, archaeology?" I asked Glück.

"Yes, pyramids, and all that shtuff," Glück said.

"I liked it and it was good pay," Tano said.

"Then it will be nice if we find the pyramids," Glück said, "but ooooh, that will be a terrible thing. I bring an archaeologist to the pyramids." He laughed.

Maybe we told him the wrong thing.

The mosquitoes came in the night. I wrapped my head in an undershirt and made an opening for my nose. I slept poorly and once Glück woke us at "twelve and twenty-five minutes," when he shined his flashlight in the water at two gleaming orange spots.

"Hello, there is a *jakaré,*" Glück said.

Mosquitoes beat the dawn in waking me, but I stayed awhile, just to pay my respects to the day of rest. Glück got up to make coffee. I thought it would be nice if we didn't have to rush off, but the sky wasn't willing to go along and we had to hustle to get everything in the boat before the rain. As we loaded, the rain began and Tano pointed to what looked like a sunken log just breaking the surface of the water. It was shaped like the snout of an alligator. Tano thought it might be a good picture to have one of us hold his foot near it. I laughed, then bent down to pick up a cup. When I looked up, the log had moved.

In a few bends we expected to be back on the Padauiri, where we had seen empty huts, but a few bends became a few hours and we again thought we might have slipped into another river system.

"Who is the river?" Tano asked and Glück shrugged.

We reached another big tree across the river none of us remembered. I said maybe we had slipped into the twilight zone and Tano said we were going to end up in Southeast Asia. The boat slid with the current to the right bank and we pushed, pried, and hacked our way through rotten limbs. The tree had no ax or machete marks. The only way past it would have been to cut.

"Maybe it just fell," I said.

"No, look at the algae on top," Tano said. "It's been down for a while."

"Then maybe the river has dropped three or four feet," I said, a drop that could mean even bigger trouble.

We hacked enough limbs off so we could jam the boat halfway through, then stood on the tree and tried to pull the boat past.

"Ho," Glück said, and we did, and he said, "Hooo," again, and we inched farther, and another, "Hooooo," and another inch, until we finally yanked her through.

"Maybe we're on the wrong river," Tano said.

"It is impossible," Glück said in a voice that was not convincing.

"I know it's impossible," Tano said, "but this is the twilight zone."

XXIX

FOR the week or two after her escape into the Caribbean, we talked about missing the *Costa Azul,* a conversation that went something like, "I still can't believe it." "Neither can I," both statements repeated two or three dozen times.

We both wanted answers, like why the captain didn't wave to tell us he couldn't take us, or why he strung us on so long, or why we were stupid enough to believe him.

Most of that could not be answered, except the last question, so we always ended those conversations with Tano's analysis on the shrimp boat dock. "The fucker."

Lady luck had changed and to make sure we knew it, she hounded us that day until we got the message. Our boat back across the bay almost sank, we had dinner with a hog beneath our feet in a stall in the market, and every hotel owner in town turned us away. Finally, we returned to the curb across from the cemetery to lick our wounds.

"Hey." I nudged Tano who was half asleep. "It's the guy who told us about the *Costa Azul.*"

"Great," Tano said, in a voice that meant anything but.

The whistler recognized me from a distance.

"Cap'n Willoughby Fenton, by nayem," he said during the exchange of introductions. He asked where we were staying and we surprisingly answered with the truth.

"I no tink datz too goot ub a playez, mon. If eoo wan, I tink maybe eoo cum 'n stay on my bote. Iyem doeked up 'til Tuzeday" (which was three days away).

We jumped off that curb. When we walked down the end of the dock and dropped our packs on the deck of his boat, a cargo boat slightly smaller than the *El Cairo,* Willoughby said, "OK, eetz Sat'day nite. Letz go hev dreenk, mon,"

I don't remember much of how or where he took us, other than it was in a backwoods and hilly section of Bluefields, with small, wooden houses that were dark except for kerosene lamps or candles that glowed through open windows. We followed a dirt path, but partway we walked on slats above puddles and long stretches of mud, until we reached a round, thatched hut shaped like a circus tent. Willoughby didn't speak on the walk, until just before we went inside, "Deece goot playez, mon."

The playez was a bar with overhead fans, clouds of smoke, round, wooden tables, and couples dancing to reggae music coming from a phonograph player. We took a table at the front and Willoughby ordered three glasses of Coke and a bottle of rum. We toasted him and when the black girls who knew Willoughby came over to our table, we talked and drank with them, but though we wanted to, we felt out of place and didn't get up the nerve to ask them to dance. I don't remember much else, except once looking over at Tano and saying, "Well, we're on our feet again."

Willoughby leaned over and winked at us. "Myetee fine, mon."

We stayed on Willoughby's boat until Tuesday, though that had not been the plan. On Monday, we took a double-decked passenger boat heading for Rama, but we only got about two miles, out of the bay to the mouth of the Rio Escondido, when the engine broke down and we drifted back with the current and the changing of the tide to Bluefields. The way our luck had been running, that didn't come as too much of a surprise. When the engine began to gag, Tano looked at me. We smiled, shook our heads, and Tano cut me off from saying something by saying, "You don't have to say it, I know it."

When you're throwing snake eyes, they come in strings. We knew we were on a roll, though we weren't talking about it. It's not good to talk about bad luck, especially when you're still gambling and don't know where it's going to end. The three days on Willoughby Fenton's boat, we didn't talk much, though later, when Tano sent me the poem before I left for the Amazon, I realized he spent his time on Willoughby's boat the same way I did, going over our lives.

One of the good things about moving a lot of the time was stopping in between. Willoughby's boat was a good stop, except for the last night, when it rained and a thief tried to sneak on board and a dog on another boat whined until dawn. Otherwise, most of our time there was peaceful. Except for the rainy night, we slept, ate, daydreamed, and whiled away most of our three days on deck. We took turns going for walks, or to the market, or to get Dixie cups, or doing whatever we had to do on shore, while one of us always stayed to watch out for things on the boat. All of that, including the time we were together, added up to a lot of time alone.

I don't think a case could be made that we, or at least I, kept moving so we could stop, but stopping definitely was part of moving. When we first hit the road, it came as part of an urge, and because of that I trusted it, like it was closer to the bone of the matter. Still, there were visions at the end of the urge. Stopping was the sighing side of the urge, the downside of the pulse. Both the moving and the stopping went together and finally, after years, when the journeys on the outside and the inside converged, I began to see where the moving and stopping came from, then everything seemed fairly simple.

By the time we hit Willoughby Fenton's boat, I half knew those things, but that didn't help much. It was part of the same kind of feeling I would have three years later in Hoboken, right before the Amazon began, a time when I was less a character and more a part of the audience with the responsibility to put things together. A story was unfolding, and because of circumstances, it overlapped with someone else's. I was not only my own central character, but also had a simultaneous part in someone else's story, and sometimes, even more than one other person. I had to act out my part knowing it not only was the main part in my story, but it was in someone else's, too. Once I realized that, I also became part of my own audience, and with that came the responsibility to try to understand.

On the boat in Bluefields, the pieces were mostly fragments. What I thought about most was mortality, or at least, a relationship of events.

Piecing things together that led to an end assumed an order, something I wasn't so ready to assume at the time, though mortality was something that kept things in somewhat of a line. Death, if you paid attention to it, tended to whip things into a shape. It gave things an edge. I liked that. What I didn't like was that death, being the only certainty, had a way of diminishing other events, a way of lining things toward an inevitable conclusion. When I was younger and gave up on God and religion, death had a mocking neutrality about it. Of course, like the way I argued that first night in Puerto Arista with Tano, nothing really mattered, but then, the way he argued, of course just because of that, everything did. There was more to it than enduring. There was something about finishing out your story.

Up to the time we reached Bluefields, things had been going fairly well, but then as I realized our luck was changing, and I had time to think about it, the sadness came. As with other trips before the one to South America, I had left a woman. I missed her and when we stopped on Willoughby's boat, I thought a lot about her, which only made the sadness worse. That didn't stop any of the thinking. Missing a woman was part of the sighing, slow-down side of the urge to keep moving. It was a feeling I had a lot before, one that I never have been able to get used to, though I never really have tried.

The other thing I thought about on Willoughby's boat, something I have tried to get used to and overcome, was the notion I had something to chip in to the world, a leftover sense of mission from the pre–May Day days, a sense that the world is improvable on a grand scale. Part of that feeling had to do with thinking about death and part of it had to do with thinking I was smart—stupid things to be thinking about at the time, considering I was very much alive and through a series of my own choices, I wasn't so smart because I was stranded on a docked boat.

When we left Tuesday and went up river with Willoughby, I was still thinking about such things, along with telling myself I had to be able to absorb as well as withstand whatever was coming. That is otherwise known as a sixth sense.

We arrived late in Rama and missed the last bus to Managua, so we walked to the edge of town and hitched a ride in the back of a truck driven by three Chinese and filled with sacks of grain. When we climbed in the truck, we had told the driver we wanted to go to the Managua airport, but we weren't sure if he understood.

At that point, our plan was to skip Panama and Costa Rica and try and catch a flight directly to the continent. The Pan American Highway was still unfinished south of the canal, we heard Panama was expensive and, because of a tough military dictatorship, rough, all of which added up to a Panama bypass. Once that was decided, it was easy to add Costa Rica and the rest of Nicaragua as road rumors had it that any place that was safe for Bebe Rebozo wasn't safe for our kind.

I was asleep when the truck stopped. One of the Chinese opened the back flap and said, "*Aeropuerto.*"

We went up to the cab and thanked the two other men, then waved and crossed the highway to the airport. Because it was after midnight, the airport was closed, and maybe because it was in Central America, it was locked shut.

We found a thicket of bushes on the front lawn, and when the military patrol had walked out of sight, we crawled under the bushes, unrolled our bags, and bedded down.

We slept two nights in the same spot with the in-between day spent racing around Managua unsuccessfully trying to find a way out. All planes and buses were booked full. The only bright spot of the day was meeting a bearded Brazilian in his forties who said he had spent most of his life traveling. He had a series of forged passports, but still was searching for a Swiss one. He, too, had slept the previous night on the front lawn, though he had camped behind a different cluster of bushes. He recently had returned from Japan, "the worst of all countries," but "that makes no difference, the world is finished. Now, there are borders everywhere."

Next day, we left our camp at the airport and crisscrossed

224

town in search of an airline company that had flights from San José, Costa Rica, to the island of San Andrés in the Caribbean. We found one and the woman at the desk, like everyone else connected with planes, spoke English, though hers was tainted with a New York accent. "I lived there for a year," she said. "It was so exciting. I want to be a model and go back."

There was a pair of seats on a flight the next day, she said, "but even if you pay, that is no guarantee." We still paid and thanked her and she told us of a bus company that ran buses the length of South America.

Tica Bus was the Latin version of similar cross-continental hippie buses that operated in Europe and for a while, back in the late sixties and early seventies, in the States. The bus station was only a few blocks away, and when we found it, we also found the almost expected. There was a bus that day, and it would leave in twenty minutes, but it was full. We were told to try another bus company across town.

We took our time finding it, which might have been the right way of going about things in that town, because they had a bus going to San Jose that afternoon, and it had seats available. Then again, that was as smooth as things got.

The bus must have realized we were aboard, as before it reached the Costa Rican border, near the shores of Lake Nicaragua, it broke down.

All the men got out and tried to push it up a slight hill for a jump start. Tano and I didn't have enough Spanish to argue backing up, and besides we figured we were guests in that country, so we did like the Romans and pushed up hill. The bus jumped, but did not start. Then everyone gave up. It was mid-afternoon and it was hot and everyone climbed out of the bus and sat on the shaded side while the driver stared at the engine. In a few minutes, everyone climbed back on the bus, even though it must have been more than 100 degrees inside, as a brush-burning road crew scorched a ten-meter strip along the side of the road and engulfed the bus in smoke.

Instead of climbing back in, Tano and I walked across the highway, through the charcoaled shoulder on the other side, stripped down to our underwear, and went for a swim in Lake Nicaragua. A young man dressed in a white shirt, black tie, black pants, and black patent leather shoes followed us, took off his shoes and socks, and went in to his ankles. When we came out, we introduced ourselves. He was an American. I forget his name, but he said he was a Mormon missionary, and when we asked him, he said he couldn't go all the way in the water because it was against church policy to go swimming by yourself when you are a missionary.

"You might get in trouble in the water and if there wasn't anyone there to help you, you'd drown," he said. "It would be destruction of church property."

"Can you believe that shit?" Tano said as we walked back to the bus to get our gear. "Church property. I wish he and all of them like him would drown."

The bus driver had caught a ride on another bus going back to Managua, saying it would be a few hours before anyone would be out to help us. That left a lot of people uncomfortable on the bus, but by then, Tano and I were getting used to that sort of thing, so we decided to make the best use of our time. We unpacked our bags and washed our clothes in the lake.

Another bus came near sunset, giving us enough time to get our clothes close to damp-dry. The ride south was fast. We whisked through customs, then into San Jose, where, once more, we were left off at a closed airport. There were no bushes in front of the San Jose airport, but then, as far as we could see, there were also no guards. After meeting nature's call in a shallow gully in the median of the Pan American Highway, we crossed over to the airport, and as a cool breeze picked up, slept on the front lawn.

Things went so smoothly the next morning, we decided to celebrate our confirmed check-in by going to the airport restaurant and eating plates of "Desayuno Americano ... Panacakees."

"Well, this is a new beginning," Tano said as we mopped up all the syrup and were working on seconds of coffee, "and I hope our luck changes."

"Managua, Managua, Managua, Managua."

"No more, man. No more," he said, shaking his head and laughing.

"Yeah, I'm really looking forward to just laying on the beach on this island and to starting fresh."

226

"No shit."

"Then again, maybe the plane will go down."

We didn't sit with each other on the plane, a twin-engine prop that seated forty. I sat up front and Tano sat by the tail. As we rumbled down the runway to take off, the plane vibrated tremendously and the wings flapped as if the engines were about to fall off. I turned and looked at Tano, who looked at me and rolled his eyes, the way he had when the skiff almost sank going back across the bay to Bluefields. I turned back around again and made sure I didn't look at him the rest of the flight. Maybe because of that, it went smoothly.

We spent a week in San Andrés, mostly recuperating from our troubles. We spent one day snorkeling amid violet-colored fish and brown cactus-shaped rocks, and lying nude on the white sand. The day was like slipping into a watercolor painting. My outer edges washed away. The only disturbance was the effects of an overdose of spinach that had me making periodic runs into the palms, but that was mostly ignored.

We finally moved on out of necessity. The airline we took to San Andrés had issued us a fifteen day transit visa, and despite repeated attempts through bureaucratic channels to extend it, we could not. That would force Tano and me to split up. I wanted to stay longer in Colombia and visit friends of a friend in Medellín and Bogotá, while Tano said he would be just as content to go on to Ecuador. I thought it might be better if I paid my visits alone, then took off for the Andes.

I don't remember where, when, or how we decided that, so it must have come easily, though I was looking forward to going my own way and wouldn't mind a change in the immediate scenery. I doubt if we would be so quick to split up now, but back then, part of whoever or whatever we were included flaunting our independence. Besides, if we split up, we figured our luck might change.

We decided to fly out of San Andrés together, then go separate ways on the mainland. The day we left, we went to the beach before coming back to our hotel and slowly packing. We wrapped everything, tying it down and tucking it away like sail-

227

ors readying for a storm. When we got to the point of pulling on our boots and tying them up, Tano looked over at me and said in a soft voice, "You know, I feel like we're going to war." We looked at each other a second, in a look that was the exact same one we recognized in Manaus when we were getting ready to leave, but at least at the beginning of the Amazon, we didn't have to say anything.

"I know it," I said. "Let's go out and have a smoke."

On the balcony, we puffed away at stumps of cigars, while in the distance, the sea sparkled in the noon sun.

We didn't sit with or look at each other on the plane, so the flight passed uneventfully. In Cartagena, I bought a ticket on a bus to a town on the Venezuelan border, while Tano made arrangements to head south. On the way back from the bus station, I had my first run-in with Colombian soldiers. I was walking through a plaza when one of two soldiers with guns, standing on a side street, whistled and called me. I hesitated a moment, then because of the first business in Mexico, followed them. They took me to a corner building with a doorway and a dark stairway. One of the soldiers pointed upstairs. I pretended not to understand, though I entered past the door and stood at the base of the stairs. One of the soldiers closed the door behind me and asked for my papers. I handed them to him, then he searched my pouch and wallet, then frisked me. The bigger of the two, who was almost six feet, took my knife. He said, "No," meaning it was supposedly illegal, and I said, "Sí, San Andrés," meaning I had bought it in a duty-free shop on the island, a lie, but I had noticed knives in all the shops.

He handed it to his side kick, a smaller and darker man who had his rifle across his shoulders. The bigger guy then grabbed my balls and rolled them around for a second of two. I wasn't sure if it was supposed to be sexual or supposed to mean that if he felt like it, he would use the knife. The scene was going in the wrong direction. I figured one way or another those guys were out to do me in, and for some reason, I'm not sure why, other than it was panic, I became emphatic and angry and started yelling at them that the knife was mine and OK and they weren't going to get it, or me, easy. I grabbed the knife back from the little soldier and pushed the big soldier, who was grabbing my balls, back against the stairs. They both looked startled and I kept yelling and waving my arms until they stepped back, and the smaller guy pushed the door open and waved his hand for me to leave.

When I got back to our hotel, I felt rattled, but OK. It wasn't the way I wanted to start things in Colombia, but in an hour, Tano and I said our good-byes, along with a "Catch you later" I think we both doubted.

XXX

"WHO this river can be rooning?" Glück said. "Only to the Rio Negro, no?" Tano and I laughed as hard as we had at anything on the trip. I suppose Glück's statement meant everything would make sense eventually, and no matter what, we could find our way back out, but his words said more. He was admitting we could be lost, while still maintaining faith in the underlying order of the Amazon, which said all rivers eventually flowed to the sea and sooner or later, we would get out. Looking back, that may not arouse hysterics, but at the time, it came across as a crack in the old man's confidence. Tano and I were laughing because once again, we had parts in a story that went wrong.

"We go to the Atlantic," I said.

"Maybe the water is rooning into a big lake," Glück mumbled.

"Maybe we'll end up in Argentina," Tano said.

"I want to end up in a Heeltone," I said, "and I want to find out the name of the river when we get back."

"Nos Rio," Tano said.

The rest of the morning, Glück kept us going with his whis-

230

tling, including an encore of "The Daring Young Man," and his "paddling, paddling, paddling," as we passed over, by, under, and through logs none of us remembered.

"We passed by so many zings," Glück said. "We are three and no one is sure we passed these zings. You see too much."

He thought about that for a few seconds, then said, "We must be on the right river."

It felt spooky. Tano and I joked about "Who is the river?" and kept asking, "Where the hell are we?" We laughed a lot, which made the day fun, but underneath, we were edgy.

As the hours passed and none of the river seemed familiar, we overheard Glück talking to himself. "Ahh, it's impossible ..."

Tano whispered, "Now, even you wonder?"

"It's e-e-e-e-e-e-m-p-o-s-s-e-e-b-l-u-h," Glück said. "We cannot be."

Clouds blocked the sun and few birds sang, although sometimes we heard cicadas that sounded more like rattlesnakes. When we passed through one overgrown stretch of river with a log across, I said I thought I remembered it.

"Do you?" Tano said.

I said I did again and pointed to a break in the log where I thought I remembered hacking through, but when we pulled up, it was only broken.

"Well ... I remember going through a stretch like this where it was completely overhung."

"Yup, I heard that before."

"Ah, yes, I remember this grass here," Glück said. "And that one butterfly passed here."

So I laughed and sang, "Oh, where oh where is our little Heeltone" and Glück said, "When we're going up, we're thinking here is the real river. We go fast and we like it and it makes nuhzing, so we never spend attention. Now, we're coming back, and tired ..."

A black lagoon none of us recalled emptied into the river. It cut sharply into the bank. We could see the river had dropped about one and a half feet, but it was not enough to explain some of the logs.

Finally, at noon, we reached a fork we remembered and the world again made sense.

"We're back from the danger, the joongle, the Green Hell," Glück said.

The sun broke through and after another three turns, we reached a bend with long, flat rocks. We stopped, did laundry, and laid out our hammocks and sleeping bags to dry.

Glück made soup and said, "What we do? Go farther south until we find someone to tell us where we are, or go up the other [west] fork?"

"We're between another rock and a hard place," Tano said.

If we went up the west fork and realized it was wrong, we again would waste gas and finally knock ourselves out of any chance to make it up the Padauiri. If we went downriver and found someone who knows the rivers and they told us we should have gone up the west fork, we would be knocked out that way. It was the losing side of choices we were looking at, but Tano and I had grown accustomed to looking in that direction. The heavens hammered home the point.

Black clouds zoomed across the sky. We quickly collected our shtuff and loaded the boat. It began to rain as Glück finished making the soup, powdered cream of asparagus that tasted more like powdered cream of flour.

We crouched beside the steaming pot as sprinkling escalated to a hosing. Except for our hats, we stayed naked. Rain splatted on the rocks, the sky turned black, and water streamed off our skin. In the cold, our bodies smoked.

"If the rain continues," Glück said, "we'll never be able to finish the soup."

I tried to make a joke about the loaves and the fishes, but I couldn't get it right. Then I gave up jokes for metaphysics and watched Glück and Tano, who in the rain and the steam and the fog, looked like they were vaporizing.

Glück apparently also was thinking a little about anatomy. He pointed to the pendulum in our squat.

"For what you get cut?" he said.

Tano tried explaining circumcision and how almost everyone used to get cut in American hospitals. Glück said, "In Germany, it is only the Jewish people that cut this," an observation I didn't think was supposed to be anything more than an observation.

232

The rain kept falling hard, but my hat kept my head warm and I felt the soup slide into my stomach, which I rubbed when we were finished. When we emptied the pot, one of us, I don't remember who, suggested we go up the west fork. It was a big decision, one which we all mulled over, but then all agreed.

There, as in almost any section of the river, it was impossible to paddle up. No matter how Olympic our strokes, the current easily drove us back. So, we decided or were forced to use the engine.

The rain stopped while Gluck worked on the motor. It took him ten minutes to get the engine from a state of blue smoke gagging to black smoke running.

Our plan was to go two hours up the west fork, then if no mountains or rocks appeared, turn back, but we never reached that point. Fifty yards up the fork, it narrowed to ten feet and the ceiling of trees and vines dropped to just above our head.

"It is too narrow to be the Padauiri." Glück said he was positive.

The motor went back on its side in the boat, a disappointment, and we again took to the paddles.

Past the fork, down the main river, we paddled a half hour before we reached a long stretch of rapids, maybe fifty yards wide, where we were sure we had not passed. Again we speculated on how much and how fast the river was dropping, but not without more suggestions about the twilight zone. We unloaded the boat, tied it with climbing rope, and sent it down stern first. Tano and I put on sneakers and hopscotched downstream. The boat went from side to side in the rush of current, like it was in a reverse rodeo, with us trying to back it out of the ring and into its shoot.

With the rain, the current picked up speed and we shot down through small rapids before finding an old Hilton where we could camp. The hut was ten by thirty feet, the palm roof gray and rotting, but it was a great thing again to have a Hilton.

Glück wanted to make noodles, but I opted for meat and rice, which would mean more. "You boys are always hungry," Glück said. That got a stereo reply. "We worked hard."

Glück made rice and heated a can of sliced swine we didn't bother to slice.

233

We were tired and Glück went to sleep after dinner, but Tano and I stayed up and tried to answer, "Where the hell are we?" It was more trouble than it was worth. There were long pauses between words and soon it became too much of an effort to wait it out while whoever was talking pieced together a sentence. We said, *"Boa noit,"* but the jungle was not finished. First a rat crawled up a post by my feet, then I heard something crawling on the rafters above my head. I got a flashlight and spotted a tarantula clinging to palm fronds.

"Don't worry, they won't kill you," Tano said from his hammock, "only make you sick." He laughed at my sleeping between a rat and a tarantula, but he was right. The tarantula dropped on my head and didn't bother to kill me or even make me sick, so I swatted him off.

Late in the night, I heard a distant whining that sounded like generators. Three times I heard it and each time it seemed to start and stop as if controlled by a switch. The noise built to a loud, high-speed *whirrrr* and then continued in a roar that couldn't have been made by anything living. I remembered Glück's story of Tatunka hearing the underground machines from the people from the stars.

At dawn, Glück called out from his hammock, "Hello, did you hear the howling monkeys?"

Glück said howling monkeys cried because they were cold, but I had heard other versions, the most consistent that they howled to establish territory.

"Once I had a man come with me on a trip," Glück said. "In the night, the howling monkeys were right above us and when they cried, the man leaped out and screamed, 'Kurt, Kurt. We're being attacked by Eendyuns.'" At least I kept my mouth shut.

Glück was wound up and chatty that morning. A good night's sleep seemed to do that for him. The night before, when we stayed on the beach, he didn't sleep well, and during the day he was less talkative and snappy.

We left, paddling, paddling, paddling, but in many places the current was swift and when the river straightened, we let the boat glide downstream. The sun rose above the trees, we stripped, and the day became one of those "Merrily, merrily, merrily, merrily, life is but a dream" days, even when it rained.

Near noon, the clouds returned and pieced the sky closed and when they were finished, it poured. We only wore hats and Tano hooted, "This is like when I was a kid." I paddled hard to keep warm and whenever I felt cold, I tried to laugh the chill away, which only sort of worked, in that it required constant laughing.

In twenty minutes, it let up and in the distance, we heard what sounded like a rush of wind through the trees, only there was no wind.

"Waterfalls."

In five minutes we were on them, big rapids, maybe sixty yards wide and as far downstream as we could see. We swung the boat to the right, all of us paddling, and tried staying close to shore, but the current slammed us through clumps of hanging vines and bushes. We tried to slow the boat and grab something on shore, but the river pushed us into a low-hanging tree. We smashed into a branch that wouldn't break and it knocked me into Tano. The boat tipped, the left side lifted into the air, and Tano screamed, "Zalis, my paddle." The boat made an aching sound, like the aluminum was bending, then it splashed back down. Glück hung from the side and tried to grab the paddle, but it slipped inches from his grasp and the current carried it swiftly down a channel through the rocks.

We grabbed a vine from the tree while the river cracked into waves as it rushed by us.

No one spoke for a minute, then Glück said maybe we could find the paddle dowstream. We unloaded. Glück chopped down a tree, cut it into thirds, and trimmed the limbs, making it into roller bars so we could try and slide the boat over the rocks. It again began to rain hard. We were getting cold so we wrapped the tarps over our shoulders.

We took the boat along the shore to the toughest part of the rapids, then tied a rope to the bow and tried slipping it through and down the river. We set up the logs across a jetty of rocks, lifted the boat onto the rollers, eased it out into the current, across a breach in the rocks, and down a six-foot drop in the river. The passage was accomplished with the help of ants who were all over the rollers, then all over our hands and arms and ankles and legs.

After we repacked the boat, we took the binoculars and

235

searched inlets and bays at the base of the rapids, but no paddle. Tano stood like a periscope in the middle of the boat. I felt bad about knocking into him, and he felt the same about dropping it.

"Bonbons?" Glück asked.

We broke out the candies, gooey suck-em, crack-em balls wrapped in different colored plastic for supposedly different flavors, but they all tasted the same. As I said, Glück brought them to give the Indians, but as the days passed and lunches got skimpier and there weren't any Indians, we began breaking into the candies. They became a treat, expecially since Tano was running low on cigarettes, and when we knocked off some work, like going over a log or through rapids, Glück would say, "Bonbon."

The usual dose was two, but I gave Tano three.

The next hour passed quietly. It rained and we rotated the remaining two paddles. Trying to look on the bright side, I said, "At least someone will always be fresh."

We could have stopped and made a paddle, but with knives and a blunt ax, it would have taken awhile, so we pushed on.

"Two o'clock," Glück announced. We had planned to find a Hilton and stop by noon to make up for the previous days' missed rest, but we were moving slowly and passing through the rapids had eaten up time.

The river had dropped six to ten feet in some places, and instead of a continuous winding ribbon of water, now the river was broken by waterfalls, rapids and rocks. No one spoke about the paddle, but Tano continued to search the shore. We paddled for hours, but no Hilton, and once more, we talked about how the river looked strange and not like what we remembered. Maybe we were still on the river of no return. I shifted into automatic pilot, took long, deep strokes with the paddle and let the rhythm clear my mind of thoughts. That took about four strokes.

We passed an island I remembered, with two trees that looked like sentinels, and midafternoon, we met another, bigger river running into ours from the east. On a hill, high above the confluence, an empty, thatched house, with a ladder to the river, crowned the rocks. Tano climbed up and in a few seconds yelled down, "It's beautiful." Glück and Tano remembered the house— actually it was the ladder they remembered, the house could not

236

be seen from the river. I had a vague recollection of the ladder, but it was the river, coming in from the east, that had us stumped. I remembered still water and thought it was a lagoon.

"How could we have passed the other river?" Glück said.

The river from the east was a mystery, and Tano and I once more unraveled the aerial picture. On one of the maps, high in the left corner, we found a fork in the Padauiri, with the left side winding back and forth, then going off the map, and the right, eastern side, leading to another section of pictures. Maybe that was the fork where we were camped.

Tano suggested that the next day we could follow the river with a compass to see if it matched the map. Although we didn't trust the nine-year-old map, it seemed as reasonable an idea as any, and Tano further reasoned, "We've got to use every bit of information we got."

We were beat, and Tano said he wanted to take the next day off. It would be our twentieth day out of Manaus, the midway point, so a break seemed a good idea to me. Glück came back from the river with his fishing line but with no fish and said, "We should take a day of rest tomorrow," so the decision was unanimous.

Glück said he wanted to go up the east side of the fork for fifteen minutes the next day and see if it was OK. I didn't want to waste gas, but Glück said, "It will make nuhzing. Beside, I want to troll for a fish. I want to fish all tomorrow. It was in the calculations. Then, tomorrow night, we can charbroil a big Christ's fingerprint, with nuhzing else." The "nuhzing else" was supposed to have a purity about it, but it didn't come across that way. It only seemed to emphasize the nuhzing.

Tano went back into the jungle to collect seeds and flowers and came back in an hour with a red-yellow hot dog–shaped seed. "Man, you're going to have to check some of the plants out sometime."

With evening, a storm rolled in from the northeast, and I went down to the rocks and watched the world change. Above the fork, the sky exploded with light. For a moment, the sun found an open seam in the clouds, near the horizon, then everything turned indigo.

I sewed in the morning, piecing together my disintegrating straw hat with fishing line, then at 10:30, we made a run up the east fork. For a quarter hour we motored northeast, the river turning sharply in a couple of places that, according to our compass and estimates of distance, matched exactly with the map. Tano shouted, "All right, all right," and Glück sat in the back of the boat, fishing, and said, "Yes, I zink zis is ze right river." We paddled back down. Twice Glück's line snagged on a rock and we had to paddle fast and hard against the current to retrieve the hook. A hard paddle stroke would give us an inch against the current and each time we backtracked the fifty-foot line, we felt like collapsing.

We estimated that as the crow flew, we still had about sixty kilometers to the pyramids, a distance we would at least have to double because of the curves in the river. We had twenty-five liters of gas left and Glück said we could get five kilometers to the liter. We might still make it. But there were variables—the current, the weight in the boat, the wind, and how many rocks, logs, sandbanks, or whatever we would have to dodge. Even so, the angels seemed to be smiling. We had come back from the River of No Return and ended up with a Hilton on the fork of the Pa-dauiri. We almost had given up making it a few days before, and suddenly we had a second shot.

XXXI

ONE of us figured it had been nine days since we had seen anyone else on the river, and that felt good.

I had been reading the book about the Amazon, with chapters describing how dense and complicated the life ladder was in the jungle. That got me thinking about how insensitive to most of it I was, how I was seeing it as green walls and odd sounds. That got me thinking about me, then even worse, got me thinking about everybody. Living seemed to be too much like traveling those rivers, not giving in to the jungle, only taking obvious turns where the current flowed swiftly, slowing down when the water was low, pushing up a river until it made no sense, then drifting down, getting hung up in bushes, remembering where you had been before, then paddling out until you found a high point for a rest at another fork.

I didn't think about that stuff long, though, as stupid questions led to what I got, the kind of things you put on posters in greeting-card stores ("Today is the next day . . .") or zen answers or no answers. That left me feeling all the stupider for having asked them. Anyway, life didn't make half as much sense as any of those crazy rivers.

Before supper, we took stock of our food supply, an inventory that prompted Glück to cut our rice ration in half. We had six days of rice and three days of macaroni left, along with other odds and ends, meaning we had nine days of food left for twenty more days in the jungle. We were out of ketchup and crackers and low on everything else, except sugar. Glück said that was fortunate. "Zucker is good for you. The athletes in the Olympics, they inject it, zucker from the grapes."

To calm us, Glück said, "We won't die, I zink."

In the evening, we tried forgetting about our food situation and went down to sit on the rocks. Across the river, two hundred yards in, smoke rose above the trees.

"Maybe Eendyun," Glück said.

No one said anything about going across and seeing what it was, inaction we could have blamed on being low on bonbons. Instead, we just sat and watched the smoke, and talked about other things.

"Who are we? Who are we? I kept asking myself while we were up the other river," Glück said. "Everyone says, 'Stay to your right, only to your right, and you cannot get lost.' Sometimes when it rains, the rivers change completely.

"When we go up, I think we cannot get lost, we just follow the current down. Then we come down." He stopped and laughed.

"In the joongle, sometimes it's crazy. The Eendyuns, they say this. They believe in the ghosts and shtuff and sometimes the ghosts..." He stopped and tried pronouncing the Portuguese word for ghosts, then gave up and changed story directions.

"The Eendyun...I know an old Eendyun for eighteen years. He tells me a story about going somewhere on a trip that he has been on hundreds of times before. He knows it completely, but he gets lost. The Eendyun..." Glück chuckled at how ridiculous it sounded to him. "The Eendyun, he get lost."

"The Curupiras, where we're going," Tano said, "are there supposed to be a lot of ghosts there?"

"Yes," Glück mumbled, as if he didn't want us to hear. "The Curupiras...There are stories the Eendyuns have of places there, one of a lake that no one goes to because it will turn you around and around.

240

"All these people that nature builds," Glück said, "the niggers, the Arabs, they have these stories."

There were few stories between us that night. Most of the time, we sat and listened to the river gurgle over the edge of rocks. There was no moon, and Glück said that heading into a new moon, there would be bad weather.

Cut rations debuted at breakfast, as the Quaker lost weight and became a milky soup with a sprinkling of oats, like seasonings.

We left in the rain and told Glück to go "slowly, very, very, slowly," to conserve gas. We crossed into a part of the river covered by a corner of the last of Glück's maps, where a black water tributary flowed in from the west. Glück said it might be Lacerda's, the piacaba king, so we veered off the Padauiri and paddled into a black-water lagoon.

Black water, like the night, can be eerie or tranquil, and that morning, with the rain cracking big rings on the surface of the river, and the mist hanging from the trees like Spanish moss, the jungle seemed haunted and black water a crack in a world we did not know.

No one spoke. The forest was quiet and even the rain, though we saw it fall on the river, hardly made a sound. The only thing I heard was the slip of our paddles stirring the water.

We paddled two hundred yards and passed through a notch between piles of square-shaped boulders when Glück pointed to Lacerda's house, a long, thatched hut, shaped like an airplane hangar, tucked in trees fifty yards in from the rocks. We docked the boat and walked up.

Like every other place we had seen in the last couple of weeks, Lacerda's was deserted, but unlike every other hut we had seen on the river, Lacerda's was palatial though like almost all the others, empty. It had six rooms, some completely separated with palm frond walls, and even a closeted area with a table Glück said Lacerda had used as his shortwave room.

"I cannot understand," Glück said. "Everyone is gone. When I was here, there were many people, and many Eendyuns bringing in the piacaba."

Tano and I said maybe Tatunka's story had scared everyone away, but Glück said, "Lacerda is a strong man," referring to his power over the cabocolos and Indians.

I had seen a picture of Lacerda at Glück's house. He was a Brazilian in his mid-forties, with dark hair and a bit of a paunch. In the photo, he wore a khaki shirt soaked with sweat. He looked like he had just come back from a bivouac with commandos. Although he had treated Glück well, he was a king of sorts, controlling the river economy above Allianca.

"What we do?" Glück said. "Stay and eat, or move on?"

Since the decision to turn back on the lost river, most decisions about movement had become Tano's and mine, but the decision to leave or stay at Lacerda's wasn't easy. The hut was dry, outside it was raining hard, and the thought of eating was tempting, but we opted for a middle course. We would wait until the rain eased and then leave. Glück said he remembered one or two huts upriver, where in the early afternoon we could stop.

The rain continued for a half hour, long enough for us to gather treasures. Tano found bright blue and red parrot feathers, and I found the head of a tapir, from which I removed a couple of teeth and gave one to Tano. Glück made the only important find, a lemon tree filled with fruit.

Above Lacerda's, the river contracted and began turning back on itself in thirty-yard intervals. We lost it on the map and passed a branch to the east. Glück said we must remember to go right on our return and not follow the downstream left branch.

The river tightened. Curves sharpened and became more frequent, but the narrowness only forced the current to run stronger. On shore, vegetation changed. Trees thinned until there were none and we were surrounded by bushes with pale, yellow-green leaves that shimmered, like chips of glass. The sky cleared. The wind died and in the brightness of early afternoon, the sun stalked us as the river and the leaves knotted us in a gauze of white light.

I remember that kind of light and time in the afternoon from when I was a kid in the Florida swamps. The light would come at the same time, in early to mid afternoon, when the sun

242

felt like it was nesting on my head, and heat settled like sludge. There was never a wind, but sometimes a palm might rustle. It had nothing to do with a breeze, but was a matter of air squirming under the press of the sun. Otherwise, nothing moved.

It was different in the morning and late afternoon. In the morning, when the sun rose and the night slipped to the west, past the Gulf, and the insects still were whining and the birds sang and the temperature started to rise, everything moved. Then again, late in the afternoon, when a thunderstorm would rise out of that heat and moisture to rip open the sky, more movement. Between those two times, there was dead space. Everything would stop, and sometimes, maybe me.

It wasn't good to move when the day packed that white light. It was like walking across loose and rotting floorboards. The world creaked and you risked waking the dead. Sometimes when I didn't move, my thoughts would, a wandering that seemed dangerous because there was nothing else in motion, nothing quite alive to hold me in check. When things moved, the world and I defined each other by where we touched, but when they stopped, and I felt that space, I was nobody or everybody, a problem I was smart enough as a kid to know not to tackle. Instead, I had the sense to realize I felt off during that time of day, and I never argued much when my mother told me it was time for a nap.

That was what Glück and Tano and I should have been doing. The jungle might have stopped for a breather, but we didn't.

The sun bleached the bushes and the air tasted like steam. Everything seemed deader when we lost ourselves on the map. The river was zigzagging wildly, and we were going in an easterly direction that didn't correspond to anything on the aerial photographs. We guessed we might be in an empty space between where two of the photographs were supposed to overlap. That would have fit perfectly.

"Who is the river?" Glück asked. I was having enough trouble with my own who's and where's and why's and what's and how's and Glück's appendices were getting on my nerves. He often mumbled about how he couldn't calculate where we were on the map, and to compensate, he kept the engine roaring. Tano and I had to turn around constantly to tell him he was going too

243

fast and we had to conserve gas. Tano and I took turns saying, "We have a long way to go," to which Glück would pucker his lips and half nod, then slow down for another ten minutes before his hand started twisting the accelerator again and we would have to turn around and start all over again.

"Who is north?" Glück asked a dozen times while looking at the compass. "If this is north, then this must be right and east. East is always to the right of north." Again and again he would reorient himself and check the compass, each time ending with an "east is always to the right, and west is always to the left."

I stopped listening and just nodded my head, yes or no, when he asked questions like, "Are we still on the middle map?" I would say, "No, we've moved on," and then an hour later, he would ask the same question and I would give the same answer.

"This cannot be," he would say, referring either to the map or the river, I was never sure which, but in any case, I always had the same answer, "But it is."

Then he would ask, "Who is the mountains?" and he would have me stumped.

Actually, as the trip grew longer, the mountains became more important, a promise the land would rise and lift us out of the choke of jungle.

By two o'clock we rediscovered ourselves on the map after going up a long, northeasterly stretch where the river widened and the trees again grew along the shore. Although we had motored more than five hours, we had gone two inches on a map where we still had a foot to go.

"If we make it, it'll be just," Tano said.

We had agreed in the morning that if we didn't find a Hilton before 2:30, we would stop and hack out a camp, but minutes before deadline, we found a Hilton on the west shore, on the edge of a ten-foot palisade of rock. We lashed the boat to a ladder and climbed up to a long, open-walled hut that looked like a meeting hall. It had benches along the side and back, and it was separated from smaller huts by a lagoon. The lagoon had been bridged by a log that was axed in half.

"It looks like someone didn't want someone else to get someplace else," Tano said.

Inside the main hut, we found woven baskets and a fan,

244

things that would have taken hours to make. Once again, we wondered why they were left and we wondered about the Tatunka scare. We built a fire and settled in for the night.

Glück was up at first light and Tano and I were right behind him. We figured we had two days of gas time left, maybe twelve hours, and with the sand dwindling from our food time clock, the earlier we got moving, the better.

Soon after we left, I lost our position on the map, where I thought we should lose it, on a stretch of squiggling lines I could not follow. The river narrowed and about a hundred yards into the jungle, smoke rose above the trees.

"Maybe the Eendyun is having his breakfast," Glück said.

Midmorning, we pulled over and changed spark plugs on a sandbank. Then Glück broke bad news. We had used half our gas since leaving the fork on the Padauiri. We still had more than a day and a half traveling time to go on a little more than a half tank of gas. I got a ruler and the map and tried to project how far we could go on fourteen to fifteen liters, but I came up with us running out of fuel at least twenty kilometers short.

My heart sank.

Glück sang, "It's a long way to Tipperary"—solace that didn't help much.

The edge of the river was as green and thick as it had been since we left Manaus, with vines and bushes and trees squeezing for a swatch of light along the edge. I asked Glück what the jungle was like near the pyramids. He said it was the same. He said that when he was with the Austrian, at the end of the river they cut their way through the trees and into the mountains. That gave Tano and me another idea.

First, we had to run out of gas, though, and how close we got would tell the story. It would be another matter to find our position on the map.

We didn't have food for lunch, but Tano made sugar water that masqueraded as lemonade.

"It's good for you," Tano mimicked Glück. "The Olympians, they inject it."

We had no idea where we were on the map or on the river, which most of the time was going west and northwest and that didn't jive with the map. I was hungry, my mouth was parched

245

and gritty from the drink of Olympians, and I tried not to think about food, but thinking about anything else seemed irrelevant.

The sun stayed away in the afternoon, and late in the day it began to rain as we pulled into a black water lagoon on the east side of the river. I was down and near out. The day had been the worst on the trip and it was looking worse for the pyramids. Tano and I talked about trying to cut our way through the jungle, but first we had to convince Glück, who was in the river cleaning a piranha he had caught in the morning.

Glück came back and boiled a packet of soup and threw in the piranha, which had a lot of triangular-shaped bones and not much meat. Glück said he once had one of the bones wedge in his throat and it took a week before it rotted.

"What we do about tomorrow?" Glück said. "We only have one and a half hours of gas left."

Tano called him on that. "I thought we had one-third of a tank."

Glück hedged and mumbled something about the gas gauge not being balanced. He wasn't sure. "Maybe we have as much as three hours, but we still have not reached the big log and rocks I remember from with the Austrian, and from that point, it's still two hours."

"Let's try walking through the jungle," I said.

Glück hesitated, then said, "If we reach the fork by the pyramids, we can drag the boat."

"If we don't reach that," I said, "I'd like to try trekking through the jungle."

Glück tilted his head and pulled his lips into his mouth.

"Hmmmm . . . Maybe. We have one rucksack," he said. "We bring the Quaker and the can of peaches and eat that."

Tano suggested bringing rice with a pot and building a fire, but Glück thought it might be difficult when it rained. He said we could bring hammocks and a tarp and maybe go two or three days. That would give us two weeks to get back, Glück's way of saying that was as much as he got paid.

"I think, maybe we can do this," Glück said, and stood up and walked into the jungle to take a piss.

"That was pretty easy," I said to Tano.

When Glück returned, Tano told him he really wanted to make it to the pyramids.

246

"But, I zink datz booshit," Glück said.

"But it's a goal," Tano said.

In the morning, for the first time in what had been weeks, Glück whistled "The Daring Young Man on the Flying Trapeze." That might have had something to do with his fishing line swinging back and forth across the river. When he fished, the boat had a tendency to drift from shore to shore and Glück would try to circumvent obstacles by yelling "oooopah" and whipping the line over a log or a rock. Tano sat in the bow and tried to guide Glück in, staying to the side of the river with the least current. That usually was the higher or more northern bank, as the river flowed and carved into the lower, southern shoreline. We felt those curves as if we had climbed a steep hill. Every curve and rush of current cut into our gas, subtracted from how long we would be able to run the boat, and added to how much we would have to walk.

Wherever we did run out of gas, it would be a long trek through the jungle and one we would do partially blind. For more than a day, we had been unable to find ourselves on the map.

During the night, the river had dropped a foot, weakening the current. If it continued to drop, we thought we might be able to pole our way up, Volga-boatman style, or if it dropped very low, wade and drag the boat.

Once, Glück turned off the motor and we tried "rooning against the current," first with paddles, then with small, thin poles, then with longer heavier poles. None of it worked.

When we paddled, we dug into the river as fast and hard as we could, but the current was too strong and threw us back.

Our first set of poles were six feet long—too short, as at some points we had to reach down into the water to push at the bottom. When we cut longer poles, they were too heavy. It was like trying to twirl trees. We moved in inches, which when added together after a half hour, came to little at all. Then, trying to cross the river from one backwater to another, the main current quickly brought the Volga boatmen to their knees. Our poles bent and gave way, and the boat spun downstream like a pinwheel.

247

We retreated to mechanics and gas. We ran the motor around the first bend in the river, and at the next curve, a tree blocked us. The lower trunk dammed the river, but on the far left, the tree spread into a tangle of limbs we tried to cut. I was at the point and hacked a hole through, while Glück gave the engine enough gas to stalemate the current. The river pressed us into the mud along the shore.

I had cut under water, and three times I lost my grip on the machete. The first two times I grabbed it before it slid downstream. The third time, I dived into the river and swam underwater but came up smiling with the knife.

"You have much luck," Glück said.

Before we reached the next curve, the engine gagged, though it was only fouled spark plugs. We squeezed another hour out of it, but by 1:30, the gauge on the gas tank hit empty and we pulled to shore.

We found a black water lagoon, twenty feet back into the jungle, beached the boat, and slashed open a camp. The jungle was thick with vines, needled palms, fire ants, mosquitoes, gnats, bees, and a swarm of other winged things I couldn't identify. It was the kind of spot that if it had hands would have choked us, and at that point, if it wanted to, I probably would have let it.

After we set up our pods, Tano and I jumped into the river and swam out to the middle to search the shore for a tall tree to climb. We didn't have any idea where we were on the map and thought maybe from the top of a tree we could spot the mountains. The tree we were looking for was downstream, about forty yards in, towering over the rest of the jungle like a parasol with its wires tangled.

It took us twenty minutes to make the fifty yards. We had to carve through webs of vines, dead trees, and needled bushes, a passage we accomplished as if we were floating. We never touched the jungle floor. Between us and the bottom, there were roots and dead trees and vines. A few times I slipped through, but it was something like crossing a horizontal ladder. Even hanging through the rungs, my feet didn't touch ground.

We cut separate paths, with each of us trying to find an easier way, something we couldn't do. We crawled under, around, over, squeezed through and between trees. Ten feet away, I couldn't see Tano, the jungle was so dense, but I could hear him hacking, breaking, untangling bushes and vines and webs of dead limbs. When we reached the tree, Tano tried climbing it, with me pushing him up from his waist, then his legs and his feet, but he couldn't get far. The trunk was slick and the lowest branch, thirty feet high, as everything jammed the roof of the jungle for a glimpse of light, just like we were trying to do.

The way back to camp took almost as long. I was surprised we didn't get lost.

Glück was working on piranha soup. I don't remember what Tano and I said, but it had something to do with astonishment. The forest couldn't have been thicker and there couldn't have been less light and it still be day. We were covered with scratches and bites and it had taken us forty minutes to go a distance some men in the right place could do in less than ten seconds. The encounter should have left us humbled, but the river already had us in that state of mind, so the jungle moved us farther down to depressed. We combated that by wolfing dinner and thinking what good it would do us.

"I think eating piranha all the time would make you tough," Tano said.

"What it makes?" Glück asked.

"It would make you tough ... tee--oh--eeyoo--jee--aatch .. tough, because it's so mean."

"Hmmm."

Tano and I drank tea and watched the light fade from the river, while Glück rummaged in his mechanic shop for a candle.

"Oh, look," he said, holding a balloon he found in the chest, "we can fly out of here."

We all laughed, but I think the joke hit a sensitive spot, as flying probably was the only way we could get where we were going.

"What do you think we should do, Kurt?" I asked.

He was counting a roll of bills, "one cruzeiro, two cruzeiro, three ..." and he acted like he was sideswiped by the question.

"Huh? Ahh .. What we can do? We can, ah, yes," as if he just had stumbled on the perfect answer. "We can go back."

I don't know how long that one hung, but Glück didn't let it hang long.

"We can go to the mountains north of Manaus. We have the time and for you, it's interesting, for the sloths. You can make pictures."

I didn't even look at Tano. Maybe the piranha soup was taking effect, as the next thing I said came blurting out from wherever I keep desperate statements.

"What do you think about walking?" I asked.

Again, Glück seemed to be caught by surprise.

"If we know it . . . walking, it's not nice. It's terrible, t-e-r-r-y-b-l-u-h," he repeated, just so we understood.

That did not move me. I doubt if it moved Tano, either. After a fifty-yard walk in the jungle, we knew it would be terrybluh.

"We don't know how high we are on the map," Glück said, "or what place we are. It can be that we will be there in two days. It can be that we will be there in eight days. Then, we never come . . ." and his voice trailed off and I wasn't sure if he said "back."

I felt some dark, shadow figure join us then. He sat down between Tano and me and I knew he would be there for the rest of the conversation, maybe the rest of the night, maybe until all this business was finished.

"It's hard work, walking," Glück said. "You have to clean the jungle and mark the trees."

"What if we tried the river again and made longer poles, thin ones?" I said.

"To go down?" Glück said.

"Up," Tano said.

"Up? Against the current? We'll make nuhzing," Glück said.

"We can leave our heavy stuff here," I said.

"What we leave would make nuhzing," Glück said. "We need the hammocks, the tanks are empty, and without knowing where we are . . ."

We tried to figure our spot on the map by comparing our upriver running time, which was very slow, to what Glück said he and the Austrian did the previous year. It took us awhile, but using a string and compass and Glück's recollection of how far he had gone each day with the Austrian, and where I thought we had made our first two camps on the map above Allianca, we could make a guess. Mine was probably optimistic. I could not take into account all the river's switchbacks, but I thought we had made it on the third and final map, near the bottom. On the map, and written vertically along the river, the word "Padauiri" covered the last photograph. According to my guess, we were at the final *i* in Padauiri.

Tano immediately took to that.

"In the eye of the Padauiri," he said with a smirk, like it was being in the eye of a hurricane.

Actually, the *i* was encouraging. As the crow flies, we were seventeen kilometers from the southern tip of the mountains.

"That's only ten miles," Tano said.

"That's straight," I said.

"In the joongle, we have to open it," Glück said. "Maybe we can do it in three days, one way, five to six kilometers a day."

"That still would be a long haul, without much food, one rucksack, and if it rains..." I said.

"It's bad if it's raining in the joongle," Glück said, "then if it's sunshine, it's bad, too. It's too warm."

No one said anything for a bit, then Glück said we could spend the morning trying to find a tall tree we could climb, and survey the terrain.

"In the joongle, everything goes up, up, to the light," he said. Then he spun around, like he just had finished a pronouncement, and went to his hammock.

Tano rolled each of us a cigarette and didn't say anything until he was finished.

"Every day is a day of reckoning, and every day we could get wrecked. I think we just ought to fuck this tree climbing and go for it. Then, if we don't make it, what the hell, we really have given it our best shot."

I don't know what I was looking for at the time, but I was looking straight up, and through an opening in the trees I saw the Southern Cross. I pointed it out to Tano, but he acted as if I didn't say anything.

"Well, it's just gonna be us and the jungle now," I said.

"That's right."

And just in case the jungle was listening, I said, "I respect it." I said that loud enough for the shadow between us to hear.

"I can't really say I look forward to it," Tano said.

"I don't either."

"It's gonna be hell."

The shadow moved.

"We could end up lost," I said. "We could end up dying."

"Oh, yeah, easy," Tano said.

"That's why we have to mark our trail really well."

"Sure, but you get ten feet away from something, you can't see it anymore."

"Well, we can tie markers to the trees and slash them."

"Boy, this is going to be hell, just going to be hell."

"If we do get lost, we can always head due west until we find the river and then float down."

For a while, each of us kept to himself and thought about other end-of-the-line possibilities. I was pretty sure we would get lost and less sure we eventually would find our way out. I had a vision of Tano and me crawling on hands and knees, the standard Hollywood scenario, then realizing it was over, propping ourselves against a tree and laughing away our last gasps, but I didn't feel like talking about that vision.

"Christ, I think it's worth a shot," I said.

"You know, for myself, I don't feel like I've got any choice in the matter," Tano said. "I just gotta do it." Then, after a gap, where I knew he was putting his own last gasp scenario together, but wasn't saying, he said, "and I sure ain't looking forward to it . . . Gotta try, though."

By then, I thought we had talked ourselves around the plan as much as we should. Any more talking and we could back ourselves into the proverbial corner, so I went to my pack and took out a present.

"Now, you're talking," Tano said.

"There's a time for everything," I said, unwrapping a pair of cigars.

"Yeah, now you're talking. No use saving them anymore. Save it for your deathbed," he said in a tone I wasn't sure was a prediction or a description of current circumstances. Either way, I didn't want to know.

XXXII

I felt dawn coming long before the forest shifted from black to gray, before the cicadas began to buzz and before the mosquitoes stopped whining, but I was unable to stop it.

At breakfast, I faced the river. We had double rations of the Quaker, a bowl of oatmeal I let slide down slowly, making sure it had plenty of time to get to wherever it was needed. We were very much awake, but we talked little, each of us working out how he would fare the next few days. I think I watched the river because I didn't want to face the jungle, at least not yet. The jungle was the house, its cards were marked, and if I stared it in the eye, I was afraid I might blink.

I had got to know the river some, and I wasn't ready to change foes. Maybe that was the feeling that made me change my mind. How long I stared at the river I'm not sure, but sometime near the end of the Quaker, I said, "Here we've got a pathway to the pyramids."

No one said anything right away, but they both knew what I meant, and I think they were glad I said it, at least that's what I told myself.

While I was watching the river, I had been telling myself it was crazy to try and hack our way through the jungle. It hadn't rained during the night, the river had dropped, and the sun was out, so it seemed to make more sense to try paddling or poling north. After I said that out loud, Glück jumped at it, and after some hesitation, Tano agreed.

We unloaded everything unnecessary out of the boat—the motor, gas tanks, empty cannisters—covered them with a tarp and camouflaged it with tree limbs. We cut long, thin poles, then as we slid the boat back into the river, Tano turned to me and said what I wished he had not said. "I don't know about this paddling."

That seemed to shift the responsibility of choice and the river back to where it started from, to me, while I wanted it to be unified. I was rationalizing, but the jungle felt like a fool's decision, one we all knew we would lose, but we were doing it anyway. With the river, I still felt a chance. Maybe Tano saw things the other way.

Tano and I stripped to our sneakers. I took the middle, with the big paddle, Tano took the point with the pole, and Glück stayed with a paddle at the rudder. We crawled upriver. We stayed to the leeward side, the side with the least current. I paddled on the river side of the boat, and Tano poled us along the shore and tried to keep our nose pointed upstream. Gluck stayed at the stern and tried to keep us off the shore, but moving.

We had a hell of a time making thirty yards to tie surveyor's ribbons on trees to mark our motor hideout, and the rest of the day was just as rough.

Tano would push off, I would paddle to push us in, and Glück would get slammed into the bank of thorned bushes along the shore. I paddled like hell, partially to prove the river was the right decision, but we inched upstream. We pressed along one shore, then as the river swung in another direction, we paddled wildly against the midstream current and crossed to the opposite side, pressing along that shore until the next bend, when we would cross back.

"Faster, faster, paddling, paddling," Glück shouted as we crossed to the other side, where again, Tano would push out, I would paddle us in, and Glück would do whatever he could to keep us straight. We carved slices off the bank. Showers of ants—

254

red and black—ticks, spiders, vines, thorned palms, and a tarantula fell into the boat. Once, a thorned tree limb knocked off my hat and snagged my hair. The boat spun around, the vine knotted in my hair, and without paddling, the boat started to slip downstream. My scalp was about to be torn off. I reached into the tree, pulled vines into the boat, and found a sturdy limb to hang on, while my feet hung on to the boat. Tano dived into the river and swam for my hat. I unknotted my hair and pulled the thorns out of my arms and legs and scalp, and Tano swam back with my hat and we pushed on.

I got angry with Glück once for not keeping us straight, but he paddled as hard as he could and I never saw him let up. The trip and the river seemed to have little to do with him anymore, but he had a lot of heart and never said no.

In some stretches, the river dropped and we got out and pulled, but the current was strong and it was like walking against double gravity. We would drag the boat until the river climbed to the level of our chest, then back to the paddles and the pole.

By the middle of the afternoon, the jungle changed. Although the banks still were a hedge of green, inside the forest thinned, and we could see blue skies through the trees. The air was cooler and so was the water, and we thought maybe we were getting closer to the mountains, a thought that fueled us for another couple of hours. Then the jungle thickened and we sagged and decided to stop for the night. We cut a camp in a thicket of palms, and I took a swim and dotted my cuts with iodine until it looked like I had on war paint. Actually, I was surprised at how strong I felt. We hardly stopped paddling during the day, and like Bob Richards, I attributed my strength to breakfast, which only made me feel bad again as I thought we could go on forever if we had enough food.

We had rice and split a sardine-sized can of swine for dinner, and I thought about going back on an empty stomach, so I chewed slowly.

"Good morning," Glück called from his hammock at dawn. "Do we keep going or turn back?"

I was stunned and answered, "We go on."

"Sure," he said in a tone that if English was his native language, would have been mocking. He said that even though we had come upriver, paddling and poling for six hours, it would take us only one hour to return to the camp we had left yesterday morning.

"One hour? We've done more than that," I said in a tone that since English is my native language, meant shaky disbelief.

"I don't zink so."

I untied my hammock and let what he said bother me, then sat down and had a cup of coffee. I steamed for a while, then Tano asked me, "Maybe we would've done better to walk, rather than pull a couple hundred pound boat upriver?"

"We threw in our lot with the river, and now we have to go for it," I snapped.

It was a sign I was going crazy, but I thought that if Glück or Tano believed we were wrong, they could give in and let the river prove them right. Tano must have sensed my pressure valve weakening. He said, "There's humor in all this. We're just thrashing ourselves against this river to prove we can make it."

I laughed, because it was true, so some of the steam escaped, and I thought, one way or another, it will be over soon.

The day was a ditto of the previous day. I played river wheel with the big-bladed paddle and tried to keep us going forward, while Glück paddled us away from the shore and Tano pointed our nose toward the center of the river, nudging us out just enough so the current would not spin us sideways. There were long, rough stretches. I paddled as hard as I could, until sweat was dripping off me in puddles, while trying to keep my eyes off the shore. It reflected what I didn't want it to reflect.

At noon, Tano and I switched positions. The point man's job was to jump out and drag the boat forward when we hit a shallow spot, and when we clung to shore, to nudge the boat from the bank, just enough to balance the paddling force of the man in the middle.

By afternoon, the river was dropping and sometimes I had to drag the boat a long way. My arms were weary from paddling, and in the beginning, it was a relief to walk against the current and use my legs, but as the afternoon dragged and the river pounded, my legs got wobbly. My hands were blistered and cut,

256

and gravel was getting into the bottom of my sneakers. At first I didn't take my sneakers off because of the palm tree pins and stingrays, though by three o'clock, after constantly having to empty my shoes, I kicked them off and went barefoot.

Once, I saw a mountain. It looked close, but it also looked vapory, like a mirage.

Four o'clock, when the water was up to my chest, instead of hoisting myself into the boat, I threw a leg up, hung on the edge, then rolled over and in, and fell to the floor. At least for the day, we were finished.

The jungle was a knot, but we hacked a hole through a bank of bushes and vines, pulled the boat up, cleared a spot for the kitchen and hammocks, then because the mosquitoes and flies were bad, went down and sat in the boat by the shore.

"What we do?" Glück asked.

I said let's look at the map and talk about it, but that wasn't much good as we had no idea how far we had come. We still had not reached a log Glück crossed with the Austrian, nor the fork in the river, both of which, Glück said, came a full day's running time with the motor before the pyramids. We had three breakfasts and dinners left—some Quaker, rice, and two cans of swine and a can of fruit.

We sat and talked awhile, but we all were beat and whatever we said must have sounded like mumbles. None of it stuck, and I can't get at it now. The only thing I remember is lying quietly for a long time and watching the sky pass above us.

It rained during the night. I stayed covered in the pod, which changed to bright blue with the dawn as the rain continued to fall. I knew enough not to bother to look for golf course sprinklers. Through the night, my hammock soaked up water, and by morning, I had slipped down and curled into a fetal position in the only dry spot, at the bottom of the bow. I laid there for a long time, while the water kept coming and pushing me into more of a curl. After it reached me, and my back and feet got wet, it refused to give up and still kept coming. No one else moved, although somewhere behind the bad weather, the sun climbed high in the sky.

A puddle formed on my tarp. It sagged until it was three inches from my nose, then water ran down and dripped off. I was cold, and outside, I knew the river was filling.

"What we do?" Glück called through a muffle of plastic.

Tano and I lifted our pod covers and Glück stuck his head out.

"Do we go up or down?" Glück said.

Tano pointed a thumb down.

"OK, we go back," Glück said.

"Wait a minute, convince me of that," I said

"What we do? We have no food. I think we go back," Glück said.

Tano ignored Glück and looked at me. "What the hell you been doin' in there?"

"Biting the bullet."

"Well then?"

"Talk to me," I said. "I need it."

"It's too wet to climb trees. I'd have to do it in my long clothes, and I won't do it. We're wasting our time paddling upriver and you know it."

"What about walking to the mountain?"

"We would have to walk through the jungle and every vine or tree we chopped would rain down water on us. Our sleeping gear is wet, so we'd have to come back at the end of our day's hike with soaked clothes and soaked gear. Without climbing a tree, we might walk past mountains, anyway."

He stopped for a second and tried to let it sink in, but it wouldn't.

"Talk to me some more."

"Jesus Christ, what do you want?" he said. "I'm packing it in. This is the end of the line for me. Play what you're dealt, man. This rain is the last card in a bust hand."

For what seemed like a long time, no one said anything, though the rain and the jungle continued to *rat-tat-tat-tat*. Tano looked at me. I knew everything he said was true, though I didn't want it to be. Then I let go.

"OK," I said.

I heard Tano climb out of his pod and I lifted up my tarp and we both started laughing. We laughed for a long time, hard

258

and then hysterical, until we were almost crying. Glück must have thought we had gone mad.

We took down camp and split a can of peaches for breakfast, then packed the boat. Just before we left, Tano and I went back and notched a tree.

All she wrote.
Tano and Zalis
May 19, 1980.

BACK

XXXIII

I knew the adventure was not finished then—it was too long a trip back for that—and I was right. But I was wrong about something else. I thought we had blown the chance to discover the pyramids, that like just about everything else Tano and I had done together, we were going to come back beat and empty-handed. Thinking that way turned out to be a big mistake.

If I had known that when we turned around, maybe things would have started off easier.

As we loaded the boat, the rain let up, so we took off our clothes.

"It will take us an hour to make our last camp," Glück said. That probably was the worst thing he could have said, but I let the remark hang. Still, he was right. The jungle zipped by, like it was laughing at us for trying to push-pull-paddle against it.

Just after we got in the boat, I turned and saw the mountains. At the time, they looked touchingly close, but as I think of their image now, they probably were still many miles.

I should have known how to deal with losing by then, but I didn't. Like on Willoughby Fenton's boat, there are times when you are moving that it's good to stop. If we could have, I would have liked to stop then, but the wave we rode in was racing back to wherever it came from, and I was caught in a riptide. For a moment, there was a sense of panic, an urge to swim like hell to the shore, but I didn't know where shore was. I remembered what swimming instructors had said when I was a kid, "Go laterally, until you get out from the undertow."

I tried going sideways, but the current kept pulling me out.

I wanted to try and make sense of things, a seemingly foolish enough notion that had managed to screw up enough people before me. I should have known better.

Like the time I argued with Tano in Puerto Arista, life was indifferent. There were no final rewards. You're here for a while, and things might work out, they might not, either way, it didn't make much difference if you saw things only in terms of an end. Perhaps that was why it was a good thing not to have made the pyramids. It forced us, or at least me, to look at other things besides all the ends we never reached.

In an hour and a half, we reached our camp of May 16. I didn't say anything and, thankfully, Glück didn't either, except to announce we had arrived and the time. In another hour and a half, we reached the five red markers tied to trees and our May 15 camp with the outboard and gas tank. Glück had been right, but I tried ignoring things, and went back to remembering.

The summer I turned eighteen, I began to think my life might have a fair degree of disorder, which I saw in terms of movement. It wasn't that I was attracted to the purity of movement, as later I would be, but because it seemed to be the consequence of something else. I fell in love that summer.

A week after I graduated high school, I went with my soon-to-be friend Bill for a summer job in Maine. Bill and I were not high school friends. We only knew each other a little, yet through a variety of circumstances and other friends, we had summer jobs together at a hotel restaurant in southern Maine, called the Cliff House, a rambling old hotel and restaurant on the coastal road. We were to be the only two busboys on a restaurant staff of twelve. Bill and I wrote away for the job and were accepted on the basis of one of those applications in "How to Find Summer Jobs" books that had a listing for the Cliff House in its "Places to Look for Jobs" appendix. Bill and I sent a snapshot of ourselves and were hired for close to the minimum wage, $1.60 an hour then, less a chunk for room and board. The deal also included our buying our own uniforms. I picked up mine at a discount store, Two Guys From Harrison, where I bought a pair of Korean-made white, short-sleeve shirts and a pair of black chinos. I borrowed a snap-on bow tie from my father and the Cliff House supplied us with cummerbunds. So, we were set.

A Mr. and Mrs. Weir, an old Maine couple, operated the Cliff House. Actually, it was Mrs. Weir, an ex-WAC sergeant, who ran the place. Mr. Weir had the misfortune of having a garage door fall on his head a year or two before Bill and I arrived, so everyone affectionately described Mr. Weir as "slow." Besides the garage-door story, he also was pursued by another story that made him into a minor legend. The year after he got hit by the door, he spent the winter alone at the family house on a cliff at the edge of the Atlantic. A nor'easter clobbered the coast one night, and, as the story goes, waves came crashing through the Weirs' bay window overlooking the sea. In the middle of the night, the roof began to sag, and still as the story goes, Mr. Weir got under a central beam and throughout the night, and despite a thrashing by the Atlantic, held his ground and held up the house. Next day, when the storm broke and neighbors came out to check on Mr. Weir, they found him standing in ankle-deep water. There he was, like in that song about Big John, but with a happy ending. Mr. Weir still was holding up the roof.

Mr. Weir was a sweet man, but unfortunately for Bill and me, we had little to do with him. It was Mrs. Weir we dealt with mostly and she was tough. She spent much of her time yelling and complaining that things were awful, or else at how we all were eating up the hotel profits.

The crew lived in a reconverted barn, with a row of dormitory rooms built over the garage with the door that knocked Mr. Weir on the head. The crew ate at a table in the kitchen of the restaurant, but what the crew saw as eating, or actually subsisting, Mrs. Weir seemed to see as wolfing.

Mostly, Mrs. Weir fed us things like beans and hot dogs or hot dogs and beans or, occasionally, treats, like macaroni and cheese. She probably saw meals as mountains of food, while the crew saw them differently. Since I was part of the crew, I saw things the way the crew did, and that was as bad. In fact, after a while, things got so bad we had scouts carry scavenging information in from the dining room. Once, when things were really bad, I remember Bill coming back into the kitchen and saying, "There's a couple of T-bones with meat left on them coming in soon from one of the window tables." As soon as the people at the window tables dropped their forks, Bill was back out. He quickly pulled their plates from the table and triumphantly swung back into the kitchen, with the bones in a gray plastic bus tray he carried above his shoulder, the way a waiter might carry a Christmas turkey under glass.

Bill and I took the plates, sat down, and gnawed the bones close to clean, until one of the waitresses ducked her head through the door and said, "Here comes old lady Weir." We tossed what was left and rushed back out with our bus trays.

That was a watershed event. After that, all plates, if not picked over, at least were looked over. Bones with meat, or even some decent fat, were prized, and we were not beneath eating used baked potatoes, salad tomatoes, or unsucked lobster legs. Dinner rolls were reheated, so we never got to them, and vegetables, like string beans or peas, were canned and we had enough of them with the hot dogs and beans, so they were skipped.

During my stay at the Cliff House, I remained a busboy, although I was given a brief chance at advancement. Once, when one of the waiters had a night off and the dining room was particularly crowded, Mrs. Weir had me wait on the Staff table. The Staff table differed from the staff table in the kitchen on the basis of age and position. The staff in the kitchen was under twenty-five and occupied the lower rungs on the Cliff House work crew, while the Staff in the dining room was mostly more than fifty-five, headed the various crews, like the chief groundskeeper and director of maids, or had white-man-face-the-public jobs like hotel clerks, bookkeepers, bartender, and even the cocktail waitress (because she was engaged to the bartender).

Being told to wait on the Staff was a chance to kibbitz some, and that was what I was doing, kibbitzing some, while serving salads and drinks, and perhaps buoyed by the situation, I still was kibbitzing when I began serving the main course, roast beef. The cook had layered the meat on a platter and drenched it in gravy,

266

a drenching I didn't notice. When I reached the chief book-keeper, who just had been talking about the new lemon-colored cashmere sweater he was wearing, I leaned forward, and while dishing off a couple of slices of meat, also dribbled gravy down the front and back of his new lemon-colored cashmere sweater.

"Oh, God," his wife shrieked. I echoed her cry, though the bookkeeper stayed completely motionless and silent. I ran to the dishroom and got a washcloth and when I came back out, he was still frozen silent in the position he had when I first doused him in gravy—leaning forward, his right hand pointing and his left on the corner of the table, and his mouth stuck midway through a sentence.

His wife and I sponged what we could off the sweater, while I kept saying I was sorry, which was something like praying before a statue. It took him a minute or two before he moved, but then he spoke.

"It's all right," he said in a tone that meant it wasn't.

At least he was talking and I was glad I hadn't killed him. Then, to my relief, he began to move freely again.

Mrs. Weir had seen it all and when I walked back into the kitchen, she walked by me and said, "Get your bus tray." I was finished with waiting.

It had been a rough day. At breakfast, I overheard a conversation I was meant to overhear, between a crippled teenage girl and her mother.

"Well, call that boy" (me) "and get yourself something else to eat," the mother said.

"But he's a man, mother," her daughter answered.

On a better day, it was from near the bun-warmer post that I first spotted the girl I would chase back and forth across the country for the next year. At lunchtime, instead of rolls and sour cream, Bill and I were refilling coffee cups and water glasses when I noticed her walk quickly past the door of the dining room. I hadn't seen her before, but she wore one of those white styrofoam, spongy-looking maid uniforms that meant she was one of us. From a distance, she looked tan and pretty. Later that afternoon, I saw her drive away in a sportscar with California license plates, and next day, to my delight, she came in and had lunch with the staff.

She had been a blur going across the doorway, but it is a blur I still can see now because I somehow knew it was the first scene in the next section of my life. It was like life was beginning to block itself into those things in sophomore English class we had called "themes." Up until she blurred across the doorway, life had been more or less a progression of sorts, but after that, chunks fell into separate, almost self-enclosed parts, with different characters and plots that were distinct, yet tied together, the same way the Padauiri is its own river, yet still a part of the Amazon.

XXXIV

WE split a tin of goiabada jelly for lunch. It was supposed to make us feel better, but it didn't, so not feeling better, we re-packed the boat.

Tano and I took hour-long shifts with the paddle, while Glück guided us from the stern. Glück wasn't much of a rudder. We danced downriver, our tail end sashaying from side to side. At a sharp curve, we sideswiped a tree filled with oriole nests surrounded by nests of wasps. Immediately, the wasps formed a cloud and began chase. Glück screamed, "Faster, faster," and I paddled as hard as I could, but looking over my shoulder, I couldn't stop laughing. Glück was bent forward and the swarm hung three feet above and behind his head. He looked like some Yogi Bear cartoon I remembered, where Yogi swiped honey and then got chased by a swarm of bees. Glück yelled again, "Faster, faster, paddling, paddling," and I did, we did, while also leaning forward, but I couldn't help turning around again and seeing him try to duck from the cloud.

With the help of the current, we finally outdistanced the wasps and when I asked Glück if he got stung, he said, "No," in a sharp tone.

269

Something broke inside me that day, but with the laughing, I had popped open a parachute and I began to think I would come down OK.

The afternoon dragged and I wandered in and out of memories. By early evening it was beginning to take forever to reach each bend in the river.

"There must be a Heeltone coming soon," Glück would say, but it didn't come and finally we stopped at a sandbank. Tano and I rolled out sleeping bags and almost as quickly rolled them back up as clouds swiftly covered a crescent new moon and it began to rain.

"This may be one of those long, hard nights."

We sat under tarps as Glück boiled water for tea, and decided to postpone the rest of the meal until the rain passed. I had been angry at Glück all day, but with the sky turning against us, I worried about the night and conducted one of those "Don't be a jerk" conversations with myself. The night could be awful and we had to pull together. I told everyone how good I thought it was to sleep on sand and watch the stars, a pretty stupid thing to say when it looked like the sky would stay covered and we would get drenched. Still, everyone concurred, the way a bunch of loonies would tell each other they really were sane, and Tano and I went so far as to tell each other we actually preferred sleeping on the bank to finding a hut. By then, the rain was coming down hard and leaking through the tarp, so we were talking crazy, but the harder it rained, the more I felt it was necessary to keep talking.

"Kurt, I hope I'm as strong as you when I'm sixty-six. You do OK," I said.

He shrugged and sipped tea that looked like it was erupting from splashing rain drops.

"Makes nuhzing," he said.

Tano and I split his last cigarette, nothing more than a dusting of tobacco rolled between paper, but as we finished, the angels smiled and the rain stopped and the sky cleared and I felt good for all the crazy talk. Glück opened a can of swine and made some rice and even though it was skimpy, we feasted. Tano and I finished dinner off by smoking the stump of my last cigar. It was acrid and hot, but I took deep drags. When we finished, I crawled into my sleeping bag, but the mosquitoes had beat me to it.

Glück was beside me and covered his face with a net. I covered mine with the turpentine. That did the trick.

In the middle of the night, I heard Glück's voice. It didn't register at first, but then it repeated.

"Hello, the boat is gone."

Then he said it was four o'clock, but I still was stunned by his first statement. I looked up, but there was nothing to see as we were covered in a thick fog.

"Hello, the boat is gone."

I thought I still must be dreaming and was in a scene from *Huckleberry Finn* where the Mississippi is fogged in at night and Huck and Jim are run over by a steamboat.

"Oh, look at the crocodile," Glück said, pointing with his flashlight as he stood in the river.

I tried again to grab for my dreams, but I couldn't hang on, the tug of whatever new trouble we had got ourselves in was too strong.

"No, it can't be," I said.

"Oh, shit," Tano said, then did what I couldn't do, rolled over to go back to sleep.

In the mist, Glück looked like a ghost cut in half by the river. Then he said it again, and any hope about still dreaming was finished.

"The boat is gone."

"Christ, it never stops."

If I had been more awake, panic might have set in, but, instead, I turned around quickly and saw our machetes sticking in the sand above our heads. At least we could build a raft and float out.

Glück waded downriver until the night and the fog swallowed him. For a few moments, I heard him wading in the water, then nothing.

Maybe the Huck Finn scene came back to me because it was like we were in a kind of reverse, something like a photographic negative. There was the image of Huck and Jim on a foggy night on a river with a steamboat running over them, then there was us on the same kind of night, but without the boat.

Our losing the boat was a mistake like many others we had made, yet it was a little different. This time we could end up dead.

Tano and I hadn't spent much time talking about that possibility, but at least with me, it was not because I didn't think about it. We were there, on the river, through the magic of a point in time, which could just as easily lose its magic. Generally that is an acceptable situation to me, except that there are times when I'm off balance. Moving, or being moved, you have the urge to keep moving, and the possibility of losing a finish is like being robbed. Going back down that river there was a rush of stories pushing me, and they seemed to be tangling with the story of Glück and Tano and me. Then again, all that seemed to be on top of a black hole. The thought of us getting sucked through to oblivion gave my gut a twist.

For a while, things had seemed as if they were slipping out of control, maybe ever since we left the Rio Negro, maybe since Barcelos, maybe long before that. Destruction has a way of sneaking up on you. I thought I had kept it at a good arm's length, but now it seemed to be on my throat. If I could have seen the fates then, I would have howled at them, howled in a way that might have sounded like the voice we had in Daytona, only this time I would have pleaded to let us finish.

Then I heard Glück call.

"Maybe it's hung up on the bend," he said.

I picked up Tano's penlight, and followed Glück into the river. At the end of the stretch of sand we slept on, I saw Glück for a moment before he disappeared. The fog was like cotton and even though I felt my feet sliding along muck in the riverbed, I couldn't see anything below my waist. It was difficult to take it on faith I was all there. It was more difficult to take it on sight that the boat was gone, but I stopped myself from thinking that way and kept going into the river.

I held up my light and down around a bend, I thought I saw something like a cloud hung up on a log.

"Is that it?" I shouted.

I heard swimming, though I couldn't see anything. The cloud disappeared.

272

"Is it the boat?" I called out, but no answer.

I was up to my chest in the middle of the river and held out the light. I heard what sounded like paddling and thought maybe I saw Glück's light.

"Is it the boat?"

"Yes, I come, but the current is strong."

Glück paddled up and out of the fog and we pulled the boat to shore and tied it with mountain-climbing rope to a bush in the jungle.

I brushed sand off my feet and tried to dry off before climbing back into a clammy sleeping bag. I laughed at Tano. "You just rolled over and went back to sleep."

"Well, it's four o'clock," he said, and laughed. "And we wouldn't be able to do anything until morning." He stopped laughing. "God, I can't believe how careless he is with his boat. We're just dumb shits, but he should know."

I lay back and looked through the fog for stars, and I giggled, and Tano giggled, then I found my dreams.

"Good morning, good morning," Glück called. I waited a second. He didn't add anything else, so I figured things were OK. I was beat and I couldn't get the energy to answer or open my eyes.

"Coffee is ready," Glück said.

I heard Tano peel himself out of his bag. I lay in mine awhile, unable to move. It took me a few minutes before I could prop myself on my elbows, where I hoped the sleep would drift out of me, but it didn't. Instead, it helped shape a sour mood and I thought I had to get up and fight sleep, too.

I took off my clothes, stowed them away, sat on a crate, and sipped coffee. Glück stared at Tano putting his contact lenses in at the edge of the water. Tano's arms were hanging, his hair was in knots and his left eyelid and sack looked like someone had punched him out. He looked the way I felt I looked, but I didn't want to go to the river and see.

I started out paddling, hoping the rhythm would shake me awake and get things flowing. It didn't and when my hour at the paddle ended, I switched with Tano and tried to write in my journal. That didn't work either. Somewhere outside my head a sparkling day was going on, but I missed it.

Early afternoon, we found the long meeting-house-on-the-cliff Hilton, and decided to quit early. The river was down four rungs on the ladder and after chaining the boat to the lowest rung, we staggered up the steps.

Glück made noodles and sawcheechez from Vienna. I licked the corn oil off my plate and Glück said, "We've got enough food."

I disagreed.

"You two eat a lot," Glück said.

Here we go again.

"How could we?" I said. "Aside from the goiabada, yesterday, we haven't eaten lunch for weeks. When we did, it was only saltines. We have a couple of bowls of soupy oatmeal for breakfast and for dinner, it's a little rice and a slice of meat. Besides, we're almost out of things like sugar and oil, and that can't be because of us."

Glück shook his head. "People, old people, on my trips have done as much and don't eat as much."

"Kurt, we could have made the mountains if we had enough food."

"Of course, it's your money. I could have brought more. My wife tells me I should bring plenty of things for the people on my trips, but I never need it. All I need is water."

"Listen, Kurt, you have to know what to bring."

"Of course, I bring and plan what I always do."

"It just would have been more enjoyable," I said.

"Yes, but this is the way it is now. What can we do?"

I took a deep breath. That was right. I was tired of complaining and worrying about the food situation. It was enough.

After dinner, I went down the ladder, sat on the lower rung, and watched billowing white clouds until evening, when Tano came down and the stars came out.

"I'm so tired and hungry, I'm still spaced," he said. "Now I know what it feels like to be stupid."

I knew what he meant. The past few days felt like my brain had a ball and chain anchoring it. I just wanted my thoughts to

274

bounce around and forget about the river. That night, with the big sky and the big dipper and the rest of the stars, it didn't feel as heavy.

"What do you want to do when we get back?" I asked Tano, a question that was supposed to be a way of reminding the fates we were going to get back.

"I think we oughta have a hell of a bash," he said.

"With Scotch," I said.

"Boges."

"Ice cream."

"Carouse."

"Sleep late."

"Big breakfasts ... and long, leisurely coffees."

"Now you're talking," he said.

"I'm not sure how far we'll get tomorrow," I said, "but figuring paddling versus motoring time, maybe we'll make the house on the hill with the hot chile peppers, the one at the fork. Maybe we could reach it by afternoon."

That made us feel better, and on that note, we decided to turn in.

I rocked in my hammock. The night was warm, warmer than the late afternoon when there was a good breeze, and I didn't need the sleeping bag.

Glück called out in the night, "Do you hear music?" I heard him and not the music. He didn't have anything else to report, so I didn't answer.

We wanted an early start the next day. Glück obliged and had us up at five. We had our last Quaker and hoped with a good night's rest, we would go far. I was wobbly, but not too bad. We downed coffee that somehow got wax in it. Glück said, "This is shit coffee," and I immediately said, "Well, we're lucky we even have this," so I broke the previous night's truce, but after that, I shut up.

I volunteered to paddle the first hour. Again, I wanted to break my drowsiness and get into gear. It was cool, with high clouds and a violet dawn. Glück chattered away about the boat, I don't remember what, but I do remember him saying, "We dance down the river," which was true.

"We make good time," he said. "If we get food in Allianca,

we can paddle down to the Rio Negro and then motor to Barcelos. Then, maybe if we can, all the way back to Manaus."

I said nothing, but thought it was a bullshit idea, and expected Tano did, too.

"There are many beautiful archipelagos on the Rio Negro," Glück said, "many beautiful archipelagos."

Through much of what he said that day, I got lost, or ignored, except for one story about the English woman, Elizabeth Forester. "We would go out looking for birds and whenever I would try to talk, she would say, 'Shut up.' " That was one of the funniest stories Glück told on the trip and had Tano and me in hysterics.

By then, Glück's chatter had become incessant, but Elizabeth Forester dealt with him more directly. With us, going back down the river, it was as if he were unraveling. He would say things like "makes nuhzing," or "now begins the adventurra," which sounded cavalier, but for what seemed ages after his pronouncements, he would babble about where we were and how we had got lost and how "this cannot be." The longer we were in the jungle, the more Tano and I had to assume control of the trip, making decisions about where to go, how best to follow the current, and where to camp. Glück switched from being a guide to being chief cook and bottle washer, which, since we figured we had paid him handsomely, we let him be.

Despite Glück, I felt better that day. It was cool, with a high ceiling of clouds and I pleaded with the angels to keep away the rain. They listened. By midmorning, the sky cleared and the sun began to pound, which made me woozy, but it at least quieted Glück.

I wished I had money that morning. Being up at dawn, seeing the new sky, reminded me of airports I had been in at sunrise and the excitement of getting ready to move, as if I was tied in with the spin of the world.

The time in the San José airport in Costa Rica, just before Tano and I flew to the island of San Andrés, we were sitting in the lounge when a woman announced over the loudspeaker an Air France flight to Paris was ready to depart in forty minutes. Tano and I sat for a moment, then Tano said, "Why don't we cash it in and head to France? Quit this beating our heads against a wall. All we ever seem to do is get wiped out. Let's enjoy ourselves for a change."

I didn't answer right away.

"I don't know," I said, a delaying tactic to give myself time to think of a reason why we shouldn't go. It was a great idea, but somewhere back I had developed a notion to stick things out. Taking off to France felt like it would be a surrender.

"Man, it's a great place," he said. "We could drink wine and eat cheese and bread and live like kings. Whatdya say?"

"I don't know," I said again, in a panic, "I don't know," because I really didn't have a good reason not to agree with him.

"Man, you'd love it."

"I know I would. That's not the point."

"Then what is?" he said. "To keep this shit up?"

I laughed. "Yeah, actually ... I guess it is."

XXXV

"WATER is jelluf, now," Gluck said.

And the river winds and the river winds and the river winds.

The sun broke through clouds and we shed our clothes and one of us said we would have to be sure to drink a lot of water and hope it would help keep up our strength.

We reached Lacerda's in three and a half hours, the same time it took to motor up, and we stopped to pick lemons. Walking out of the boat, I felt weak and dizzy, the same as the night before, but worse than the night before, I was getting anxious.

"I feel like I'm reining in a race horse," I told Tano.

"Take it easy and enjoy the jungle," he said.

"I don't like doubling back over the same ground, and besides, my mind is on other plans."

"You mean what to do with your bones?"

"Yeah."

At noon, we arrived at the fork in the Padauiri. The sun was bright and hot and we sat in the shade as piums and mosquitoes lunched on our skin.

In less than an hour, we left, and by early afternoon, the jungle folded back and the river opened wide and the day felt south-

278

ern and muggy. The light had everything shimmering and me floating somewhere between the water and ground and trees and air. Birds stopped singing and everything stilled except for the trickle of water against our paddles.

"In Mexico, they say only gringos and donkeys move between one and three," Glück said.

The night before, I dreamt about the girl I was after when I was eighteen and in the quiet of the afternoon, the dream came back to me. I thought how I probably never would see her again. Of course, that was part sentimental, but it was also part astonishment. There was a time, ten years earlier, when I couldn't have imagined not seeing her again.

At the end of our first week at the Cliff House, a few days after she first blurred across the doorway, Bill and I decided to take in some culture, so we bought a pair of tickets to see George Gobel in Woody Allen's *Play It Again, Sam,* being staged at the Ogunquit Playhouse. We got our tickets through the entertainment director at the Cliff House, who also happened to be the bookkeeper, who, in about ten days, I would spill the roast beef gravy on, but of course he didn't know that at the time, so he was cheery and wished us a good time. As fortune would have it, the seats were in the same row, and a few down, from a pair of tickets he sold to the girl in the blur.

Bill and I arrived a moment before curtain time and we spotted her and she spotted us and we all waved. My eyes went from boots to a headband she was wearing, then stopped at a figure beside her, a male. The theater lights dimmed and I felt a pang of jealousy, which was the first sign I was getting into something.

At intermission, I exited out the opposite end of our aisle, then coming back from the men's room, I caught sight of her gentleman friend. He was almost as tall as me, stocky, and at the time was losing a battle in the lobby. He was trying to shake loose the phone booth door, behind which he seemed to have locked himself. I walked quickly past him, pretending not to notice his banging, and with bolstered confidence, reentered the theater on her side of the aisle.

After greetings, we talked about the play, with her making seemingly astute observations and me bluffing about what I had

279

not paid attention to, until the telephone booth prisoner returned.

"This is Tom," she said. "My brother."

Things happened quickly after that. The next day, Bill and I met her and an exchange student friend of hers, at the beach. The girls either talked about California or in Spanish, so there was little memorable, other than once, when they both pranced away to take a dive in the sea, Bill commented on the girl I was after's loose-fitting two-piece batLing suit.

"She's got small tits," he said, which at the time I interpreted as his lack of interest. Only later did I realize that Bill was even more adept at making excuses and dawdling away opportunities than I.

A couple of days later, I asked her out to the movies, and afterwards, we went to a greasy spoon where I had a hamburger and fries and a shake, while she sipped water.

"It's bad for your digestion, heart, everything, to eat before you sleep," she said. I assumed her remark had something to do with growing up in California. It would be something I would have to break her of, and was something I ignored while I finished eating what was bad for my digestion, heart, and everything.

"The most I ever have before bed is Ovaltine," she said. I thought about the guy in *Play It Again, Sam,* and wondered what Bogart would have said next.

She stayed with her grandmother, who wanted her home before midnight, which I accomplished along with a bad joke about her having enough time to make a cup of Ovaltine, but she didn't seem to mind. As I left, just before she closed the door behind me, she stuck her head out and let me kiss her.

Three weeks later, I left Maine, which if I wanted to avoid falling in love, should have been almost three weeks earlier, but it wasn't and I was, though I wasn't complaining.

I had to leave Maine to go to a college orientation in the Midwest. Because the college business would take a week, I had to give up my job.

The day before I left for the Midwest, she and I drove to Cape Cod. That may seem a silly thing to do when you are on the coast of Maine, but I never had been to the Cape and she

280

hadn't either, and besides, the water was supposed to be warmer there, though I didn't get much of a chance to find out. It rained so hard that day I had to pull off the road a couple of times because my windshield wipers kept legato time while the rain fell at allegro. On Bill's advice, we went to a place called Wellsfleet, where, he said, there were sand dunes like in *Lawrence of Arabia*. With the rain, they looked more like waves of porridge. Still, we danced across them. I got the bottom of my jeans muddied and my hair wet and though she didn't, I took off my shoes and rolled up my pants and waded into the ocean. I wanted the rain to stop, but it wouldn't, though that didn't matter much, because it was only a fake wish. What I really wanted was the world to stop, with me and her the only people on the beach, with the wind coming off the Atlantic and the rain falling harder and the waves thundering to shore with muffled secrets about an ending, an ending that kept replaying itself, an ending that eventually would become permanent and infinite. It was if the sea was saying, "If you walked in, right now, if you gave up the fear and walked in and let it swallow you, it would take you in and keep everything just the way it is and hold you forever in the sound of the waves."

When I came back out I held her. I ran both my hands down the back of her hair and when we kissed it was like it wouldn't stop, though I knew it would and she did, too.

A breeze picked up midafternoon and we skipped through a series of rapids. I had heard running water for maybe a quarter mile. It sounded like a train, the way the rain did, and I watched the trees and hoped it was only the wind rustling leaves, but it wasn't. We worried about how difficult the rapids would be and whether we would have to unload the boat and carry de shtuff, but they were mild, with only a few rocks breaking the water, and we shot through, and then I shot back to Maine.

For me, Maine led to a lot of different things, but it also was a break from the past. With that, there were losses.

A couple of days before I left for the Amazon, I visited my folks and however many of my five brothers were at the house at the time. We had dinner and talked awhile. My father told me about my uncle, who upon hearing I was going to the Amazon, said, "What's he going down there for? Doesn't he know that was where that Rockefeller kid disappeared and got ate by cannibals?"

I told him it had happened twenty years before, on the other side of the world, so he calmed down.

Around eleven o'clock, one of my brothers called from a tavern in town.

"Hey, Schplitz is down here," he said. "He wants to see you."

Schplitz was an old friend who otherwise went by the name Steve Schwartz. He got the name Schplitz in high school, after he went out for football in his freshman year, played defensive end and, I think, split end, positions he described as "schplitz."

In high school, Schplitz was in my class, though he was a couple of years older than me, but there were more ways he was ahead of me than that. Early on, Schplitz had become a rock 'n' roll afficionado, and his taste ran to loud, acid rock. Baseball helped him develop that taste. Schplitz was a pretty good ball-player (he was a catcher), and during the summers he would go to the boardwalk at the Jersey shore, where he would play games to win record albums, games like throwing a baseball at a stack of rubber milk cartons, or tossing a ball in a peach basket, or even pitching pennies. He was good at them, especially the one with the baseball, and at the end of the summer, he would come back with the records of Lead Zeppelin, and Cream, and Janis Joplin and Big Brother and the Holding Company, and Canned Heat, groups no one else had heard of at the time, but by mid-fall, they were big hits and Schplitz took to wearing tie-died shirts and became a kind of seer.

When I saw him in the tavern, he didn't look as big as I remembered, but he still looked older.

"A long time," he said, "a long time since I've seen you." He took my hand and shook it, the hippie/brother way with the thumbs clasped, and we patted each other on the back and Schplitz turned to the bartender. "Get this guy a beer."

We talked awhile and then Schplitz said, "Let's get the Whale down here."

The Whale was Victor Lindholm. Victor grew up around the

282

corner from Schplitz, played football and baseball in high school with him, along with basketball with me, and skipped school and went on beer runs with both of us. I hadn't seen Victor either for about nine years. The last time was in college when Victor came home for Thanksgiving break and told me he was taking a philosophy class. Philosophy had an effect on Victor.

"For all we know," he said back then as we walked into a local diner after midnight, "right now we could be at the end of some big turd being flushed down a giant toilet in the universe."

Victor was called the Whale because of his size. He was somewhere in the six-foot-four range, and at times, quite a few bricks more than two-hundred pounds. He was blond and Swedish and although he hated the comparison, lots of people said he looked like Wayne Newton, though calling Victor Wayne was not something you would do in his presence.

We usually called Victor Vic.

Vic drove a convertible, a red Chevy (I think it was a 1960), the kind with fins. For a while, it had a hole in the muffler, so it rumbled like a boat, but it had all the push buttons on the radio keyed to decent stations, so you never had to listen to a commercial, and it had a hole in the back floor in case of an emergency, like when you were going over the George Washington Bridge and had to piss.

On weekends, and sometimes during the week when we were supposed to be at the library, we would go cruising. There was a regular route that included the bowling alley, The Nest (a cheap hamburger joint), Friendly's, the YMCA, a gas station where Steve sometimes worked, and if there was something going on back at the high school, the high school. Later as the same nothingness came up, we expanded the circuit to include similar stops in similar towns, but inevitably we ended up with more of the same nothingness. Then, we would go out and race.

"Yeah, we had good times together," I told Schplitz at the tavern. "Go ahead, call the Whale."

The Whale still lived with is parents, and by the time Schplitz called, it was midnight, so we knew he would wake up the Whale's mother or father.

Schplitz exchanged pleasantries, then cupped the phone.

283

"It's his mother. I think I woke her up, but she's going to get Vic."

When Schplitz got Vic on the phone, Schplitz told him where he was and who he was with, but Vic said he was tired and had to go to work the next day.

Finally, Schplitz waved to me. "Come here. You talk to him. Try to get him to come down."

I got on the phone and said my hellos and told Vic he should come down, "for old times' sake," which apparently was the wrong thing to say.

"Why?" he said. "You went away."

I didn't know how to answer that, so I let things die and said, "Maybe some other time."

Schplitz and I stayed in the bar until closing, then we bought a couple of six-packs and went out into one of our cars, in a nearby parking lot, between an old brick building where Frank the Italian used to sell pizza for fifteen cents a slice when I first moved north; and the Community Center, a tiny gym with a record player where the black kids played Aretha Franklin and The Supremes, and basketball; and Leroy Oridge's house; and the Acme Market, where I got my first job when I turned sixteen, after I quit caddying. Frank had moved his place, and the Acme was gone, replaced by something called Wawa Market, which sounded like a George Harrison song during his Ravi Shankar–India days. I didn't know what happened to the Community Center or those old 45s. I heard Leroy Oridge, who was the only black kid (until he quit) on the school basketball team, got married and fat, although Schplitz said Leroy still jived around.

Schplitz and I got good and buzzed and told old stories and laughed. He told me about his wife and his home in Pennsylvania and a long commute he had to make to work, and I didn't feel right telling him much about what I had been doing or where I was going, but he didn't seem to care. When we were tired of talking, one of us threw a beer bottle at the brick wall where Frank's Pizza used to be, and the other one of us threw one to match. We went back and forth until we had finished all the bottles and laughed and Schplitz made me promise that next time I came back east, I would call him and we would try to get the Whale and go out, "for old times' sake."

284

For some time, I thought about Vic's "You went away." High school meant different things to different people, and to me, it didn't mean too much. I learned to type there. Also, through no fault of its own, it taught me about memories. It was a lot better to remember things as funny, otherwise they might never rest in peace.

When I still was in grammar school, I remember my mother once looking through her old high school yearbook pictures and telling me I should try and get the most out of things when I got to high school, "It's the best time of your life. You'll never be as free." That made me feel awful. I had to gear up for four years, and if I blew it, I blew it. I would be chained the rest of my life to bad memories.

My father never talked much about high school, other than one story I remember, the same story my friends' fathers told them, about how he had sprained an ankle at school and had to walk miles through a blizzard to get home. That story was supposed to explain how I should enjoy walking without sprained ankles, and not always complain about not getting a ride.

My mother had been a dancer and around the time she graduated from high school was asked to join the Rockettes, but her father would have none of it. "There aren't going to be any show business people in this family," he said. My mother took it hard. From what I remember hearing she locked herself in her room for days and cried, and for many more days wouldn't speak to the old man. Anyway, she got over it, I guess. She gave up dancing and after high school got a job. By the time she was twenty, she married my father and they were on the way to raising a big family, so maybe that explained things about the way she saw high school.

XXXVI

THREE o'clock, we found a meadow on the west bank, beside a black water stream. We had stopped there on the way north, at a similar time of day, but had decided to push on and find a Hilton. We remembered the spot because Tano had discovered a trail of leaf cutters.

Although it had been a mild day and the paddling easy, I staggered to shore, reeling from what was becoming chronic late-afternoon knockout. The heat was booshit, so I took a swim ("Black water, man, I like this stuff," Tano said), put on a shredding white shirt, and felt OK. Glück mumbled to himself. "Why does he always do it in English," I whispered to Tano. "Oh, *sheiss*, look what happened, now the water is boiling over ... Ohh, look at the butterfly ... Ohh, we must have a fish. *Sheiss*, this is hot."

I wrote in my journal about talking baseball in the afternoon with Tano, and because of the mosquito turpentine, my pen stuck to my hand. Besides melting, it also was running out of ink and I thought how when it was finished, I would toss it over my shoulder and into the jungle. I suppose that was terrible. I wouldn't have done it back in the States, but on the river, tossing

286

cans or plastic or pens on sandbanks or into the jungle gave me some kind of satisfaction, as if by depositing my garbage, I was marking the jungle, like a cat or a dog pissing to mark his territory. Actually, at night I had got into the habit of pissing near my hammock, telling the rest of the jungle I had cut a section of ground for the night.

While I rocked in the hammock, Tano and Glück were down by the fire, trying to figure out where the food had gone. The next day we expected to be out of everything, though we also hoped to make Allianca and hoped there would be supplies there, at least manioc. I felt weary to my joints and didn't want to walk down to get tea, though I knew it would taste good, and even better, cut into my appetite. I knew it had to be cut into because in the war against supper, appetite would win. So I went down, after marking my place in my journal with a parrot feather Tano had found. When he gave it to me, he had said, "It's good to have purty things to look at."

We had schnoodles and split our last can of sawcheechez from Vienna, then drank more tea. After, because Glück had soaked everything in the end of the oil, to the point it was soupy, I went down and washed in the river. I was startled to see my face.

"Ugly sons-of-bitches, ain't we?" Tano said behind me.

I dunked my head and kept it under, like I was bobbing for apples, until I heard Tano shout.

"What?"

"Look," he said, pointing downriver, the way home. A rainbow split the sky in half. It was the first since the day we left Allianca, and it was just the beginning. The sky kept it up, replaying Genesis that night. We were camped on the west bank of a long north-south stretch of the river, with the sun setting behind us. To the north, the sky lit up, glowing as if the upper river was on fire.

Glück came down to watch and said, "I wonder what's going on?"

"It's fallout from the nuclear war between the United States and Russia," Tano said.

To the south, the sky turned the color of nickel. The rainbow looked like it was driven into the river. Across from us, beyond the east shore, thunderheads rolled in like schools of giant whales cruising through a surf of bubbling, brilliant blue, with shavings of white clouds. The rainbow faded and a new one appeared above the whales, stretching across more than half the sky, reflecting in the black water in front of our camp, then wrinkling with the ripples into the milky green of the Padauiri. The whales kept coming, rumbling at us as the sky shuddered with flashes of lightning. The whales dragged in the night, while behind them rain rushed over the jungle.

"This is all going to be hard to remember," Tano said, "these past days ... weeks. I've felt so tired, it's been like I've been stoned, like I got haze over my brain."

Me, too, and sometimes it was unclear if I was moving in reality or memory or imagination.

I couldn't sleep that night. Maybe it was just that after breakfast we would be officially without food and from there on out, we would be on borrowed time. Whatever was bothering me, I couldn't put a finger on it, other than my brain kept replaying the refrain from an old sixties tune by Quicksilver Messenger Service about nature letting you know something's wrong. As Tano had said, it felt like I was stoned, but as the night wore on, it was more like psychedelics. Lying suspended in a hammock above phosphorescent leaves was something like taking a second hit. To combat that, I started thinking about women, then about the past.

Thoughts about women centered on thoughts about deprivation, and that was not very centered at all; it spread out over years. Some of that time I shared with Bill, with whom I had grown close since that summer in Maine, though he often seemed even more deprived than me. Maybe that had something to do with his going to school at Dartmouth.

Bill was a good guy to go looking for that night. I would have talked with Tano, but like me, he seemed to be feeling pretty miserable. Besides, Tano was tucked away between other trees and psychedelic leaves, a safe distance from kvetching, so I let him be. Instead, I went searching for good travel memories, even if they were tangled with deprivation. That brought me back to Bill, who, as I said, knew a lot about deprivation, but I picked things up and started with good memories, about him and me and the first time we went to Europe.

Bill arrived in Europe three months ahead of me. A few days before he left the States, we went cross-country skiing together at a golf course in the night. It had snowed during the day, but by evening, the clouds had passed and the moon had risen and the skiing was a dream.

The golf course was hilly and we had to herringbone and sometimes we had to climb sideways up hills, but going down was a straight shoot and on some of those hills, we flew down. I skied fast enough to make me scared and think about snowplow-ing, but it was one of the first times I had been on skis, so I wouldn't let myself snowplow. When I fell it didn't hurt much and after Bill whipped by and I wiped the snow out of my mouth, we both laughed.

We skied for an hour or two and although I had fallen a lot, I always brushed the snow off fast, so I stayed dry.

"Want to go to O'Brien's?" one of us said. The other one said, "Sure," so we packed our skis away and drove down to a local Irish bar.

Bill ordered beers, but I wanted a brandy, so I had one and then some girls I knew came in and we talked to them for a while. It was fun coming back from skiing in the moonlight, go-ing into a place that was warm and a little noisy and smoky, then drinking and getting to talk to some girls.

When the girls left, we talked about stories we had read. We had gone to different colleges, but we studied the same things and read many of the same stories and many of the same stories seemed to have a similar effect. We talked about two Hemingway stories, "The Three Day Blow," and "Cross-Country Snow." There were two guys in both stories, and in each, they drank together and talked about things that mattered to them, about how their lives felt important and manageable and open, and I think Bill and I both fancied those guys were a little like us.

We talked until it got late. The bar quieted and I ordered one more brandy and Bill ordered another beer. We talked some more about stories and we talked some about girls, but mostly we were quiet and thinking about how our lives felt important and manageable and open.

In a couple of days, Bill left for Europe. I told him I might meet him there, if my plans didn't work out. My plan was to go to Australia.

When I first went to college and met Tano and we decided we wanted to get out of the States as quickly and permanently as we could, we thought Australia might be a good place to go. We heard it was still wild and there was a lot of space. That sounded good.

After I finished college, and just after Bill left, I made a few visits to the Australian consulate in New York. I wanted to swing an immigration visa, or some kind of visa that would let me stay longer than three months, but I didn't have any luck. That threw a hitch in my plans. I had hoped to get to Australia and maybe find some work. If I had to put down enough money for a round trip, right off the bat, which was what the consulate wanted before they would grant a tourist visa, I would have almost nothing to spare. I was in a bind.

Around that time, I got a letter from Bill. He was skiing in Switzerland and would be in Paris by the time I got his letter. That was fill-in stuff. The brunt of the letter was that he thought we both could get jobs teaching English in Iran. He was running out of money and if he went to Iran, where he had a friend, he could stay afloat, save some money, and travel some more. If I came and met him somewhere in Europe, then we could travel overland together. That would be an adventure. Also, I could lend him some money.

I met him in Athens. As my plane landed, I wasn't so sure Bill's idea had been a good one. When the plane touched down, fire trucks and police cars raced down the runway alongside us, and when we stopped in the middle of the blacktop, away from the terminal, soldiers with tommy guns surrounded us. The plane was supposed to continue to Tel Aviv, and apparently the PLO had said they had packed a bomb on board.

We landed in early morning. I was supposed to meet Bill at a downtown square at noon, but the soldiers said they would keep the plane isolated on the runway for three hours before we could get our baggage. It wasn't until three o'clock that I got into downtown Athens.

As I crossed Syntagma Square, I saw Bill sitting at a café where he said he would be sitting. His face was dirty, he had a stubbly beard, and he was drinking a beer and smiling the biggest, widest smile, the kind of smile he would have liked to have had when I dropped the roast beef on the Cliff House guy's cash-mere sweater.

When we shook hands and slapped each other on the back, Bill said, "I had enough money left for one more beer. After that, I figured I was screwed."

I bought him another beer, then he took me to our hotel, Diana, The Huntress. Diana was a series of furniture-less rooms, with people our age, dog-eared books, transistor radios, and sleeping bags sprawled across the floors. We went upstairs and claimed a corner of the roof.

"What were you going to do if I didn't show?" I said.

"I didn't want to think about that. Maybe wished I had taken the credit card my father offered."

"Well, I said I was coming. I would've done something," I said, which was my way of trying to tell him he could count on my word.

That night, we celebrated at a restaurant. We came in through the kitchen, past long wooden tables mounded with squid and octopus and trays of moussaka, while the cooks laughed at us. I assumed that was because we were so tall and looked like we would eat a lot.

We got a table with a tablecloth on it and I took off my beret. We ate moussaka and drank Domestique and Bill told me about his adventures.

When we went to sleep, I was drunk, but it was good to be in a foreign city and have troubles half a world away, and it was especially good to be in a city and lie down and look up and still be able to see the stars.

Two days later, we took a ferry to Crete. I wanted a vacation and Bill wanted some time off the road, so the plan was to stay a week on the beach. The idea to go to Crete was Tano's.

At dawn, our ferry docked beside a Russian freighter in the port of Iráklion, on the northern coast of Crete. We walked into town as shopkeepers unfurled canvas awnings in the market, and when they were finished, we bought bread, oranges, peanuts, and a salami, and went to a café called the Omnia.

At the Omnia, the coffee came in a cup the size of a shot glass, which at the time was something new to me, and was served with a glass of water, something like having speed boiler-

291

makers. The coffee was strong and sweet and thick, and when we got to the bottom, we found a layer of mud, which surprised me as much as the size of the coffee cups.

"You supposed to drink this stuff on the bottom?" I said.

"I don't know," Bill said, which disappointed me and made me think he hadn't learned everything in the three months he had been in Europe.

"Maybe we should leave it," I said, and Bill agreed.

The bus we planned to take to the southern coast wasn't scheduled to leave until midafternoon, so to kill time we took another bus out to the ruins at Knossos. They didn't look like much to either of us, and when we returned to town, a thunderstorm hit. We waited it out in a card house with square wooden tables and walls with pictures of soldiers with swords. There were maybe a dozen men there and it was obvious that was the only gender allowed. The men had jet black hair, thick mustaches that curled at the end, dark eyes which I would have said were black except I had never heard of black eyes, and mahagony-colored skin with wrinkles and creases and lines that were not wrinkles and creases and lines, but trenches.

They wore billowy, baggy pants and black leather boots up to their knees, and either Bill or I said, "These guys are the hand-somest toughest-ass guys I've ever seen." If there's a heaven for real old-time macho guys, it must be something like that card house.

Bill and I sat by the window and had a cokaah-coolaah, but watched faces inside. Sometimes they watched us, but then they went back to their cards and I felt good, thinking how we all had sized each other up and everything was OK.

We stayed until the rain stopped and sunlight split our table and the place looked a little less tough.

Our bus to go south was in a yard with twenty other buses, but as the ticket agent described with a wave and a wiggle of fingers, like he was reading something invisible, our bus was easy to find. It was covered with tassels and decals of birds, ducks, chickens, flowers, places around the Mediterranean, and other things I didn't understand. On the dashboard there was a female doll dropping her pants, and above the front window, a billboard

292

of what looked like family pictures. Along the inside of the bus, there were more tassels and bunting and a decal of Christ exposing his heart. We sat near the back.

The bus driver climbed on the minute the ticket agent said the bus would leave, looked at his ten passengers, and said, "Oh, la laa."

The bus driver's name was Harry. He was six feet tall, muscular, with a black goatee and tiny dark eyes. He wore a Dutch seaman's cap and looked a little like Popeye's buddy, Bluto, only not as stocky.

As Harry drove the bus out of the yard, two other bus drivers yelled, "Hey, Americanos," at Bill and me, then they made the sign of the cross, crossed their fingers, and laughed. Harry saw them, then looked in his rearview mirror, saw us, and laughed, "Oh, la laaaaaa."

As much as Harry could, he kept the gas pedal pressed to the floor. He drove with one hand on the wheel, the other hand out the window, one eye watching for something in the countryside, and the other eye watching for something on the mirror or on the road. He drove through, around, and over mountains, spraying gravel and kicking up clouds of dust while all the passengers gagged and bounced on their seats. In a couple of hours, when Bill and I were the only ones left on the bus, Harry turned down a rocky, narrow road where there was a sign, LEDAS 17 KM. Harry drove a kilometer or two, then pulled off the side of the road into a field of olive trees. He looked into the mirror at us, laughed, and said, "Oh, la laa." His weasely sidekick ticket agent, who had sat in the front seat, laughed, and reached up to a shelf above Harry's head, took down a rifle, and handed it to Harry.

I turned to Bill and said something appropriate, like, "Oh, shit."

Harry must have seen the look on our faces, but he only laughed and rolled down a window, took aim, and shot at a bird. He missed and cursed and his sidekick shook his head and took the gun. Harry started up the bus again and headed down the road for Ledas.

"Your friend said this is a good place?" Bill said.

"Yeah, don't worry."

The shooting interludes occurred whenever Harry saw a bird stationary on a wall or a tree, but he never hit one. He always punctuated his misses with curses, until we got to Ledas, where he laughed and held up his hands, as if saying, "Well, what can I do?"

As Tano had told me, Ledas was a tiny fishing village, but he'd left the scenery as a surprise. Bleached mountains dropped straight into a turquoise Mediterranean, one sea rolling into another, and as we arrived, the waves sparkled.

Tano had said the best place to stay was a little east of town, so just before sunset, Bill and I hiked over a mountain to a long, barren beach. We found a spot between some evergreens, ate salami and bread, drank wine, and fell asleep.

We spent the next day swimming, talking ethnography— "Do you think the people here are called Cretans?" Bill said—and walking down the coast. In the afternoon, we found a cove above a five-foot beachhead of layered seaweed that felt like a sponge. Bill went for a long swim and I lay on the rocks and watched goats come halfway down a crack in a forty-foot cliff, then watch me. That got me thinking about hippies who were supposed to be living in caves fifty miles west of us, and how I would have preferred watching naked girls to goats.

We ate dinner at the town's only restaurant, a balcony on the beach with a cypress tree next to it. An old woman named Maria lived there and cooked one meal, fried fish with a salad of tomatoes, onion, and olive oil. She also served wine that went by the same name as the stuff in Athens, Domestique. When we ordered Domestique, it seemed like we were asking for tea or lemonade. Maybe too, because a woman served it, drinking Domestique we never felt so wild.

Harry came to dinner with weasel, the ticket taker, and taught us a new word, *"Asperbotto,"* which after a quick demonstration, I understood meant, "Bottoms up." Throughout dinner, Harry yelled *"Asperbotto"* at Bill and me, and since we knew Harry had a gun, we did what he said. After we were all good and drunk, Harry took out pictures of his family and told us he was crazy.

He didn't give us much time to let that sink in as the next

second, he took out a pair of wide-barreled pistols he had tucked away in his vest. He laughed, and said, "Oh, la laa,... Me, cowboy," and shot the pistols out over the beach. They triggered with a loud crack as two rockets whistled over the surf, exploded bright red, and fizzled down into the sea.

"Fourth of July, Harry," Bill said.

Harry heard him and probably understood it to mean something like loco, so he laughed and said, "Me, cowboy." We echoed, "You, cowboy," and laughed and we all *asperbottoed* some more.

When we'd had enough, Harry gave us a flashlight and we stumbled up the mountain, with Bill occasionally falling straight forward on his face, like a tree, but then immediately bouncing right back up again, like a ball, which is a mixed metaphor, but Bill was so drunk, he didn't care. He kept falling like a tree and bouncing back up again like a ball, while I laughed until I thought I would piss in my pants.

"Man, the ground shakes when you hit," I said as he bounced up again and said, *"Asperbotto."*

We planned to leave Ledas on a Monday. On Sunday night, we decided to go to town and have dinner at Maria's and celebrate, just the way we had done every night. We had a final fish and salad dinner with Domestique, then probably because we were usually the only ones who ate on her balcony, Maria brought us plates of rice pudding as a send-off. After we finished, she sat down to talk, or actually make gestures with us. I think we talked about war and Turks, because she kept wanting us to say something bad about "Keysencher," so we said, "Bad man, *malo.*" Then Harry arrived. We had told him we would see him at dinner that night and he had told us we should bring our gear and sleep on the bus because he left at dawn. We had our gear with us and he was there for dinner, so we all had kept our side of the appointment. Harry was up to more than that, though.

He told us to wait. He disappeared for twenty minutes and returned with the weasel and a bunch of their pals from town, along with a butchered goat. We all went down to the beach where Harry's friends already had built a fire and had let it die to coals. They set the goat on the spit and took turns turning it and running back to town for more Domestique. We drank until no one was bothering saying *"Asperbotto"* anymore. For Harry, that might have been a sign.

He took out a transistor radio and found a station with bouzouki music he said was "Kriti music." Then, with the moon almost on top of him and the sea breaking behind him, Harry stretched out his arms, slowly lifted his feet, spun around, and showed us how to dance.

XXXVII

IN the morning, I slugged coffee down, but it didn't work, so I tried psychology. When I went to wash my face at the edge of the river, I told myself I would try to ignore how tired I felt, or at least look at it with a detached eye. My inner conversation was like talking with someone you didn't trust, someone you expected sooner or later would turn on you.

There were moments when I felt clearheaded, like times the night before, in between the psychedelics, when I bullwhipped my brain into spots of clarity, but most of the time fatigue dulled it. I tried washing my face twice, but I couldn't clear the cobwebs, so I gave up and went back to coffee.

Sitting, waiting for Glück's milk rice to boil, he told us a story about how he used to sell caterpillars for $50 apiece to a clothing manufacturer in Germany.

"Later, I find out they were worth maybe six hundred dollars.

"Then there was the time I sent a packet of air to Germany."

I didn't feel like listening, but I didn't feel like talking, either, so I listened.

"At the post office, they wanted to open the packet. I told

them it was air that was supposed to be tested for pollution in Germany. They still wanted to open it. 'But it will escape,' I said. They say, 'We must open it.' So, I take the package away and bring it to a German boat in the port. *Sheiss*."

I laughed, but then Glück's coffee buzz struck him and he broke into gibberish I didn't hear, other than its drone. Tano actually made himself look like he was half listening, so I got up and wrapped my pod, slowly, until breakfast was ready. When I returned, I got a bowl of warm powdered milk with the last sprinkle of rice, and walked down to the river to eat in peace.

We left at 8:15. Neither psychology nor coffee had worked, so I decided to take a third strike and sit out the first hour of paddling, which sent me back to daydreams.

On the train from Athens to Istanbul, Bill and I shared a second-class compartment with a Greek soldier, a Syrian commando, and two Pakistanis.

It took thirty-nine hours to reach Istanbul, enough time for at least some of us to get acquainted. The two Pakistani men, in their thirties, with pencil-thin mustaches that still looked too big on their faces and rumpled serge suits a few sizes too big, never said anything. They either stared wide-eyed or stood outside the compartment and drank tea from tiny cups, then drank what spilled off on the saucer. They may have talked, but I don't remember if they did or what they said. I supposed the Syrian and the Greek made up for that. Each of them spoke some English, and it was the Syrian who eventually got the ball rolling.

The first night we left Athens, no one said much, other than exchanges of pleasantries. Bill and I unsuccessfully tried to sleep squeezed straight back on the benches, but then gave up, went out in the corridor, and slept on the floor. The move apparently had been a good one as everyone else in the semi-emptied compartment also got some sleep, and in the morning, for our night's sacrifice, we were heroes of sorts. That helped get conversation going.

We all talked about ourselves, with Bill and I not having too much to say, other than we had spent most of our lives in schools. Justifiably, that didn't interest anyone else.

The Syrian told us about a vacation he had taken recently in London, showed us a knife he had bought there, and proceeded to demonstrate its sharpness by peeling an apple in one peel. As he cut, conversation shifted. He talked about a raid he had joined against an Israeli radar base, where he slit the throat of a guard, then tossed a grenade into the barracks. One of the Israelis survived and stabbed the Syrian, but one of the other commandos killed the Israeli. The Syrian had finished peeling his apple by then, and while he held it in his mouth, lifted up his shirt to show Bill and me his stab wound. That got the Greek soldier, in the seat across from me, excited. When the Syrian finished his apple and his story, with tales of how tough and disciplined commando training was, the Greek soldier told us he, too, had been in battle.

"I fight Turks," he said. He told us about fighting on Cyprus, where he was shot in the neck, and blood came "shpurting way out." He said "shpurting" while he pulled down the collar of his shirt, and when we saw the scar, he demonstrated "shpurting" by putting his hand on his neck, opening his palm, and throwing his arm out in an arc across the compartment.

"My blood shpurt a meter," he said. "But, I live."

I don't know if the Pakistanis understood what was going on, but after the stories ended, they went down the corridor and I never saw them again.

Istanbul came on us the way I wanted it to come on us, after dawn, with the wail of muezzins, and mosques and minarets gleaming golden in the sun.

We found a dollar-a-night hotel, bunk beds in a communal room, near Ayasophia, then went over the Golatta Bridge and had lunch at a café near the docks, where we met a French truck driver. The trucker was heading where we were heading, Iran, and going over much of the same route, the trans-Turkish highway, a mostly dirt road. Although we planned to miss half the highway by taking a boat across the Black Sea, we asked the bus driver about the road in eastern Turkey.

"Très dangereux," he said. *"Les Turcs sont fous."*

He said he knew another truck driver who, a month or two earlier, was driving at night along the highway in eastern Turkey when bandits on horseback attacked. They ransacked the truck, robbed and decapitated the truck driver, and stuck his head on a spike at the front of the truck's hood.

299

The French truck driver shook his head.

"Allez par avion," he said.

"Nous sommes pauvres," Bill said. *"Nous n' avonsqu' un peu d'argent."*

"Vous allez encore?" we said, which was our way of saying he must be just as crazy as the Turks.

"Oui, mais c'est le temps final."

"Mabye he's right. Maybe we should take a plane," I said. "But it'll cost too much, and besides, we'll be on a bus."

"Yeah," Bill said. "Instead of a decapitation, they'll call it a massacre."

Probably to clear our heads of their possible removal, that afternoon we went to a Turkish bathhouse, where I sprawled on an octagonal marble altar. Actually, it was more like languished. Whatever, between languishing and sprawling, I watched steam drift up past archways and through splays in a perforated dome, while old men with towels around their waist lolled like walruses on steps and marble benches, a frieze of straight and sagging lines. On the beach at Crete, when Bill was eating peanuts, he had said, "Whenever I eat peanuts, I think of how we're still like monkeys," a comment that made me smile at the way he was thinking then, but it came back to me in the bathhouse, with the fog of steam and all those bodies and loose skin that looked so mortal against marble.

When we finished sweating, we got rubdowns from short, turbaned men with muscles that looked like ropes. Actually, they gave us less of a rubdown and more of a beating. Bill called his man Abdul, and laughed when Abdul pounded him, which made Abdul smile, a big, toothy smile, and pound Bill some more. I tried to look indifferent.

When they were finished, Abdul and my man, Abdul's twin, showed us to wood-paneled closets with curtains, and inside, mats with sheets. I laid down and soon another man in a turban knocked and served us *chai* in tiny cups and saucers, the kind the Pakistanis had on the train, but I only finished what was in my cup and left what remained on the saucer, on the saucer. Then I melted into sleep.

That night, we decided to head uptown to the new city, to a nightclub called the Folies Bergère, where we hoped to see belly dancers. For a drink, the Folies Bergères charged what it would cost us for a week at our hotel, so we nursed one awful drink through twelve awful acts, while almost as awful-looking women, employed by the house, came and briefly sat with us and tried to coax us to drink more. By the last act, I had one pea-sized ice cube left and a sore arm from waving barmaids away, even though they had given up by the third act. There only were eight other men in the nightclub, which could have seated two-hundred, but none of the Turks were drinking, either. Midway through the show, the barmaids retreated around an old blond hag in the back who looked like she owned the place. Occasionally, she stood up, looked across the club, and snorted, as if Bill and I and the eight Turks were scum, while her attendants smoked cigarettes, crossed their legs, and dangled their high-heeled shoes in rhythm.

While the first eleven acts included acrobats, jugglers, and magicians, the last act was what Bill and I came for, though presented not in the fashion we had hoped. A large woman, who looked more heavy than muscular, bared her breasts, which weren't more than nubs, so I wasn't so sure she was a woman, and danced what was supposed to be a provocative belly dance in front of a guy with a beard and a crown, whom we understood to be King Herod. The woman, Salome, stumbled around a few minutes on stage, then reached behind a curtain, and someone handed her a plastic head on a platter. We understood the head was supposed to be John the Baptist's. I'm not sure what the Turks in the audience understood, but they hooted and the old hag in the back stood up and snorted at the Turks. Before trouble started, Bill and I left, not appreciating being reminded of decapitations.

The next day, we took a ferry up the Bosporus and for the first time I stepped into Asia. We met a Turk called Fahti on the ferry and joined him for a picnic of olives, peppers, tomatoes, mussels, and goat cheese on a hill outside a small town. It was cloudy, but from where we sat, we could look across the Bosporus and see the European side, and across the straits, sloops with sails that looked like feathers.

Fahti talked about Turkish life and told us some of the history of Istanbul and the Bosporus, and while sitting there, listening and eating olives and feeling the breeze off the water and watching sheep on another hill, I knit myself into a tapestry, like the ones I had seen in the Cloisters, only better, one I could always carry and piece together when I felt like it, like on the river.

A few days later, we took a boat across the Black Sea, from Istanbul to Trabzon, thereby avoiding most of the bandit road. The Black Sea lived up to its name, as a few hours out of Istanbul it began to storm. Our ship tossed and tumbled and Bill and I laughed a lot when we went up and down steps or actually stairways, in one step, and slid down banisters, but soon, I wasn't laughing. Bill still was when he looked at me and said, "Hey, you're turning green."

We had booked the cheapest class, which put us in the bottom of the hold, on bunk beds in the midst of dozens of peasants with heavy woolen clothes, mounds of burlap bags, crying babies, smoke, and a light bulb or two. It was like a rocking version of the Mexico City train station, an image that helped me look greener and stay hunched over a bucket.

There was an Englishman down there, too, a man in his early thirties, who didn't talk much, but made me hope that in ten years or so, when I was his age, I would have enough money to go second class.

XXXVIII

MAYBE twenty minutes after we took off, we hit a wide stretch of rapids. The hull of the boat scraped against rocks, but we sped through; then, just past, we heard a motor.

"It must be a plane," Glück said, but it wasn't, and got louder, coming from the southwest. It was nine o'clock. The sky was almost clear, but there was no sign of the sun. It should have been three hours in the sky.

"Are you sure it's nine o'clock, Kurt?"

"Yes, nine and three minutes."

"Something's going on."

"Where is Lacerda's house?" Glück asked. "Above or below the fork where we made the wrong turn?"

"Above," I said and turned to Tano. "Remember the joke you told Melnick before we left."

He smiled. The last thing he'd said to Melnick was, "Don't worry, we'll bring Glück back safe."

I switched to paddling. The motor sounded closer, very close, maybe just around the bend. Then an explosion, or shot, echoed upriver. We had been joking, hoping the motor was the police to arrest the people who went to the pyramids, but the shot turned the jokes sour.

We took the curve and saw a dugout with five cabocolos. One of the men was standing and putting a gun away, while behind him a puff of smoke hung near the edge of the jungle. We stayed down and waved, not much more than a nod, as if we had been out for a walk and passed a neighbor we knew only by sight. One of the cabocolos, a short, dark-skinned man, I recognized from Allianca. He returned our wave, yelled, *"Raso,"* and pointed right. The river was low ahead and we would have to stay near the west shore. We thanked them and waved again as we passed, glad to be going in the opposite direction.

For two hours, we kept going, not talking much, while the river got wider, the clouds, high and distant and hazy. Something about the sky made me think that would be the way it would look when the world ended, indifferent, something like "not a bang, but a whimper." Without the sun, the jungle looked as if its colors had drained. A parrot squawked, then an egret flapped downriver, swooped into a perch high in the trees, watched us get close, then skipped farther downstream, like he was leading us down the Styx, all of which, despite our seeing people for the first time in weeks, made me feel as if we were the last ones on earth.

"Man, I don't know what's going on today, but something is," I said to Tano. "Do you feel it?"

"Yeah, I don't know what it is either."

At noon, we saw a cluster of huts on the east bank, with people. Glück said we should stop and try to get eggs, and we slipped up through the rocks. There were a few Indians by canoes. We waved and a man with glasses came out of the house nearest the river.

"I know him from Allianca," Glück said. A short, barefoot man with a big forehead followed and waved. He was a man we had asked to store some of our gas. Then more men and women and children came out of the huts and waved and shouted. The children ran to the river's edge and helped pull us to shore.

The man with the big forehead asked us what happened. Glück told him we took the wrong turn at the fork in the river.

The man squatted on the boulders and laughed, rocking on his haunches.

We asked him the name of the river to the left, and he said Rio Castanha, the Nut River.

"Oh, man, it figures," Tano said.

We bought provisions from them, including tobacco, and after a magnificent lunch of wild boar, fish, and *fejoaida*, they tossed in extra farinha for our trip and offered us three liters of gas to get to a house where they said they had left the rest of our supply. They said they brought the gas upriver because everyone had left Allianca.

Tano dubbed the afternoon "Christmas in the jungle."

By the time we left, the sun had appeared, so we figured we were back from the end of the world, though we weren't sure.

We cruised downriver under the hum of our own engine. The hut with our gas was supposed to be two hours paddling time, but it took us an hour and a half motoring time, almost enough time to run out of fuel.

The hut was on the west shore, and a man and a woman were standing outside and waved for us.

Along with our gas, they had eggs, which we exchanged for vitamins, multiples and B's, which seemed like a fair exchange all the way around. I asked the man about the Indians and why everyone had left the upper Padauiri. He said he had stayed after everyone left in November after Tatunka made his speech about an impending Indian attack. Then, in December, ninety Indians, Xingu, Maku, Tukano, and Uiaka, from reservations in Araca, came down by land to Allianca. Three had guns and the rest bows and arrows. They took all the canoes in Allianca, including his, the man said, then escaped upstream. He said he followed them and got his back, although he didn't explain how he managed.

"What a bunch of shit that Tatunka spread," Tano said.

We thanked the man and woman for the gas and eggs, then left, cruising down wide expanses of river that seemed to have little current, like they were a series of connected lakes. Just before sunset, we pulled into the piacaba hut behind the ring of rapids at Allianca.

We took everything out of the boat, figuring we again would have to carry it overland, then went in for a swim/bath in almond-colored water that was almost still. Tano and I swam until we smelled Glück cooking onions and meat.

"We're gonna have full bellies tonight,' Tano said.

We did and when we were finished, we settled down to greasy *jakaré* tobacco cigarettes that were almost as good as the meal.

For a while, things kept up that way. Glück made joongle pancakes for breakfast, then went through the path in the jungle to Allianca to see if he could find someone to help us with the boat.

Tano and I packed camp, sat down, unbuttoned a notch off our belts, and burped.

"Looks like we're over the hump."

"Yeah," he said. "But I learned from South America not to fly too high. We could tip the boat over and lose everything."

"All I'd like to hang on to is my journal," I said.

"Even that, South America really changed my ideas about all that stuff. When I was down here before, I got to like Indian sand paintings. They make something beautiful in the sand, then puff, just wipe it away."

Planes of sunlight slid through the roof and Tano rolled each of us a cigarette. We smoked awhile, then I had something to say.

"About the trip ... I've thought some but not that much about turning back, and when I do, all I think is, 'What if we just cruised up with plenty of gas and food?' The way it really was, if nothing else, the trip had heart," which was a roundabout way of saying I didn't think the trip was only another rough time.

"Yeah, our best would've been good enough," Tano said.

XXXIX

GLÜCK returned in the rain and said Allianca was empty, so we cut thin logs and rolled the boat through the path in the forest.

"Like they did in Egypt," Glück said.

We motored down for a while after Allianca, then paddled. We had twenty-two liters of gas left, including ten liters we planned to save for when we reached the Rio Negro.

At four o'clock, we found a Hilton on a hill on the west shore. The hut had been DDT'd, had a panoramic view, and behind it there were overgrown fields of bananas, which combined for a four-star rating.

Glück made coronet beef and rice for a near perfect dinner, except for his constant "Ah, so now who is the fork? ... Ah, yes ... Oh, *sheiss*, the rice is boiling ... Ah, now who is the fork?" which we didn't let bother us. Afterwards, Glück went down to the river to wash and shave, while Tano and I stayed on the hill and talked about other rough trips we made, which kept us up late into the night and didn't help our dreams.

I woke during the night and heard animals drinking in the river and some crossing. One sounded like it was human, going up for air, breaking the water with a puff, then going down again. It must have been a dolphin, though it could have been something having trouble crossing. The puffs sounded like gasps.

I rocked in my hammock, half dreaming, half remembering things, though I was awake enough to recognize how my mind felt like the river. Memories were going up and down on my river like the rocks that surfaced and submerged under the rule of the sun and rain in the Amazon. Sometimes, when the sun was out, and I could see clearly, it was like I could waltz up those rocks, though I didn't know where they would take me.

Once, when I was nineteen, I went ice skating on a river in New Hampshire. It was mid-December. The night before, I had seen the girl from California, the one I went chasing after across the country. She told me something that I thought was the saddest thing I ever had heard. Though I didn't right away, afterwards I cried. It wasn't one of those sobbing things, just a leaking out at the eyes, something I couldn't control, my chest squeezing water out. The next day, I went skating on the river. The river had a dusting of snow, but underneath it looked black and I skated a long way up, trying not to think about things, seeing black strings of trees, feeling my cheeks and nose get icy, then not feeling them, hearing the carving of the metal in the frozen river, turning and seeing slivers of tracks and all the time just trying to see and suck cold air into my chest and keep from thinking, though inside, I knew I was beginning to learn about dying.

I woke before dawn and watched the sun rise behind trees, changing the color of the jungle from steel to copper. I faked sleep and watched Glück put coffee on and walk down from the hut, through a path toward the boat. He was best silent, and I thought that when I couldn't hear him, I liked him and would miss him. Then he returned.

"Ah, so, you are awake. I make the coffee. When in Manaus, I drink coffee ... " and on and on. I said little, trying not to encourage him, and instead stared at the river, as if I were looking or listening for something, but Glück didn't notice.

"And then, many times, my wife, she says to me ... "

We had farinha for breakfast, something like having sawdust

soaked in warm evaporated milk, powder on powder with a water lube. The manioc had everything from bark to wood shavings and flies in it, a kind of jungle granola that wasn't bad.

"A little interior decorating along the digestive tract," I said.

"Wood paneling," Tano said.

The day was cloudless and dry, the way I thought the day before might have been. Still, it dragged. Glück seemed to want to take his time. At first, he wanted to stay at our camp and wash clothes, but Tano and I overruled.

"We still have eight or nine days at least before we can make Manaus. Maybe we won't even make it on schedule," Tano said.

"Ach, it will be no problem," Glück said, "and if we have to, sometime we can paddle at night. It is b-e-e-y-o-u-t-e-e-f-u-l to paddle in the night. The moon is out and it is lazy and nice. You will like it."

The racehorse looked like it was going inside Tano, too. He told Glück he thought it might not be a bad idea.

A half hour before we left, we heard a boat that sounded like it was a short distance downriver.

"Yes, I hear," Glück said as I turned to ask him. "Maybe we can catch it. Maybe it goes to Manaus and we can go with it the whole way."

We loaded and paddled down to a hut where a small riverboat had docked. The boat was heading north, to Allianca, and Glück talked to the captain. He said it would take four to five days to reach the Rio Negro, but suggested we try and catch the boat we had heard earlier that morning. It was bound for Manaus.

"Let's go for it," Tano said.

Early afternoon, we caught the *Walma-Manaus,* a piacaba boat, as it stopped at a hut on the east side of the river. We pulled alongside and Glück chitchatted with the crew, but didn't ask if we could tie on, he only asked if they had eggs so he could make pancakes. I told Glück to ask about being tugged behind and he said, "Ah, yes, we must ask the captain."

The captain was a middle-aged man with a shadow of a beard and a cigar. He acted like he was annoyed when one of the deckhands asked him to come and speak with Glück. The captain said he was going to Manaus, but would be making many river stops, loading piacaba and castaña nuts. Glück asked when he would leave and the captain said ten minutes.

"OK, let's hitch on," I said.

"Ten minutes can be two hours. I don't think we should wait," Glück said.

"What's going on? I think we should wait," I said. "Why don't you chime in?" I said to Tano who was holding our boat on the rail of the *Walma*.

He didn't say anything and I turned to Glück.

"We can paddle down," Glück said. "Then when the captain comes by, he can pick us up."

"Why not just wait? I don't understand. Tano?" I turned and tried giving him the Perry Mason stare. "What do you think?" a question I immediately knew I shouldn't have asked as his poker face was not so blank. I knew he was turning up his cards and siding with Glück.

"Let's just paddle and get picked up."

We paddled. We got a hundred yards from the *Walma* when it started up and pulled away. It came up alongside us when we reached a fork in the river. A boy, tightroping along the rail of the stern, yelled and pointed at us to go left, even though the boat was going right. He said we could tie on at their next stop. As the boat turned sharply into an inlet on the right, the deck-hand waved and shouted he would see us downriver. At least that was what we thought he said. I also thought the captain probably was pissed at Glück for being impatient and not waiting the ten minutes.

I had a terrible feeling, something like the way we felt after the *Costa Azul* left us at Bluefields, that grafted on the jungle. It was a collage that came out blank and I thought we were in for trouble.

We headed downstream, we thought. The river split into three channels, one looking like it was draining into us, and the other two flowing down. We took the middle one. It seemed to be flowing south. We were running the motor, using what little gas remained. The jungle changed from giant hedges of tall trees to lower scrub, marshes of reeds and grass. We kept going, passing many side channels, tributaries and lagoons, while the jungle flattened, mixing the water into a web of options.

I turned and looked at Tano, but there wasn't any need to

310

speak. I guess it's called that awful sinking feeling, the way there is a direct line between your brain and the bottom of your stomach and something starts rolling.

We pushed on. "I don't remember this section, do you?" Glück asked, mostly to himself. "No, it cannot be ... I don't know ... Maybe ... Who is the river?"

No one remembered that section of the river. It didn't have the high, leaning trees. It was more like a swamp, and though it kept splitting, like it was undergoing some kind of mutation, we always tried to stick to the middle channel of the split. Then, we began to lose current.

We turned off the engine to save gas in case we had to figure our way back upriver. Paddling, first we went swiftly, but as the river broke up, it lost force. Soon, partially submerged logs and rocks were causing only a trickle in the current.

The river got wide and glassy and we followed a channel into what looked like a lake—long and broad and almost still. Clouds came up from the south and the wind picked up against us and if there had been any current helping us, it finally gave out. We had to paddle, deep and fast, to make any headway, fighting both the water and the sky.

We paddled until we were short of breath, then checking to see if we completely had lost the river's force, we stopped and the boat stopped and the wind pushed us back, north.

Then Tano said what his face said before. "I got this sinking, rotten feeling."

"Man, I know.... Life is cheap here."

He shook his head.

"That captain and kid probably just sent the gringos down a series of lost lagoons. 'They can't wait ten minutes. Fuck'em.' "

Against the wind, there didn't seem to be current, but when the wind faded, there still was a trickle.

"I've seen lakes with current," Tano said.

Then I said what I shouldn't have said, but I was in a call-a-spade-a-spade mood. "Well, there's a good chance we're lost."

I tried to remember things about the past hour or so, twists in the river, where it widened, and which channels we took.

Glück kept checking his compass. Most of the time we paddled south.

"If we keep going south and don't see huts," I said, "I may

311

be up for just hacking our way through the jungle south. Sooner or later, we'll reach the Rio Negro, but once again, the problem will be lack of food."

The wind stopped and the clouds thinned to a haze. Then came the piums. We put on long shirts and pants, but that only made the pium attack more centered, on our face, necks and hands.

We passed a pair of empty huts on opposite sides of the river. The huts were immediately interpreted as a good sign.

"I doubt someone would build huts on a lake. The only reason people build them here is for piacaba and rubber, and for that, they need up and down access on a river," I said.

No one said anything, so I wasn't sure about their faith in my assumptions.

"Wait a second," Tano said and reached over and held my paddle. "I thought I heard a motor." We stopped, but no one heard anything.

"Now you're hearing them, huh?"

We paddled on, which I suppose was something like keeping moving when you are lost in the woods, even when chances are you are going in circles. Movement has its own logic, and when you don't have much else to hang on to, it gets independent and self-perpetuating. You keep going because you have already gone this far, and you got this far because you said the same thing a while ago, the kind of thing the Greeks thought made for good stories. Sometimes it's known as doom.

"So, now begins the adventurra," Glück said.

I wanted to pop him.

"Man, I'm burning," Tano said, looking straight ahead at the horizon.

Glück took out his compass and talked to it. "If this is south, that must be east ... We must be on the right river." For the next hour or so, he must have held the same conversation with the compass a couple of dozen times, with only slight variations. "Now, if that is north, and this is south, then that must be west and that must be east. Yes. We have to be on the right river. Yes, we must be."

About the twentieth time Glück talked to the compass, the current picked up and we saw a hut on the west shore. It was broad and high off the ground, on four stilts, and looked like it could have been a school or church. In front, there was a board on a post that looked like a sign. We were near the opposite, east side of the river, maybe a hundred yards from it.

"Let's go over and see what that sign says," I said. I don't know why I said that, other than I half expected it to say something like "Moscow 48,000 km" but everyone else must have been thinking the same because no one protested.

As we neared the western bank, we had to paddle hard as the current seemed strong and dragged us down and away, which five minutes earlier would have felt great. Now, it fought us and we tried to stay even with the hut and not be swept down. The sign was posted high in the sky and I couldn't see it in the glare. We had to paddle closer. I stood in the boat and cupped my hands over my eyes to try and block the light. The sign was directly between us and the sun, like an eclipse, and my eyes ached as I tried to focus.

"I think I can read it ... E ... S ... P ... E... R... A... N... C ... A... *esperanca*, what does that mean?"

"Hope, man, hope," Tano shouted.

We paddled more, maybe ten minutes, before we heard a distant *put-put-put-put.*

At first, we thought it might be the *Walma,* but the sound came from the south and grew stronger. We reached a bend and hugged the inside corner just as a double-decked riverboat, the kind I would have imagined on the Mississippi eighty years before, freshly painted white, swung around the turn, gliding upriver like a bull on skates.

"Hey, it's Bozo Big Nose" (the Allianca bossman we met on the way up), Tano said.

"Damn, we're on the river."

The boat churned by and we waved and Glück nodded, like he knew it all the time, and Tano said, "Let's have a cigarette."

"Best idea I've heard in hours."

When we looked like we were screwed in the marshes and I was getting nervous, I told myself to wait until evening, when we could sit down after dinner, smoke cigarettes, realize we were lost, bad, then, in relative peace, really got worried. So, the cigarette offer hit a responsive chord.

313

Tano rolled them, laughing about how the tobacco looked like pubic hair, but curling them into svelte, elegant cylinders. We quit paddling and let the current take us down, while Glück worked his oar like a rudder, trying to keep us midstream.

"It is good to smoke, now," Glück said. "When I was younger and I had my pipe, all day long I would smoke . . . " and on and on, but I didn't even care.

"Man, this feels unexpected and great. I thought for sure we were screwed."

"Man, this South America has taught me a lot," Tano said. "When I get high now, it's not like a kite anymore. It's like a hawk. I'm up there, but I'm stable, keeping my balance."

I watched him as he spoke, which was not so much to me, as it was to the land and the river and the sky. His head was leaning forward, his eyes were squinting, just a bit, and staring, and he looked like he was hundreds of feet in the sky, with his back skimming the bottom of clouds.

XL

FOR a half hour, we drifted downriver, then more good fortune. The *Walma* came *put-put-put*-ing, hell, it came barreling down on us. When the captain saw us, he looked indifferent, and waved for us to pull up. He slowed the *Walma* down. We threw a rope to the deckhands. He tied us on and we were in tow.

The *Walma* whipped us down the Padauiri, and we saw the jungle the way a water skier might, only with three of us on one ski.

"Well, at least the engine drowns his mumblin'," Tano said. "I can't hear a word that damn guy is saying, though every time I turn around, his mouth's moving."

We stopped a few times and loaded piacaba and, by early evening, reached the leper's hacienda, where we loaded for an hour in a light drizzle. As the sun set, it broke through the clouds and in the soft light and rain, the trees and palms glistened, like they were draped in tinsel.

Early evening, the rain stopped and a sliver more than a half moon shone through the fog. I sang, "Another Saturday Night," which Tano told me he had been tuned in and waiting for.

By 6:30, the clouds were back. It was midnight black, but

we shoved off, even though earlier in the day the captain had said he did not run at night. *"Muito perigoso."*

In thirty minutes, we passed the teacher's house where we had stayed.

"This is icing on the cake."

I put on a wool shirt, and lying against my pack, I watched the clouds crack and the moon reappear. A warm breeze washed over us and I felt like I was on my back, swimming, though with the *Walma* exhaust it was more like urban municipal-swimming-pool swimming. I pulled a tarp to my nose and passed out.

Two hours later, we docked on the non-current side of a curve. The captain came around and said he would stay for the night. We should go across the river, to a cluster of shacks, and sling our hammocks in an empty piacaba hut.

We paddled across a stiff current and tied beside a trio of boats that looked like sampans. Glück wanted to go to sleep, but Tano and I said we would wait and make cold farinha.

"For what?" Glück said. "Tomorrow morning you can eat. It is so much trouble now, and this farinha, it is shit. They give it to dogs."

"It's no trouble," I said, "and if you're worried about us leaving the boat uncovered, don't worry. We'll cover the boat. Our stuff is in there, too. Go to bed and we'll take care of it."

Tano and I helped him carry up the gear, then walked back to the moat.

"Man, sometimes I feel like nailing Glück," I said, which made Tano laugh in a way that said, "It's about time Glück was getting to you because he got to me that way a long time ago."

We made poison milk—powdered milk with iodine water—but it took ten minutes for the manioc to absorb it. I tried to be patient and let the manioc, which was like gravel, turn to mud— I didn't want my stomach swelling into a balloon—but I was too hungry to be patient, so I was into it when it still had plenty of crunch. We sprinkled on sugar, plenty of sugar. "At least it's raw," I said, "though I've got enough to make my blood tingle."

We cleaned up and repacked the boat, then Tano and I sat on a hill above the dock, smoked cigarettes, and wished for lawn chairs.

316

"The life."
"The life."

We were up with the crowing of roosters, a sound that normally might have been followed by Tano moaning something about syphilization, which for whatever reason, he didn't moan that morning. Glück went down to the river to make coffee, while across the river, the *Walma* awoke with a blast from its radio. The piacaba hut where we slept was thirty feet from another one with a family that in seconds had their radio blaring with matching volume and station, so we had stereo.

"You know," I said to Tano, "I woke in the middle of the night. My hammock was rocking, and the source of that rock was your hammock, which kept rocking for a while until it stopped when I heard a sigh. Have good dreams?"

"The best."

We left when Glück announced, "Seven o'clock. Z'good."

Once again, the captain put the *Walma* in high gear and we cruised down that river.

"Icing on icing," Tano said.

The farther south we went, the faster the river ran. Trees danced up and down in the flow, their crowns shaking to the rhythm of current. Sunlight was patchy and oblique, like an autumn sky.

Being tied to the boat felt good. We made many stops that day, one at a village with a man with two elbows on one arm. He got some Indian boys to climb mango trees and shake the limbs, and the fruit dropped to the ground in a pounding that sounded like someone playing bongos.

At midday, we passed south of the equator, an event the *Walma* deckhand marked by letting his toilet paper fly out the back of the hole in the plank-banho. The paper floated above our bow, then landed at Tano's feet.

"Appropriate," Tano said as he lifted it off with his paddle.

Near evening, we went up an oil-slicked black water channel, "like the sixties, tie-died." Indians paddled up in canoes loaded with piacaba, which they exchanged for soap, coffee, and pinga. We smoked cigaretes and watched, then after they unloaded, they sat and smoked cigarettes and watched us, then Tano suggested we trade them Glück for something.

In my hammock that night, I was thinking about old people and slow deaths and was half asleep when I heard four musical notes off in the jungle. They sounded over and over again and Tano asked if someone was playing the flute, but I said it was a bird. The notes stopped and I went back to thinking about old people.

My father was transferred and my family moved from Florida, up north, when I was twelve. Although I knew I had seen snow when I was very young and lived in New York, it had been years and I didn't remember it and couldn't wait to see it again, or what felt like would be the first time. In Florida, for cold days, I had a red sweater my mother knitted me, but on days I could see my breath, I didn't wear it and instead rolled my sleeves to just above my elbows, which sometimes produced the desired effect.

"So, a tough guy," a priest who came to visit our school said to me. "You don't feel this cold."

"It's nuthin'," I said.

When we moved north and winter hit, even before the snow came, the windows in my bedroom iced and if I pressed my lips on the pane, I would stick, which wasn't like anything in Florida. My mother got us long underwear and heavy coats and gloves and my grandfather helped in dressing the three older boys for winter by getting us fedoras. I was the oldest, but still thought I was too young for a hat like that, but I agreed to keep it in a box and wear it on Sundays.

The first Sunday I wore my fedora, I spent a long time in front of my mirror trying to get the right tilt, but it didn't help. When I went to church, a bunch of the guys were standing outside on the front steps, but instead of staying out and talking with them, I walked through the laughter fast and got inside where I knew I was supposed to take the damn thing off.

I didn't think my grandfather understood what it was like to be twelve. When he saw me with a pair of white socks on with dress slacks he had a fit, and one time when I was visiting him and he made a Salisbury steak for dinner and I asked him how come he didn't give me a bun, he picked up the phone and called my mother.

"How you training this boy?" he said. "He wants to slap a bun around ground sirloin, his pants are so tight he barely can bend down, and he reads the paper backwards. He licks the ink off those sport pages. I never saw such a thing."

Apparently he felt my parents had let things slide, so after that he took more of an active part in my education. He had been more involved during the first four years of my life, before we moved from New York to Florida. Although I don't remember it, not too much after I learned to walk, he started taking me to the racetrack. He had a lot of friends there, and spent much of his time along the backstretch, where he liked to go just after dawn and watch the morning workouts. His friends were mostly trainers and jockeys, including a jockey named Pete, a Cajun from Louisianna, who, for a while, rented a room in our house.

Before Pete came to live with us, my grandfather would dress me up in a suit and a cap, and take me to see Pete and the other fellows at the track. Although I'm glad I don't remember, I am told that when my grandfather brought me to the track I would be inspected as if I was a yearling. The first thing, the boys there would lift up my lips and check my teeth. Then they would tell my grandfather I was going to be healthy and strong, which I bet always made my grandfather beam.

When we moved away, I guess my grandfather thought things might slip. On visits south, he tried to maintain a progression of things and would bring my brothers and me Garcia fishing rods and Mitchell spinning reels along with a shrimp net and baseball mitts, Spauldings or Wilsons, from a Manhattan store he said was "the best."

Then, after I came back north and I wanted to put my dinner in a bun, he decided he had better pick up where he left off.

While we waited for our house to be built in New Jersey, we stayed in New York with my aunt and uncle, who lived in a Polish neighborhood in Queens, in the same house where my father grew up. My father commuted to work in New Jersey and took my brothers and me to school there. We usually didn't get back home to New York until after dark, but on days off and weekends, I played touch football and stickball in the streets with some of my cousins and the local kids, until my grandparents called. They usually called Saturday afternoon and asked if I wanted to come over for the rest of the weekend, an invitation I always accepted. They lived close enough for me to ride a bike, and when I got to their house, if it was still early, I went shopping with my grandmother to stock up for the rest of the weekend.

Sometimes on Sunday my grandfather and I would go to dinner together. My grandfather's favorite restaurant was a place called the Triangle Hofbrau, run by two or three brothers from Alsace-Lorraine. My grandfather told me that was the French side of the Rhine, the cooking was French and German, and, he would add with a wink, the food was "all right," which might have been his way of teaching me about understatement.

When we arrived, we walked in through the bar, where my grandfather talked to a bartender who said, "How are you, Mr. Briggs?" and then said something else about the days when my grandfather would come in after midnight and order steak tartare at the bar. My grandfather laughed and then we went inside to a dark, paneled dining room with maps that looked old enough to be used by Charlemagne. Before we sat down, my grandfather talked to the maitre d', who said something about a Hofbrau brother being sick, or another one dying. My grandfather and the maitre d' both shook their heads and my grandfather said he would like a table for two, and then he told the maitre d', he wanted a bottle of sparkling burgundy and a "glass for the boy."

Other than the wine, I don't remember what my grandfather would order, but I always ordered the same thing, roast duckling à l'orange, followed by two plates of strawberry shortcake. I liked the duck more for the spectacle. It came to the table covered in blue flames, which I thought was a grand way to serve a meal, even if I did have a tough time sawing through the skin.

For dessert, I always had room for a plate of strawberry shortcake that was so big and whipped-creamy, it came in something like a giant soup bowl. Then, because I had done it before, and because the waiters were watching again, I ordered and ate another strawberry shortcake, even though I was stuffed.

As we walked out, my grandfather and the maitre d' marveled at my appetite and the strawberry shortcake, and my grandfather told them the same thing he told them every time he went there. "I used to like to go to Lüchow's, but you fellows got them knocked."

Then we went back home and took a nap.

Although he missed it by a few decades, my grandfather was and still is very much an ante-bellum man. He was born and raised in Georgia, which he described as "the South" though the raising part was cut short, as he ran away from home after sixth grade to join the merchant marine. By the time he was twenty-five, he decided he needed a wife who would not run away from him, so he chose a Catholic woman, who because of the laws of the Church and the threat of eternal hell, was forced to stick with the "till death do us part."

My grandmother had lived on the Lower East Side of Manhattan and her parents were immigrant Lithuanians. To make ends meet, her father worked the docks and kept a still in his bathtub, though I'm not sure which bit of enterprise brought my grandfather first in contact with the family. My grandfather was not Catholic, but was Welsh and a sailor, all of which, I am sure, did not enhance his appearance with my grandmother's family. So my grandmother and grandfather eloped New Year's Eve, 1925, and shortly afterward, my grandfather went back out to sea.

My grandfather got what he wanted and during the times he was away, my grandmother kept the hearth burning, though maybe it was back then she developed the philosophy, "What he won't know, won't hurt him."

When my grandfather was a boy, he had an accident, something about a cave collapsing on him. He damaged his eardrums, and he ended up hard of hearing. My grandmother made up for what he missed, but she also filtered out what he needed to miss. She explained the filtering as "being for the best."

My grandfather liked to paint and what he painted most were pictures that involved the sea, and when he was painting the sea, he talked a lot. Being from the South, he had an accent, which he had hung on to even though it was near the beginning of the century when he left the South. He didn't talk in twangy

321

sing-songy Southern, but in more of a hoarse farm-boy voice that sounded as if it had been gurgled through mud and cotton and tobacco and pecans. The closest thing I ever heard to it was Muhammad Ali, but when I mentioned that to my grandfather, he said, "Whaaaat?" and lifted his fist like he was going to swing. It wasn't only his accent my grandfather kept from the South, but all her old ways, which he talked about in reverence of a bygone era, something similar to the way King Arthur spoke of Camelot to young Will at the end of *The Once and Future King*.

When my grandfather was not talking about the South and the "thin gray line" (Civil War veterans who were dying out when he was a boy), and why J. E. B. Stuart was the best general and why Abraham Lincoln was the worst president and how we had an uncle who participated in the firing on Fort Sumter, he would be saying something about "nigguhs" or "headhunters." The last part I ignored. He was the most adamant racial separationist I ever knew or, for that matter, heard about. A comparatively mild example of that had to do with baseball. My grandfather loved baseball. Whenever he docked in New York, his first stop was to buy some new clothes and his second stop was Yankee Stadium. He would quit jobs if they interfered with a chance to see a game, but all that changed in 1947. The day Jackie Robinson broke into the big leagues, my grandfather quit going to baseball games and he hasn't gone since.

Aside from baseball, and when he wasn't talking about "headhunters" and he wasn't talking about the South, he was talking about his trips to sea. I liked those the best. He would tell me stories about what Guinness beer from Ireland tasted like, "thick as molasses"; and how his best friends on the ships were Basques, but during the Spanish Civil War, "They went out of their minds, crazy. When they started throwing firebombs, I had to say that was it"; and South America, "You could live like a king for nothing in Argentina"; and Havana, where he would drink at Sloppy Joe's, "that fat son-of-a-bitch, with that stupid hat of his and that nasally voice" (which he would imitate in a kind of a snort). "He once tried to charge me tourist prices, but I pulled him across the bar and said, 'Look, what the hell's going on here?' Then he charged me the right price. Son-of-a-bitch."

Despite the fact he only made it through six grades, and despite the "nigguh" business, my grandfather held a great respect for education. He said he educated himself on the ships, where he had a lot of free time, so he read, "not that poenogrephee stuff everyone else had," but "good books," like Faulkner and Hemingway and Rourke. "Who's Rourke, Grandpa?" "Jeez, don't anyone teach you anything."

Still, when he talked about education, he most often talked about his fourth-grade teacher, and some of the things she taught him filtered down to me.

Sometimes on Sunday, my grandfather and I would get dressed up and he would wear a cap and I would get out of wearing a fedora because I said I forgot it, and we would take the subway into Manhattan and go to The Metropolitan Museum of Art. It didn't matter what exhibition was there at the time, we were interested in the permanent collection. We would climb the stairs and turn right and spend most of our time with paintings from the Renaissance to 1900, but mostly he liked the nineteenth century. His favorite painting was Rosa Bonheur's *Horse Fair*. When he reached it, he would take a step or two back and clasp his hands and stare at it for a few minutes while I wandered on. *Horse Fair* is exactly that, though a little on the wild side, with big, muscular horses almost charging out of the frame. They come at the viewer in a wave, and my grandfather liked to stand there and get washed in it. His fourth-grade teacher had first showed him that picture and told him about artists in France and other parts, and I understood the picture was a key to the world for him. So, when he was looking at it, I never said anything, and left him alone until he was finished.

Then we would move on. His second favorite picture, and probably his favorite artist, was *Gulf Stream* by Winslow Homer.

"That nigguh ain't got nothin'," my grandfather would say about the fellow in the boat in the picture. "There's a squall coming and the sharks are about ready to get him, and his mast is busted, but that Homer, he left the nigguh some sugarcane on the deck, and way off at the horizon, there's a schooner."

One of the times when we were at the Metropolitan and we had finished with the paintings, we went down to the library in the basement and bought a book on Homer. When we got it home, we showed it to my grandmother, and my grandfather and

I looked at *Gulf Stream* all over again and we talked about other pictures, like *Crack the Whip,* which got him going again about the South, and some pictures about the Caribbean, which got him going again about sailing, and a picture called *Prisoners from the Front,* which got him going again about the Civil War.

In *Prisoners from the Front,* three Confederate prisoners, their guns thrown to the ground, are standing in front of a Union officer. They are in a field, and behind them, there are some Union soldiers keeping guard, and farther behind, more Union soldiers, cavalry soldiers, who look as if they are waiting to mount their horses. Of the three Confederates, to the far left, there is a youngish rube-looking fellow, then moving right, an old man with a white beard and his hands folded, and at the center of the picture, a red-haired Rebel, with hair down to his shoulders and boots to his knees, staring into the eyes of the Yankee officer.

"The old man, he's pious and meek, but that red-haired guy, he's an arrogant son-of-a-bitch," my grandfather said.

Later, when I grew my hair down to my shoulders and my grandfather would shake his head and say he would "just as soon shoot me," I showed him *Prisoners from the Front* again. My grandfather said the same thing and laughed, "Yeah, he's an arrogant son-of-a-bitch, isn't he?"

XLI

"HELLO, the coffee is ready."

I pulled the side of my hammock down and, through the DDT-powdered door of the hut where we had stopped, watched the sun rise, a violet lid of clouds lifting for a peach-colored sky.

I downed my coffee fast and went outside to avoid Glück's chatter, which was worst after he had a night's rest.

"He's dangerous in the morning," Tano said.

The captain of the *Walma* came up and waved for Glück to walk with him down by the river. When Glück came back, he said the captain wanted a thousand cruzeiros for taking us.

"That price is bullshit, Kurt."

He shook his head. "What I do?"

After cornmeal mush, we told him.

"We think you should go back and talk to the captain. Offer five hundred cruzeiros."

I thought it might be better to go along until we were dropped off, then figure how much we owed, but Tano said we should figure things first.

"In South America, you settle on price first, or later there's a big stink."

To some extent, the captain already had passed up that rule by earlier saying, "We'll fix later," but now I thought Tano was right.

Glück went back and offered five hundred. Captain said he had spent a thousand in gas, but Glück countered we had made many stops. Captain said six hundred cruzeiros and Glück agreed, at least that was what he told us.

When Glück had settled, he bounded up to us, smiling like he had done right. I was at first silent because I was still pissed at his original acceptance, then Tano said, "You did good. That's twelve bucks," and persuaded by that, I chimed in.

We loaded up, tied on to the *Walma,* and left at 8:30, an hour and a half past the appointed time, but "makes nuhzing."

Two hours later, we broke down in the middle of the Rio Negro. Tano had seen smoke coughing out of the chimney, and the bilge pump stopped spitting out the river. In ten minutes, the engine died. We had been talking about making it with the *Walma* all the way to Barcelos, but now, adrift, the wind blew us west, backwards, and the shore was a kilometer to either side.

Glück whistled "The Daring Young Man on the Flying Trapeze." If anything had served as the refrain or chorus for the trip, it probably was that tune. Maybe because Glück whistled it so much, I thought there must be more significance to it, something that was eluding me. Oracles could be speaking and we were missing it. Then again, that could be one delusion on another. Still, I went looking. Glück was lying behind me, his back resting against the engine, his feet up against the side, his skipper's cap on, and his eyes masked with aviation goggles; the captain of the *Walma* was yelling at his boy in the engine room; Tano was smoking a cigarette and staring at them; the wind was pushing us back, and waves were lapping against the side of the boat and keeping time for the Daring Young Man. It was one of those William Carlos Williams red wheelbarrow moments when everything vibrates, yet I was listening and looking, but feeling like I was missing something.

The deckhand pumped water out of the bilge for forty minutes, then got the engine to sputter to a start and cough itself up to a semiroar before it cleared out its clogged throat and droned into an off-key howl. He climbed up on the deck, gave us a thumbs-up sign, and we were cruising again, ignoring the wind and the waves and looking at the distant shore in terms of minutes.

As on the way up, the Rio Negro was big sky country, Texas over the Everglades. Tano and I had thought we would hate being back on it, retracing steps, but, instead, it felt like home. Maybe that was because the Padauiri, with the jungle practically at our ears, was getting to us, even if we hadn't talked about it. In contrast, the openness of the Rio Negro, with us being dragged carriage-style, was heady, daydreamy stuff. So, as long as we were moving and the jungle was half a river away from us, I thought about other, smaller jungles.

When I was fifteen or sixteen my grandfather bought me a gun. "How come your old man never got you a gun?" he said. "I grew up with guns. Jeezus, sometimes I don't know what's wrong with that family of yours."

Perhaps as an answer, my father made sure I took a safety course with the state before I got my hunting license. The last day of the course, after I took an exam, the eight or nine of us who were in the class went to a trap and skeet range, where, because it was late in the day, we were told we only had enough time to take two shots apiece. It was the first time I shot my new gun, a Winchester 12-gauge pump my father kept triple-locked at home.

I loaded it like I was handling my mother's china, gently sliding the shells into the magazine and sweating while I squeezed the gun and made sure it stayed pointed to the ground, the way my instructor had said. When I was ready, I leaned forward to keep from getting knocked over by the recoil, the way I had read you were supposed to, pressed the butt against my cheek, yelled "Pull," the way I had heard you were supposed to, swung the barrel out in the direction of the pigeon, slapped the trigger, and flinched at the *kaboom*, which did nothing else as the clay pigeon floated gently to the ground.

"Lower," my instructor said. How he made that judgment, I couldn't understand. My ears were ringing and though I still was leaning forward, my shoulder hurt from the kick, but I lined up again, tightened my muscles and yelled, "Pull," through my teeth, and when the pigeon was forty yards in the sky, I blew it to smithereens. So I knew I was ready.

One Saturday that fall, I went hunting with Lurch, my friend who lived down the block and got his name because of his resemblance to the butler in television's "Addam's Family," and his brother Steve and one of Steve's friends, Sandy Mantone. Sandy Mantone was shaped like a gorilla and was a star football player and wrestler, though I first knew who he was through baseball. Two springs before, I had graduated into the Little League's Major League, which was made up of players too old for Little League, but too young for Pony League. I had spent one year in Little League, but it wasn't enough to prepare me for the majors, where there were players like Sandy Mantone.

Baseball had been an education for me. When I was in Florida, at St. Theresa's, where Sister Margaret Mary was, lunch hours were split into ten minutes for eating and socializing and fifty minutes for baseball. The eating and socializing meant eating your lunch in three minutes and then in the next seven minutes, trying to get the girls to throw Dixie cups at you, a game in which I had achieved a limited success. Then, after the ten minutes were up, we joined other classes and broke up into baseball teams. I always was the the captain of one team, and set up the batting order so I would bat clean-up and the fielding positions so I would play third base, but my role actually was bigger. I was one of the unofficial commissioners of school sports there, deciding where the bases were placed, how far were the invisible fences, who batted first and last, what names the teams could have, and whether the girls were allowed to play (never). I also was instrumental in making the decision about what week in the year we switched from football to baseball. Those things were supposed to be decided by a committee of minds, but shortly after I arrived at the school, I won a miniature G.E. College Bowl–type tournament run by Sister Margaret Mary and staged over a month-long period. To win, I edged out Paul Mozak, who I thought was an egghead, though for sure, he was smart. I once asked him how come he was so smart, and he told me that every night he read from the dictionary and the encyclopedia, which even then, I thought was the stupidest thing I ever had heard. Still, near the end of the month of college bowling, we were neck and neck and it wasn't until I got the question about the lengths of the large and small intestines that I got ahead of him for good and won a one-pound bar of chocolate Sister Margaret Mary said came direct from Ireland.

Later, at the end of the school year, Sister Margaret Mary gave me a copy of *Huckleberry Finn*, which she engraved in gold English script and which has stuck with me ever since.

It was partially because of those victories I became the influential voice on the sports commission, but back then, I liked to think I ran the sports commission because I could hit the ball farther and catch better than anyone else.

I made sports decisions for a year, then moved on a grade, out of Sister Margaret Mary's class into Mr. Simm's. Mr. Simms liked sports and taught me something about wind. He would put a finger in his mouth, hold it in the air, and whichever side of his finger was colder, he would say that was the side the wind blew from, and during football season, the team that kicked off, got the wind at their back. Mr. Simms also knew how things were organized during lunch and sometimes he came out and played. He seemed to enjoy ball, and when spring arrived, he announced he had arranged for the school to play an exhibition game with another Catholic school down the coast. Everyone wanted to be on the team, even the guys who never played at lunch, so Mr. Simms said that one day after school he would hold tryouts.

I never doubted I had third base locked, but I went to the tryouts anyway and found that there were three or four guys vying for every position except pitcher, catcher, and right field, all the bush spots. We all got a chance at the plate, and I hit the ball solid a few times, then we went out to our respective positions for fielding trials. When it was my turn, Mr. Simms hit me a ground ball, to my right, near the bag. I backhanded it, then turning around, planted my right foot and fired across the diamond, making sure I didn't skim the pitcher's head. I didn't. The ball went twenty feet over everyone.

I knew back then that if there was one flaw in my play, it was my arm. I was wild. Although sometimes I could bullet it right to first base, there were many times I sent the ball in a fan of other directions. None of that bothered me too much, though, as I'd figured I had made a great stop on the ball anyway, keeping it from going down the line for extra bases or through the hole and into what always was a porous outfield. Still, because of my wildness, a sometimes great stop didn't mean much to the batter who made it to second on the "wild throw." If it wasn't for the ruling "wild throw," which I pushed on the commission, some-one could circle the bases by the time the ball was retrieved. In-stead, when you yelled "wild throw," it meant the batter could advance only one base.

At the tryouts, after I sent the ball over everyone's head, Mr. Simms said, "Get it down." He hit me another, a one-hop shot to my left, which I stabbed, then that time, sliding my right leg back around me in a half circle and anchoring with my left, I threw sidearm and the ball went sideways, out to right field. I was shook. I shook my head and then my arm and walked back to my position and pounded my glove and Mr. Simms said, "OK, ready?" and I nodded and he hit a pop-up over my head, forty feet into left field. When he hit it and I saw it go over my head, I just turned and took a half step, then watched as it floated out toward the guys waiting for fly balls. Then it dropped. I turned back to-ward the plate and started to crouch into position, but Mr. Simms said, "OK. Next," meaning I should get off the field, which really shook me. I called in, "Was I supposed to get that?" but he didn't answer me, just said, "Next," again, and I walked off the field and tucked my glove under my arm and stood beside some guys from my class who didn't say anything.

That night, I told my father about the pop fly and he said, "You always try for the ball. No matter where it is, you always try." I felt terrible and said to him, "But it was way out in left field," he said, "It's a hustling game. You always try."

Next morning, Mr. Simms posted the list of names of who would be on the exhibition team. My name wasn't on it. I saw the list in the morning and went back twice before the bell rang, then at lunch time, I looked again, but it hadn't been added. I spent most of the day feeling sick. Guys in my class came up to me and said, "I can't believe it," or "He must be crazy," and the girls said, "How could he not pick you?" or "It's got to be a mis-take, he'll add you," but it wasn't and he didn't

The team got to have special practices during school hours, which made me even sicker—and then the next week, my class

330

and the sixth-graders rode with the guys in the team on a bus, south, to the other Saint-something-or-other. I brought my mitt along and Kathy Morton sat in the seat behind me, and when she asked, I told her I'd taken the mitt "in case someone needs to borrow it."

I sat behind the bench, but down away from Mr. Simms, and watched our team fall behind, then in the late innings, rally and get close. I hadn't eaten breakfast, and I threw my lunch away, and even though I kept walking to a fountain to drink water, I couldn't make myself stop feeling like I was going to puke, or if that wasn't happening, keep my throat from knotting. When the game reached the last inning, we were two runs behind, with two out and two men on, and a chunky blond guy (whose name I don't remember, but I do remember he could swing the bat) was up at the plate. When he got up Mr. Simms turned, looked over at me, and said, "Grab a bat and get in the batter's box. You'll be up next," but before I even could take a step, the blond kid swung at the first pitch and lined out to shortstop and the game was over. So I never got the chance I wanted, which was somehow to show I never again would not hustle after a fly ball I knew I couldn't reach.

When we moved north, the baseball shadows followed me.

I played for a team called the Cubs in a league where fast-balls were fastballs, something I was unprepared for, so for much of the time, I rode the bench. One game, though, only nine guys showed, and I got my break. Buddy, the coach, put me in left field; he stuck someone worse than me in right, and it was from left field I got to know Sandy Mantone, Steve Cook's friend, the one Steve took hunting with me and Lurch.

Sandy Mantone played for the other team and had a blister-ing game that day, hitting a homer, a triple, and a single before the sixth inning, when he hit a high fly to me in left. At first I charged in, it looked like it might fall between me and the infield, but it kept going and I had to spin around and race for the fence. That happened in a second or two. I got close enough to the ball that I leaped and just touched it with the webbing of my glove, but it skipped off and onto the ground. By the time I got up and threw it in, Sandy Mantone had rounded second, but at least my throw was good, and he held up.

331

At the end of the inning, sitting on the bench, I overheard two old guys shouting in each other's hearing aids in the seats behind the dugout.

"Do you think it was a hit and they'll say Mantone went four for four and hit for the circuit."

"Naah, the kid didn't know what he was doing out there. It was an error. He misjudged it."

"Even so, they'll give Mantone four for four, even if the kid didn't know what he was doing."

They did and there were headlines in the local sports pages about Mantone's four hits, but I didn't care much about that, I just kept hearing those two old guys talking about me and how I had muffed it.

When I heard Sandy Mantone was coming hunting with Lurch, Steve, and me, I thought about the cheap hit I had given him, but that was only for a moment, then I didn't think about it anymore. I was two years older.

I got up that morning at four o'clock. It was the earliest I had got up in my life, but I thought it was important because I knew for sure I would get something that day. It was still dark, just before the false dawn. Nothing else seemed to be alive. It was easy to hear echoes, and since nothing else was moving, it was an easy time to take myself too seriously. I was doing that when I was putting on my long johns and triple pair of socks and two layers of shirts and a sweater and my vest with the shell loops and the bright orange back, I was taking myself too seriously and in the wrong way, thinking the day might end up with me and a couple pheasants in my hand and getting patted on the back by Lurch, like the way I would have read it in a story in one of those anthologies in English class.

I made oatmeal for myself (my grandfather had said, "What can make a plow horse plow for a day oughta be good enough for a man"), put my gun in my case, and walked down to Lurch's house, where the lights were on. I didn't knock, but waited by the car. Around 4:30, Steve came out and said, "Hey, the Polack's out here," a name no one else called me, but it got me to forget about taking myself too seriously. Steve took my gun and put it in the trunk and I helped him load things, which he did without taking a swing or two at me, which I knew meant he knew I was going to have a loaded gun in my hands that day.

When Lurch came out he said, "Hey," and laughed, meaning it was going to be funny with all of us carrying guns together in the woods. Then we all got in the car and went and picked up Sandy Mantone and headed for the Great Swamp. No one talked much. With Steve and Lurch, I figured the silence was because they were thinking about what they were going to kill, and with Sandy Mantone, it was because he said he had been out late the night before and only got a couple of hours' sleep. With me, it was because I was hoping I would be a good shot. I was going over things in my head, like leaning into the shot, squeezing the trigger, and laying my gun down when I climbed over a fence. I had been out in the swamp a few times before, but each time came home with wet boots and nothing in my game pouch. Actually, I never had seen any game when I went hunting. I had read stories in *Field and Stream* about how birds, like pheasant and quail, heard hunters coming and would run away without your ever seeing them. The guys who wrote those stories said the way to deal with birds that hid in the bushes and ran along the ground was to stop for a moment and make the bird think you had spotted him, even if you hadn't spotted him. Then, when you got him scared, you should make a sound by blowing hard through your nearly closed mouth and letting your tongue flap. That made a sound like air escaping from a balloon. To the bird, it was supposed to sound like other wings flapping, as if other birds were escaping. The tactic was supposed to frighten the bird you had cornered and make him take to the air. The three or four times I had been out hunting before, mostly by myself, I walked around in the woods cracking branches, kicking up leaves, and thinking about how all the pheasant and quail were running along the ground, hiding. I would walk ten or fifteen yards, stop for a second or two, and make the *pudadadadaaa* sound real fast, then wait for the birds to flush, but they never did. I spent hours doing that and nothing ever happened, except my mouth got dry.

The last time out, I switched tactics and gave up on the *pudadadadaaing*. Instead, I crept as quietly as I could through the woods, thinking about when I was younger and had read army books that suggested the quietest way to get through an area was hands-and-knees on the ground, with one hand and one knee moving together, then the other, each side always together so you minimized the noise. That didn't do any good, either. It was too wet to go crawling through the swamps.

I tried walking quietly, then staking myself out under a tree or in some bushes, but I would stay there only until my feet got cold before I had to start walking and again trying the *pudada-daaaa*.

All that was going through my head when we stopped and Steve pulled the car up beside a ditch. As we got out and loaded up, the sky began to turn from black to gray.

Steve and Sandy Mantone said they would take one side of the road and Lurch and I would take the other, which made me think about Steve not hitting me that morning, but then I stopped thinking about that the moment we started walking.

I nodded and headed my way, to the left. I felt for my compass, looked down at my day-glo orange vest, and thought with Lurch close by, I had better not try any of the *pudadadaa*.

I walked for hours. In the fall and winter, the Great Swamp was as dead as any place I knew, and that day, with about four inches of old snow on the ground, it was dead dead. The sun never came out and in the trees and the muck and the briars, it never got any brighter than the way it was a half hour after sunrise, a kind of speckled gray, like snow mud, not like the snow on the ground, but the stuff on the side of the road the plows throw up, snow that was more dead-fish–colored slush. I didn't see anything move in that light, except a couple of times I ran across Lurch and we talked for a minute and I wished I had a cigar, like the ones we used to smoke when we went fishing together.

Late in the morning, when I knew it was near the time we said we would meet back at the car, I heard something move in the trees. I stopped and heard a bird sing. When I looked up and saw it, I paused for a moment and saw how small it was, about the size of a sparrow, and I wondered why it was there all alone and singing, but then I thought about all that silence that day and all the other days that had been silent, and how the bird was the only thing besides Lurch I had seen alive. Then without thinking anymore, I pointed my gun and shot it down. It hit a branch once, but then fell straight to a patch of snow. When I walked up, it still was breathing, but it had a bright red blotch on its breast. I didn't know what kind of bird it was, but I can see it clearly now and think it was a phoebe. When I looked at him, his chest heaved like his lungs or his heart was going crazy and I wanted to lift him up and put him back up in the tree and tell him to sing again, but I knew it could not be erased and I knew I had done one of the most awful things I had ever done.

When Lurch asked me, I said I just had shot my gun to see if it worked. We walked to the road where Steve was waiting, but no Sandy Mantone.

"He said if he got lost, he'd shoot three times in the air," Steve said.

We waited for what seemed forever, with me thinking about how hard that bird's heart was pounding and how bright its blood was, then me, feeling sick, knowing I couldn't change things.

At some point, we heard the three shots, and every two or three minutes, three shots more until Steve found him. When he got to the road, he laughed and took three shots more, but I didn't laugh.

On the way home, just after we crossed a tiny bridge and took a bend, a pheasant raced across the road. Steve stepped on the gas pedal and tried to run over the bird, but it was too fast and Steve pulled off and ran back to the trunk. I wished I could trip him, but it didn't matter, the bird was way too quick. He got away on his own, and at least for that, I was glad.

XLII

" . . . AT this boat," Tano said. "What a mess."

"What?" I wasn't sure how much Tano had been talking, I hadn't been paying attention to much of anything, though I had noticed that houses on islands in the middle of the river were at the edge of black water. High water meant riverboats could take shortcuts through channels and miss the main drags where, after the *Walma* would leave us off, we hoped to catch a hitch to Barcelos. Sometime during my thinking about baseball and the hunting business, I remembered Glück said that with the high water, we could wait a week or two without seeing a boat. "Then, if we try to paddle against the wind on the Negro, we go nowhere."

"What'd you say about the boat?" I asked Tano again.

"I said, look at it, camera, sunglass case, short pants, knives, shoes, everything scattered everywhere like someone emptied the inside of a giant pocket..." Then he paused and thought. "Kind of like that time on the trip to Montana, the way everything looked inside your bug. Man, the two of us, cramped together, burstin' with energy. The seams of that car must've been ready to split."

All of that was an invitation to talk, kind of like when you

336

are at the beach and have had enough of staring or closing your eyes and trying to sleep. I had finished with my daydreams and was just as happy to switch gears.

The river swelled to the size of a sea, a mirror with small configurations of ripples, and we broke the glass.

"Yeah, that was a good trip. One of the few. Maybe the only one we didn't end up screwed."

"That's because the son-of-a-bitch started so badly," Tano said.

"If we had any sense, we should have turned back immediately."

"Why? Shit, man, it worked out great."

"Still, we should have known better and turned right around. We've missed signs at the beginning of enough bad trips. Same thing—only on the Montana trip, we lucked out."

What we lucked out about was my car breaking down in the California Sierras, and us spending the night, outside, fixing it in the middle of a blizzard.

It was spring 1979 and I had heard a buzzing sound in my engine as we were leaving town, when we crossed the Bay Bridge. Actually, I had heard it on and off days earlier, but wishing it away, and playing my radio loud, I had grown to ignore it. Somewhere in the hills north of Oakland and Berkeley, Tano heard it.

"What's that?"

It sounded like a cat purring, only more malevolent, a word I only thought and didn't say.

"I think it's the generator. It's been going like that a couple of weeks. I don't know what's wrong with it. The car still runs," an analysis fundamental to my mechanics logic, the kind of stuff that would have made me an out-of-touch bad guy in *Zen and the Art of Motorcycle Maintenance.* The way I looked at it back then, if it runs, keep going and try not to pay too much attention to it until it actually forces a breakdown. Maybe it will go away.

It didn't. We had started late that day and near midnight and near Truckee, California, the generator light went on. We smelled smoke, then ground to a halt. It was maybe twenty minutes after it had started snowing. We had been worried about making it through the mountains, and if we didn't, about where we would stay. We were on a broken and retied shoestring budget with no room for the comfort of paying someone for a room.

We took deep breaths, like bagpipes readying to wail.

"Well."

"Well."

A tow truck for the highway patrol came in a half hour and told us he thought our generator was blown. He was a youngish guy, with a beard and a watchman's cap, and he understood our predicament.

"I could tow you down," he said, "but if you want to save some bread, shift it into neutral, glide down this hill, and turn at the off-ramp. There's a service station right at the end of it, but they close at midnight, which is soon. See what they can do for you. Good luck."

They couldn't do much, other than sell us a rebuilt generator, the right size, though, for which I am still grateful. Then they told us to roll back on the street.

"Sorry," the bossman said, "but you can't work here and we're leaving and can't lend you tools. Insurance and all, you know?"

He looked outside and must have felt sorry for us. Snow was coming down hard enough so that we could barely see the gas pumps.

"Well, if you guys are going out there and spend the night dickering with that, want some coffee?"

By 2 A.M., after pulling, prying, and stripping assorted bolt heads and other metal shapes, we got the old generator out. Tano was under the car, doing most of the work, and I was crouched with a box of matches beside the right rear tire, reading *Idiot's Guide to Volkswagen Repair.* We probably should have got the generator out in fifteen or twenty minutes, but up to that point, I barely knew what a generator was, and Tano's, mechanical experience had been developed on a '62 Chevy truck and an old Comet he called Vomit. I was thankful for his tutelage, though; it was a new side of him I never would have predicted.

"Yeah," he said, "after a while, I just figured if you're gonna live on the outside, you better learn how to start fixing things."

Those generally were new ideas to me, and hearing him talk like that, in a detached way (all I could see were his legs, which

338

were snow covered. The rest of him was under the car; his voice sounded like it came up through the carburetor), would have been something like seeing Jack Kerouac do an American Express card commercial, "I never leave home without it."

I had learned how to change my oil, adjust my valves, and do a bit of a tune-up, but beyond that, mechanics was the magic of fuel, metal, and diagrams, something I had grown accustomed to taking on faith.

"Now, what does it say?" Tano asked.

"What?"

"What's the next step?"

"Hold on, I got to light a match." I did and read until the match burned my fingers. "It says, 'Put the vise grip on the shaft and now turn clockwise, until the nut doesn't move when you bang it a good one. It only needs forty-five foot-pounds, so don't get too tough with it.' "

"Ah, shit."

"What's the matter?"

"I'm tearing the hell out of my knuckles, though I'm probably doing worse that that, 'cause I can't feel much anymore. My hands are cold.... OK, give me that ratchet again... Man, I need a breather. Why don't you try pounding for a while?"

"OK."

That went on for most of the night. I relieved Tano once in a while, but mostly he did the work, I did the reading. "You're the one with the education," he would say, but he would do the figuring between the reading and most of the pounding, turning. A few inches of snow piled on us, the car, and the manual, and maybe because of my education, one of my jobs was to keep things brushed clean.

Near dawn, we finished. I got in the car and turned the key and the generator light went on and the car started up and then the generator light went off.

"God damn, it works." It had taken us four or five times shop time, but that didn't matter, and to celebrate, we went in and joined the bossman, who had returned to work. We had some coffee and, with the bossman's OK slept a few hours on vinyl stools beside the vending machines.

Although I had my doubts at the time, after our generator

job, we decided to keep going, a move, we figured, that would transform our jaunt into an adventure.

"We did good this time," Tano said. "Don't worry. Those forces started coming at us, but we knocked them out in the first round. Everything else is going to be cake."

The forces stayed out of our way and we got into Ketchum, Idaho, by midmorning the next day (we had rolled our sleeping bags out and slept by the side of the road during the night), where we ate sprouts on some kind of dark bread with something else mushed on it, and talked about how good Ernest Hemingway's granddaughters looked in the movies.

That night, we stopped at a café near the Salmon River where Tano flirted with a waitress who was ten or fifteen years older than he, and said something about wanting to ask her to go dancing with him. I convinced him we only had a few more hours to Missoula, "and if we don't leave now, you'll end up here all night."

Missoula was where Chris Kronberg, and old friend of mine, lived, and visiting him was the expressed purpose of the trip. For the next week or so, I visited Chris and went skiing and camped in Yellowstone, while Tano took my car and drove off into the mountains, where he found a cave and built fires, cooked rice, smoked cigarettes, and wrapped himself in his gondora. When I came out from the snow in Yellowstone, Tano was at the side of the road, waiting, just how we had planned, which though it shouldn't have surprised me, did. I knew he would be there sooner or later, but it was just that he was punctual, too. That was almost as much of a surprise as his mechanical skills.

When we left Montana, we drove through Nuclear Regulatory Commission (or whoever it is that controls the bombs) land in southern Idaho, a vast stretch of desert peppered with tumbleweed and surrounded by chain link, with me stopping every hundred miles or so to make a telephone call to an old girl friend who I had heard was living in Boise.

At each stop, the phone rang about a dozen times before I hung up, with me getting nervous each time I dialed, then feeling relieved when it was apparent no one was there.

"You sure you want to do this?" Tano asked.

"I don't know."

340

Ex's usually have wanted about as much to do with me after things became "ex" as a cat does with water after falling into a lake. Usually, I have been accused of being the cause for near drowning, a subject I have generally avoided in this story, although to some extent, it plays a part, as I walk around with a number of accusations hanging around my neck.

So why I wanted to go to a place where I surely would only find trouble, I don't know. Part of it is I have a way of dragging around my past, a stranglehold on identity, though I think a major factor that time in Idaho was the landscape. The desert, except for those nuclear peoples' fences, was wide open and wind torn. Once or twice we stopped, took a piss and a walk, and the winds felt like they would pick me up as if I were a paper cup and send me to the Atlantic.

"This is my kind of country," Tano said, his clothes barely hanging on him and his voice about three feet east of his mouth. "I like the space."

I wanted to say I did, too, but that wasn't exactly right. I liked blowing through, but I eventually wanted to get to a port. I fill out with the wind in places like that, with a great sense of size, both of myself and what's around me, but I can't always see the wind inside. That's both good and bad. It leaves me with a great sense of invisible forces, then sometimes with a sense of ache, all that because it would get me thinking I had roots that never would take.

So to combat those sorts of things, and because I was dragging blankets of memories around, and because of the ache, but maybe most of all, just because I was curious, I tried making the calls.

"You're crazy," Tano would say each time we stopped at another phone booth, to which I would answer, "I know it," and still do it.

I tried most of the pay phones between Idaho Falls and Boise. I suppose that made them accomplices with the landscape, though by the time we reached the capital and we figured our way through one-way streets and around the capitol building, I tried one more time, without luck, and gave up.

"Well, that's over with," I said.

"Good," Tano said. "Now, let's get stoned."

We headed south and had dinner at a velvet art Mexican/ Chinese restaurant. Later that night, we put our bags down on a cliff off the side of the freeway and got stoned and watched shooting stars until I fell asleep.

After a few hours, Tano shook me awake.

"Man, I've been lying here for what seems the longest time, watching this glowing thing, like a spaceship or something, move across the sky. I was too stoned to turn and say something to try and wake you. I thought it might go away."

"Where is it now?"

"Gone."

"Right . . ."

Next morning, we crossed into Oregon and stopped for breakfast at the first café we saw, but before I got to putting my powdered non-dairy creamer into my cup of swill, two cops walked up to the front of the café and stared at my car. I was parked, as Tano would say, a spit from the window. They walked around the car and stared at the license plate, then went over to the passenger side and looked at the dashboard, beneath which, in the glove compartment, Tano had stashed a film cannister of hashish.

For unknown reasons, maybe it was being out of Idaho, we both felt calm, and I turned to Tano in between a scoop of hash-browns and margarine-painted toast, and said, "I think we're gonna get busted."

"Maybe."

A minute later, the cops swung through the café doors and, like dead-sure bloodhounds, walked right up to us, like they had been waiting for weeks for just this opportunity. I took a deep gulp of air or undercooked fried egg. I am not sure which, but either the air or the eggs or the cops made me gag.

"Your car, fellas?"

"Yep," I said, trying to talk while choking.

"You know, you're in a loading zone out there?"

"No, didn't notice."

"Well, you should move it."

If I got up any faster, I would have taken the world record for the standing high jump.

"I'll get it right away."

342

"Naw, that's OK" the older of the two said. "Just move it after you're finished breakfast."

"Will do."

"Thanks."

They walked to the back of the café and ordered something similar to what we had, though we didn't stay long enough to see them finish.

"I can't believe it," I said. "I thought it was bust time."

"That's what fixin' the generator will do for you," Tano said.

Eastern Oregon is mostly high plains desert on the leeward side of the northwestern rain forests. I had driven through once before, a few years earlier, on a trip to a graduate school in Eugene. I got there late at night and bartered with an East Indian family for a motel room that smelled of disinfectant and had the shadow of one-night stands crisscrossing it. The next day, I spent an hour and a half at an orientation put on by my department members at school, and at a coffee break, I asked one of the second-year students where the Exit was, which I immediately passed through and kept going.

Seeing Oregon a second time around made me feel good, something like seeing a blind date you managed to pawn off on someone else.

"Damn, this country's beautiful," Tano said.

"I know it."

We took back roads and in the middle of the afternoon ran into a cattle drive, going in the opposite direction. There were about five hundred head, driven by a few guys with yellow slickers and chaps. When they finally made their way around us, we waved at the guys bringing up the rear, with Tano and me not having to say anything to each other. Driving away, I looked in my mirror and saw a coyote cross the road between us and the herd. I have seen plenty of coyotes since, but that was my first and something I will never forget. He was a howl come alive as he slipped behind that herd and across the road in a breeze that even the sunlight couldn't catch.

"Coyotes are the best," Tano said. "They're so wily and smart. Them and wolves."

A couple of Christmases later, I gave Tano an old painting of a wolf I found in an antique shop. The wolf was standing, with frost coming out of his mouth, on a snow-covered hill above a town, and you weren't sure if he was considering going down, leaving, or just thinking about the kind of beast who lives in places like that.

"Yeah," Tano said. "Them and wolves."

A few bends down, we stopped beside an airplane with a damaged wing that was parked beside the road and next to a middle-of-nowhere Mom and Pop hamburger stand. Mom and Pop had a big sign outside, "We Are Not a MacDonald's," a distinction that was redundant as there didn't seem to be another building for miles. Next to that, they had another sign.

30 feet from water
60 miles from town
2 feet from heaven

"My kind of place," Tano said. "Let's go in."

Mom and Pop did run the place, and fixed us a burger that reemphasized their sign. There was enough beef on it to make a meat loaf.

In between fixing, they told us a story about the plane crash-landing two days before, and also told us how they hated fast-food chains. Then they told us about how they had been there since the fifties, serving ice-cold beers and the same two-handed burgers. Once, while they were talking, Pop put his hand on Mom's and held it for a while, something Tano noticed and brought up again when we were on the river.

"You know," Tano said, "those two gave me hope."

We came out of Oregon and the northern Sierras that night and into California, a descent that unnerved us. We had gone through a mountain pass and saw a sign that said the nearest town was something like twenty-two miles or so, but it took what felt like hours to get down. We didn't have a watch and the car radio wasn't working, along with one of our headlights, and with having no other cars on the road, the drop seemed endless, made more so by each of us asking were we sure we read twenty-two miles on the sign. We would ask that every five or ten minutes, or what we guessed were five or ten minutes.

"Man, whatever it is, we've been going down an awful long time," Tano said. We kept going and we kept going, never passing

344

anyone. It was like we were in a relativity experiment with the ruler and clock getting longer. Still, we kept going down, with the dashboard lights making Tano's face glow like a ghost, and me getting the pyschological bends in reverse.

Eventually, gravity and mechanics and some semblance of intellect did what they were supposed to do and we got to the bottom of those mountains, but it was another hour or two before we found an empty parking lot in a county park were we pulled over and slept.

In the morning, we had a brunch of granola and powdered milk on a curb, a breakfast that provided creative energy we channeled into inventing the "Winter Wonderland" travel anthem "It's a doggy, dog's world..." we sang the first night in Manaus.

We sang about doggies the rest of the way home, our singing a melodic honking that only got louder the more we sang. By then, the car was a cross between a Dempster Dumpster and a tight, two-man space capsule, with clothing, spoons, wrappers from dried food, empty cans and bottles piled up shoulder high into a form-fitted garbage console, so maybe I was wrong about honking geese. The only winged creatures who could have stood those quarters, I thought, would be sea gulls or vultures, and since we were a hundred miles inland, that cut the possibility to one.

"No, you got it wrong," Tano said. "Rats."

XLIII

THE boat was something like the rat car, with a difference. The bow, where we sprawled, was a tangle of gear and junk, but the stern, where Glück didn't move all day, was immaculate, spiffy. To reemphasize the point, Glück continuously referred to Tano and me as the shitter and pisser. Tano got the former name because of the gases he produced, and I got the other because water took little time to go through me.

The afternoon passed lazily. I sprawled nude on the middle bench while Tano was across our gear at the bow. I dunked my head to keep cool, drank iodine water (which also fueled Glück's name calling), tried to make cold corn mush that tasted like cough syrup, ate mangoes, and sucked down *Walma* exhaust.

"Life on the big river," Tano said.

The ride went farther than we expected, but also like a super hitch, we waited to be dropped off in the middle of nowhere. That happened at four o-clock, when the *Walma* stopped at a hamlet with a new school. The captain told us many ships would pass where he left us off.

We waved *"até logo,"* tied our boat to a piling, and walking

346

a hundred yards to a small village on a bluff above a bay. Maybe thirty people came down to greet us. A barefoot old man, in a bright blue shirt and tattered trousers ripped into shorts, stepped out, bowed, and introduced himself as Roberto. Glück walked up and spoke to him, and Roberto pointed to a large, open-walled building beside a church. The crowd of mostly women and children parted, and Glück said, "Come on, we can stay in their fiesta hut."

We unloaded our gear in the hall, a long, thatched hut with benches, that was immediately filled by everyone who had parted before us outside, so Tano and I headed out for a swim.

We went a hundred yards upstream, tied on to the limb of a tree, took off our clothes, and dived in.

A couple of weeks earlier, we would have been diving into trees, but now it was high water, black water, and wonderful. I had to hoist myself up, jackknifing out of the water and throwing a leg quickly over the side while the current tried to drag the other leg down under. We soaped and rinsed off a few times before we stood in the middle of the boat and let the river dry off us.

"Two nude, rude boys in the jungle, ten years later," Tano said.

We each rolled a cigarette, mine stuck to my lips, then sat back and got treated to a show. The sky filled with separate skies like paned glass and all were reflected by the black river that stretched for miles.

Roberto had told Glück his village was called Céu Aberto, or Open Heaven, which also might be translated as Open Skies.

The sun set from where we had come and the moon rose in the direction we were going.

"Man, being on the equator, they're just splitting the sky," Tano said.

The sun dropped into clouds while to the north, black thunderheads rolled toward us, dragging a curtain of rain across the jungle. To the northeast, mushroom clouds sucked water from the forest, turning the moisture into a vapor that glowed pink in the sky. In the northwest, golden clouds faceted a corner, and to the east, an outline of more clouds, more skies, more worlds, broke by a wash of fading blue and through it rose the

347

moon. If there was a little less flesh and bone about me, I would have evaporated.

Everything else liquid-base seemed to be in motion—water vaporizing into the sky, then condensing, back to the ground again and down the river, everything moving, changing.

In the afternoon, I had picked up Matthiessen's *The Snow Leopard* again and read descriptions of stark mountains and icy air and crackling snow and wolves, while I was being dragged by a riverboat, with jungle walls breathing steam into the air and the equatorial sun frying us and the *Walma* spraying us with water from her rudder. In *The Snow Leopard*, Matthiessen kept grabbing for meaning, figuring out the ommm of things. For a moment, watching those skies, I had a twinge of that, the Western, Eastern, human compulsion to put it all together, but then I didn't care, it just felt good to be there.

We didn't paddle or talk. I'm not sure if we breathed for a while, as the river carried us east. The Negro wanted to take us farther, but I took a last look at the sun and said, "Let's leave before it leaves us," and we paddled to shore.

In the evening, Roberto joined us. He had a stubbly beard that glistened in the light, and he smiled at Glück's questions. Roberto said many boats cruised by the village, it was a main passage on the river, but there had not been so many since the river had risen. Glück asked him how long to Barcelos by motor, and he said five hours with a big motor and four hours with a small, which didn't make sense, but neither did we question it. I sensed Glück wanted to go on by ourselves, something I was absolutely against.

I waved to Tano to step outside.

"Listen," I said. "We have to lay down the law. We wait for a boat," which was my idea of the law.

"Shit, I know it. We don't even have enough gas to go on."

We were in agreement, though it was one I expected to be tested in the morning when I knew we would have to struggle with Glück.

It was raining when I woke and I stayed in my hammock and listened to Glück ask a female voice for eggs, but she said she had none.

I had slept poorly and felt tired and it took me awhile to get out of the hammock. When I did, Glück asked me what I wanted for breakfast and I said milk rice would be fine. He had the coffee ready and the milk rice was on its way. Then the old woman, Roberto's wife, came in, and Gluck asked her for eggs and so began the South American–gringo *tête-à-tête*.

Glück kept the milk rice going, and in a few minutes Roberto's wife returned with five eggs. I didn't want the eggs, the milk rice would be enough, but Glück asked her how much she wanted for them. She said fifty cruzeiros, an outrageous price, but she had us over the barrel, or actually, we impolitely hung ourselves over it.

"In Manaus," Glück said, "we can get them for three cruzeiros."

She shrugged and said, "OK, three." She said that in a way that was supposed to hide how she was incredulous that we, her guests, were balking at whatever price she asked. They probably were the only eggs in the village, but Glück was angry and arrogant and spoke quickly to her, too quickly for me to understand.

Tano was tying his hammock and though we weren't looking at each other and weren't talking, we carried out a silent conversation that went something like, "These people have been hospitable to us. They do think we have bucks, the way everyone thinks gringos have bucks, but we've put them in an awkward position by asking for the eggs and they answered with the high price."

The woman put the eggs on the table and waved to Glück to take them for nothing. She didn't say it bitterly or sarcastically, but in a completely dispassionate, "Take them," which was the worst way she could have put it.

"I don't like that," Tano said to Glück, who was digging through the food canister. "That's bullshit."

"I give her a tube of toothpaste," Glück said.

Then I jumped in, I don't remember what I said, but it was something about us not being able to take the eggs.

"Makes nuhzing," Glück said. "The people, they always try to take advantage of gringos."

"Well, we don't need the eggs, anyway. You're making milk rice. We have plenty."

"I like them."

"I thought you didn't like food?"

"I like it when I have it, and if I don't have it, I can go without it. I don't have to cry for food."

My arm cocked.

"We didn't cry," I said.

"Look, I've been dealing with these people for forty years." He used the word people like a subspecies. "I know how to handle them."

"You don't treat them with respect, like other human beings."

"Listen, I give them two tubes of toothpaste." He had upped the ante. "That's a lot."

Glück took the five eggs off the table, cracked and fried them. I whispered to Tano to let Glück eat them all, but then I retreated and said it would put a pall on the end of the trip, so I took one egg, just to say forget it. Tano took two, saying Glück would just scarf them down to prove a point, which Glück did do with the remaining two. I was a little pissed at Tano, but also felt self-righteous, so I was the worst of the lot.

We said no more about it, but Glück tried to justify himself the rest of the morning with tales about how people always tried to cheat him and about the good things he had done for the "people." He took a painted paddle one of the men had offered as a gift, then gave the man a shirt of his in return, and told us how good the shirt was, just to prove what a nice guy he was.

Later in the morning, maybe to help us forget what happened earlier, Glück sprang his plan on us.

"Maybe we should paddle down to Barcelos, spend a night in the joongle, do our wash on board," Glück said.

I flared up. "We've already decided to wait for a boat."

Glück said maybe we could stop at a nearby hut on one of the islands, but when he asked Roberto's wife about it, she said no, all boats pass the village and take the bend in the river close to this shore. If we went farther down, we might miss them as they swung back out to catch the main current near the north shore.

We sat and scribbled in our journals and Glück read his music box maker book until the men from the village came back

350

from an island across the bay carrying squealing pigs tied by their ankles and suspended from sticks.

A young boy in his early teens talked with us and said he and his father took sixteen hours to paddle to Barcelos by canoe. Glück leapt on the paddling idea again, and I, just as quickly, leapt to remind everyone about jungle time estimation.

"If he says sixteen hours the way people on the Padauiri do, that means an eight-day trip to Barcelos."

"He's probably the only accurate one we've spoken to," Tano said.

I waved Tano aside.

"Listen, we've been gambling and because we're alive, we'll come back on the winning side." I liked the sound of that, so I kept up with the gambler bit, and judging by the glint in Tano's eye, he liked it too. "As long as we play sure bets. A sure bet is waiting here."

I felt less convinced with that sentence. Already I was feeling antsy. Maybe it was just the expectation of another Glück vs. Tano, or Glück vs. me, or the village, explosion, but the thought, first of paddling, then of maybe getting lost, excited, then restrained me. That was something like being a racehorse and having a jockey take the whip and pull the reins, though at that point, I only told Tano about the reins.

"It's time not to mess with the river anymore. We'll only get slapped down. . . . Who knows what will happen between here and Barcelos, and then how long it will take to catch a boat to Manaus?"

The rest I said only to myself. Let's wait the afternoon, and if we don't catch a ride, I'll spend the time getting used to the idea of going out again with Glück.

"It's eleven thirty," Glück announced. "Eleven hours and thirty minutes," just to be sure we understood.

"We wait another night if no boat?" he asked.

"Might as well," I answered immediately in a tone that meant damn right.

I went down to the sewage, Maytag bay, to do my wash, which was both a statement to Glück that we weren't going to jump in the boat and head downriver to do our wash, and hope that doing something simple and mindless would work its usual trick and help scrub out anxieties of life with the old man.

As I hung my clothes on a metal line behing the church, I heard a humming sound, like a distant bee. Roberto came out of his hut and turned his head south. The motor was a drawn-out *hummmmmmm*, not the familiar *put-put-put* of a boat on the river.

"*Avião*," Roberto said. He pointed across the river, while behind us, women and some children ran out and shouted, "*Avião, avião*," and pointed to the sky.

I picked up a speck moving across white clouds, and again the children went into an uproar about "*Avião*."

Before I left New York I visited my parents and my father gave me a mirror, "Just in case you have to signal a plane." I laughed again about it at Cué Aberto. Who cares? Life was swallowed by the jungle or the river without so much as a belch, thinking about which made me stop laughing and instead got me edgy. My mind was best at that sort of thing, seeing the underside of events. Seeing a plane above the jungle meant you were in the jungle and there was still quite a way before you got out. The moon was full, but the other side was always dark. Some might say, it's the ying-yang of things, but with me, it's nothing so wholesome as ommmm. You're alive because you're not dead. That was what I thought the jungle had been telling me for days, something I had heard from other sources over the years, something I sometimes preferred to ignore, but I seemed to do best when I paid attention.

My antidote, when I feel one side of the equation more strongly than the other, is a kind of mouth-to-mouth resuscitation without the other mouth. Breathe in, breathe out, suck in the plane and the bright sun and the screams of "*Avião*," and blow out the shadows. Something I also had tried on the mosquitoes. Maybe, I thought, I had been living too long in California.

Glück talked again about the shirt he had traded for the paddle, and since kooky thoughts were gurgling inside me, I suggested to Tano that we take a walk.

We went down a path west of the village to a clearing and a couple of old, abandoned huts, where we sat down on steps, a version of stoops, and rolled cigarettes.

"When do you think we'll get a boat to Manaus?" I asked, putting the positive edge on something I wasn't so positive about.

"By seven thirty," he said, so he was doing the same thing.

Strange thoughts drifted into my head, and even stranger, they went unchecked and began patterning themselves into a plan.

"I got an idea," I said, which made me laugh when I said it, because I remembered the beach scene in San Diego where all this Amazon business began. This time, though, I didn't look at him, so I have no idea what his eyes or his face was saying. Whatever was about to work itself into my words wasn't quite stable enough to withstand discouragement.

"Maybe we can have an early supper, get a big pot of coffee going, then paddle out to Barcelos." I was too worried about his reaction even to be shocked that I said it.

"We've been talking about taking shifts, waiting up all night for a boat. Why not just paddle out? We'll almost have a full moon. It could be beautiful. It's supposed to take sixteen hours. We could be there tomorrow."

"Tomorrow" hung in the air only a second or two before he answered.

"That could be all right."

"The only question is getting lost,." I said, putting our plan in the perspective that it was actually Glück's plan, one that we had been telling ourselves would mean disaster. "Still, it's a chance to take fate into our own hands. One last roll of the dice, rather than have the house roll against us."

Tano, and for that matter, I, too, still were suckers for gambler talk.

One of us had the aerial photographs we got lost with on the way up and we unrolled it and plotted a course.

"Look, man, as long as we stay on the southern bank, avoid narrow canals that cut sharp to the south, and always look through a channel until we see wide stretches of the main river on the other side, then, it'll be cake. Just as long as we keep everything out of his and under our control."

With that, of course, Glück came walking down the path.

"OK? You go for it?"

353

"Sounds good."

"All right. Let's tell him."

He went for it, too. "Yes, I think it will be all right," and didn't question why we had changed our minds.

When we settled on everything, I opened my journal and discovered my feather missing. I immediately interpreted the loss as the fates commenting on our plan, but for a while, I kept it to myself.

We celebrated our decisiveness with a swim. When we returned, we talked to Roberto about the river.

"You cannot get lost," he said, the last word triggering me to think about a wad of our money I had stuffed in my pocket, which of course, when I went digging through my pockets, was gone. I ran down to the river to see if I had lost it when we were swimming, but I couldn't find it and when I climbed the steps back to the village, Roberto was standing by our hut and he asked me what I had lost.

"Nada," I said. I didn't want to cause a stir, and if someone found it, good, they could keep it, which was my way of trying to swing the cosmic balance in our favor for the night.

Then, just as I turned to go into our hut, a rainbow split the sky in the direction of Barcelos. I called Tano, and we howled and slapped each other on the back and I told myself I was getting terribly superstitious, but was glad for it.

"Six o'clock," Glück said after the sun dropped from the sky and, the boat loaded, we waved back at Roberto and drifted into the Rio Negro. Tano and I lit cigarettes and let Glück paddle.

"Makes nuhzing," he said.

He had managed to hustle two paddles from the villagers; one he got for his shirt and the other for an ax head, telling us, "We can paddle all the way to Manaus," when he made the trade.

"Feels good to have done this," I said to Tano. Surprisingly, it really did. "Taking the reins back in our own hands."

"You bet."

I felt even better when I found the feather Tano had given me under my seat in the boat.

For a while, we drifted, until we smoked our cigarettes and watched the light begin to fade as the current pulled us into the

354

center of the river. The Rio Negro seemed more like a sea with us going along with it and Glück paddling, until we realized we had drifted into a Little Big Horn of weather.

Black clouds the shape of dinosaurs rose from the western horizon, blotting the last of the light and knotting the sky and jungle in seams of lightning. "What a show!" I said, until Tano said, "Hey, look what's up front."

Two columns of thunderheads, one from the northeast and another from the southeast split the eastern horizon, with a small channel of sky between, where the moon had begun to rise. It's light zigzagged in a narrow line across the river and covered us, leaving the illusion of a path through the storms.

The thunderheads in the east cut off the sky in a pincer movement, squeezing the light off the river, while from behind, the dinosaurs were breathing down our neck as a wall of rain rolled with them.

"Man, if that rain don't plain crush us, we'll drown in it."

Ahead of us, I couldn't see rain, but the ripples of moonlight twisted into white-capped swells.

"Will making nuhzing," Glück said, which was something I wished he had not said.

"Now I know we're in for it," Tano said.

The storms reached us in less time than we could say it, though it only rained lightly at first as we tried to follow the line of moonlight.

Glück tried paddling toward the south shore. It was a mile away and cut off from us by one of the columns of thunderheads.

"Turn out to the middle, Kurt, toward the moon, maybe we'll swing past the rain," I said. Calling it rain was like calling a bull a male cow, which wasn't meant as a taunt, but as a way of trying to quiet things down.

"Man, I can't believe we have to tell him what to do," I said to Tano in a voice that would have been loud enough to hear a fathom below if the thunder wasn't on top of us.

We zigzagged through curtains of showers, but finally were caught from behind by a blue-black cloud that rushed over us— again with only a spray of rain, but it moved so fast it was like being caught in the backdraft of a truck on a highway. The vacuum shoved us deeper into the river, toward a funnel of showers.

355

"We're not going to miss the next one."

Tano and I stripped and packed our clothes in the food cannisters. We already were wet, so I suppose it didn't make much difference about getting wetter. It was more a statement, "If the boat goes down, we're ready to go with it." We clung to the reflected moonlight, cutting deep into it with our paddles. The dinosaurs were almost on top of us. To the southeast, the clouds got to the moon, but we paddled as if we were chasing the last of all light. My arms and shoulders and chest ached, but I kept digging into the river, with my force starting at the balls of my feet, the way you would throw a punch, only it wasn't flailing, but steady, roundhouse rights.

Once I turned and looked at Tano, who lit up in a flash of lightning. His hair blew flat out, while his body kept knifing into the wind like a metronome on a half swing. I laughed when I saw him, laughed as hard as I ever have laughed, and he turned and laughed just as hard. He looked so wild, the noble savage, with the heavens shattering above him and waves coming over the side and him blinking with the lightning and us snapping into the night and the river and the storm. But somehow—maybe it was just because of the feather—we beat it.

We shot for the southern, leeward side of an island, and in about fifteen minutes, made it. We were soaked and the boat was soaked, but we had outraced most of the dinosaurs and in the distance, again, maybe because of the feather, I heard the *put-put-put-put* of a boat.

As we neared shore, we had to make a decision, to go either left, into the middle of the river and the center of the storm, but at least a certain (according to the map) way to Barcelos, or right, around the south side and risk getting lost in dead water, but hope to catch the boat, which sounded like it might be headed in that direction. I told Glück we should hang on to one of the trees that were partially submerged in high water and wait for the boat.

"Yes, I sink so," he shouted between bursts of thunder, a statement that shocked the shit out of both Tano and me, it being the first sensible thing he had said in weeks.

We slid into dark water. Tano reached for a leafless palm and immediately got covered by fire ants, but he hung on, and we waited until we saw the boat with red and green lights, another floating Christmas package, coming puttering near us.

Glück signaled with a flashlight. For a long minute or two, it wasn't answered, but then the boat engine cut off, and we drifted toward each other.

"We ask the captain the price now, rather than fix in Barcelos," Glück said, assuming we would get the ride, but when we pulled up, the captain said, yes, we could have a ride, but, no, we would fix it in Barcelos, which we all were just as happy to agree to, seeing that thirty minutes before, it was a good bet we were heading for a black water version of Davey Jones's locker.

Although it looked like we had beat the worst of the storms, we expected more rain, and kept our clothes off. We sipped the rest of the coffee Glück had brought, and ate the end of a castaña cake called "leg of the small boy," which Roberto's wife had baked. Behind us the jungle flashed.

Tano said, "It's giving us one hell of a send-off."

XLIV

IT took only a few hours to reach Barcelos, which Tano promptly dubbed the Emerald City, but the rains followed us. Tano and I quickly grabbed our gear, climbed a bluff into the city, and found a gazebo in a park to sleep in for the night, while Glück opted to stay in the boat.

It was a good sleep on hard concrete, the kind of sleep Hemingway might have called fine. The rain still was coming down, but not so hard, when organ music and the father and mother in the sky announced six o'clock and dawn.

The gazebo was behind the *Prefeitura Municipal,* which opened with the organ music when a janitor came out and hoisted a tattered flag. From below, we heard the boat motor kick, then start and fade just upriver before cutting off again.

"He must've got clobbered," Tano said. "He's heading for port . . . Man, what a great place to wake up. There's flowers on some of those bushes. It's probably the only pretty place in town, and down there, Glück must have got the shit kicked out of him during the storm."

"Makes nuhzing," Glück said when he came to get us for breakfast. "I wrapped in the plastic."

358

We went to the market where we could find only a man selling coffee and stale bread. Glück asked him for eggs. The man said he had four. "Then put in the two between your legs," Glück said. I didn't hear the exchange, but Tano told me he was ready to punch out Glück's lights.

We drank our coffee and ate our stale bread without saying anything, then went down to the port, a few wooden docks, and asked for a boat to Manaus, but there were none. So we tried the mission with the tower and the loudspeaker that sent voices into the sky, but the padre said he knew of no boats. On the way back into town, we met the famed Tatunka Nada.

He was cruising on a banana bike, the kind with the long seat and the high, up-turned handlebars. Tatunka wore a big-brimmed white hat, a flowered shirt, shorts, and thongs, a jungle version of street wise. His face fulfilled his name. He looked like a watersnake, with beady eyes and a pointy nose and chin. Glück and he talked in German for a minute, then Glück introduced us and Mr. Nada invited us to his home.

"We will slaughter a peeg, how you say" (he snorted), ... "Yes, that's how we say" ... "and I invite you to lunch."

His home was a concrete bunker off a dirt road on the edge of town, where we met his dark-haired, dark-eyed, puffy-cheeked wife, and two blond, German-looking children. His wife seemed alternately excited and reserved about guests. When she was excited, she tried speaking English with Tano and me, telling us how she was a nurse and a teacher. When she seemed nervous, she would turn from us, as if it didn't matter if we responded to her last statement, and talk with Tatunka and Glück, who rattled away in German.

"Long lost buddies," Tano mumbled.

Tatunka took out a photo album, then German cracked into English and the talk shifted to the pyramids.

Tatunka and his wife said they discovered the pyramids in 1972.

"I don't think they're anything more than mountains," his wife said. "They are completely overgrown. Some might be pyramids, Mayan ruins or something."

Then Tatunka broke in, "But they need an excavation crew to discover."

359

Tatunka talked about some of his trips to the pyramids and his story included Brandon (the Brazilian), Peret (the journalist who didn't like Glück), and Ferdinand (the Swiss man and secretary to Von Däniken). Brandon shot himself in the arm and Tatunka broke his own arm when one of the boats turned over when they were trying to pass through the rapids.

On one of their trips, they supposedly found an old vase that dated back six thousand years, but tests were unable to confirm it. Von Däniken said that if Ferdinand found anything, he, Von Däniken, would finance it.

As to the Indian story, which was almost as pieced together and vague, Tatunka said the Yanomari were working for cabocolos and Lacerda, cutting piacaba. The year before, the Hyshu, a tribe of five thousand, came from the mountains and attacked the Yanomari and took their women. The Yanomari had been buying guns with the cabocolo money they earned, but the government sensed trouble and forbade cabocolos to give them money to buy guns. At the end of the summer, in November, the Indians wanted money or guns, and afraid that the mountain Hyshu would attack, Tatunka made his speech at Allianca, the one we had heard about, and warned that the Hyshu were ready to attack. The speech had the expected effect. Everyone left.

Tatunka did not volunteer much more information, and Glück didn't ask him about his connections with the cabocolos or Lacerda. When we asked him, he mumbled about knowing some people, then trailed off into speaking German.

Reasoning for the lines in his story was vague, which at other times might have made me press for explanations, but they didn't seem like they would be coming and I was getting itchy, feeling cramped and trapped with Tatunka and his wife in the concrete cell. We tapped Glück and told him we should go to town and look for a boat.

"Ah, yes, of course," he said and we bade a brief good-bye until lunch.

Glück couldn't remember the way down the two roads to town, so we helped him and got him back to the dock where he had tied up in the morning. We found the captain of the boat that towed us the night before, and he said he was leaving soon for Manaus, with a load of fish. He also said fish spoils fast and he

WHO IS THE RIVER

would have to go as fast as he could, so he couldn't let us tie on. Sorry.

Walking back and through town, I thought Tano was ready to explode, not about the missed ride, but about our breakfast with the watersnake.

"What a pack of lies, that Tatunka and his wife," Tano said. "They make me sick."

We returned for a brief lunch with the snake and family. He served beans and rice, but the "peeg" was neither seen nor spoken of, so the snake probably had a similar opinion of us.

In town, we split with Glück and returned to our gazebo, where we howled with the siesta incantations from the calliope organ loudspeaker. Once a dog came and sat against the wall across from us. Tano nodded to him, laughed, and said, "This is our doggie heaven."

Then our shadow returned.

"I have found a house," Glück said. "Father Frank's."

We followed him down side streets until he found a woman who took us to another street and a pink wooden house with turquoise trim.

"Father Frank's," Glück said.

We opened a gate and brushed through chickens, then climbed a ladder to an attic with posts for hammocks. It looked fine, that time not in the Hemingway sense, but in the OK sense, but it wan't enough for Glück, who climbed downstairs and wanted to sleep in Father Frank's bedroom near the kitchen.

"He grooves on electric lights and the refrigerator and stove," Tano said.

We told Glück the house wasn't ours and even though Father Frank was away, we should stay in the attic where the caretaker said we could sleep.

"Makes nuhzing," Glück said. "If Father Frank was in Manaus, my home would be his," which, because we knew it would cost Father Frank $10 a night for Glück's tourist room, was bullshit, but no one felt like arguing.

Glück said he wanted to move in immediately, but I told him to wait until later. We might get a boat and then have to cart everything back to the river. He answered, "Natyourally."

Tano and I returned to doggie heaven.

It had been hot and steamy all day and I felt washed out, though I didn't sleep more than an hour or so, in a stupor interrupted only by the gonging of five o'clock, when the schoolchildren came out and we expected a new audience, so we scraped ourselves away and set off in search of Glück.

We found him near Father Frank's, then wandered through town together in search of a woman who would cook us dinner, but there were no restaurants. In the past month, Barcelos had been hit by a typhoid epidemic, with half of the town's population of a thousand being stricken. Six people had died, including three in one family, and the one town restaurant, wherever that had been, was out of business.

I told Glück we would be happy to go back to the boat and make farinha, and Glück gave us the old routine about how he wouldn't feed his dogs the stuff we ate, so rather than argue with him, we went to the tienda above the docks where he bought a can of swine we washed down with something that came in a bottle and tasted like cream soda, street food, Queens, New York circa 1958–62.

We downed the stuff at a table next door that Glück had cleared free of a high school boy. That was enough to send another one of our meals into an ordeal of growling silence.

Soon, a pack of locals stood and watched us from across the street, but their attention was easily diverted by a drunk Indian, who had passed out on the street, with either blood or a dead worm across his face, and an old drunk woman who was yelling at everyone for yelling at her. Our table was on a ledge above cans of garbage. That put the final touches on the meal and ensured Glück he would get my share of the swine.

After dinner, we gave up waiting for the boat and moved into Father Frank's. All evening the mission megaphone blasted over, through, around, and on top of us, with incantations and the latest conversations between God, the padre, and the nun.

"Surreal," Tano said, which was the only word you could use and the only time I really thought I knew what it meant.

"This blows me out," he said. "No way you can ever get away from that. Man, this is Big Brother land."

It went on for what seemed a long time, deafening us into silence, and I suppose numbing us, too, because when it was finished we were so glad for the quiet, we didn't break it with talk.

The windows were open and outside we could see palm leaves swaying in the wind. Earlier in the day, when we first came to Father Frank's, I stuck my head out the window and saw a rainbow form in the sky, to the southeast, toward Manaus.

We lit a pair of candles and set them on a table between us, then took off our clothes, got in our hammocks, and rocked.

We talked about Butch Cassidy and the Sundance Kid and the gaps of time between when Tano and I had seen each other.

"You know, Butch lived," Tano said. "He still has a daughter." I said something about how I could see Bolivia or South America would be the only place that would blow them away, but it was something I didn't know if it was true or not, or Hollywoodized.

Talking about that stuff, and a woman who got between, made me think of women and other things and got me feeling sad and not wanting to talk any more, but still, we did, about the day before.

"A perfect day," Tano said. "We rolled the dice one last time. Took on the river and came out ahead, with a perfect night. Something about it . . . Going for it, then playing our cards right, waiting at the island for a boat, then slipping into town, the best spot, a park with dogs, lying low and beating the watchdogs, then grass and before the rain hit, we scoot inside the doghouse. Christ, how we sleep good on concrete. And we slept great that night in the storm while the old man got beat to hell . . . The ultimate road night."

"Maybe we've learned something," I said.

"Graduation."

XLV

I faded into sleep, feeling good about the last night, bad about that day, and blue about Butch and Sundance and death and women.

I don't know how much time later, it must not have been too much, I heard Tano moving. I opened an eye and saw him smoking a cigarette and standing nude by the window. Down below, someone had come running up the street, yelling about a boat. Tano spit some Portuguese out about where and when and the voice answered, "Manaus, *haje à noite.*"

"Holy shit," Tano called out.

Glück woke up and ran to the window and found out a big boat had pulled in and was leaving tonight for Manaus.

"I go to the dock and find out more," Glück said. "You pack."

Glück came running back in minutes and said the boat would leave in a half hour. It was nine o'clock. Earlier that day, Tano had predicted we would get out by nine thirty.

"If it's anything I've learned on this trip," he said, "it's trust your instincts."

The boat was big, maybe sixty feet, the same size as the *Em-*

364

erson, the one we came up on, and one of the crew was Monkey Man, the Indian who guided us upriver that first night out of Manaus.

We ran over and got Glück's boat, which coughed for two or three minutes before it started, but eventually it did, and we tied on and loaded everything on board.

Then the captain came aboard. He was a blond-haired kid, maybe sixteen years old. I had seen him in town, holding hands and teasing one of the high school girls. Glück asked him if he was the *comandante,* and he nodded. From the captain's cabin, we heard rock -n roll music.

"Christ, we're being taken home by Huck Finn," Tano said.

We waited until ten o'clock, then Huck ran down, pointed, and yelled a few orders at his crew, rang the bell, and the engine started. He dinged orders down to the engine room, then swung the wheel around and pulled the big baby out.

"Damn, the kid knows what he's doing," Tano said.

I sat up front and watched the moon for a while and Tano came up and said he was trying to remember a song about looking out a window and seeing a rainbow.

XLVI

I didn't know it in the morning, but by afternoon, the vision or feeling I had weeks before in the park in Hoboken, about discordant images and stories, about my finding the key to a picture and the world stopping and letting me off for a look, by afternoon that would happen. I should have suspected it was coming.

On the way back down the Rios Padauiri and Negro, when memories were flowing like streams, I didn't always see how they were connected, they were running so fast. My being there with Tano and Glück and going up the river and trying to find some pyramids, that was another stream, but then all that changed. By afternoon, I knew the universe would not seem quite so vacant and the streams would flow into a river and have meaning and I knew Tano and I were meant to be together in the Amazon.

The Amazon had been an answer to things. It said not only do you have your own story, a story that often can get tangled with other people's stories, but behind those stories there are forces or currents, which not only shape and move things, sometimes they comment on the stories.

Realizing you're part of a story gives things meaning. Realizing you're in the story with someone else who's got his own

366

story with threads leading up to your shared story, just the way you do, then even more than meaning, there seems to be fate. Then, when you get meaning and fate happening together, and you see your story and how it is knotted with someone else's, and you see where some of the threads begin, and you are sitting there thinking there is meaning and maybe fate in the way things happen, then, when something from the outside, which maybe was not so outside, comes and ties it up together for both of you, as if that something on the outside had been watching all along and you were right in thinking you were part of a story that had meaning and fate, then, even if you died the next second, it would be OK. You had found a treasure.

I didn't know all that was about to happen, so I slept late, and I slept with the weight of weeks and years oozing out of me. My bones ached and my joints were as taut as water. I opened my eyes briefly at sunrise when I heard bells ringing for a stop. It was a magnificent, burning sunrise and I watched an Indian paddle a canoe in the still waters, while four deckhands carried aboard a turtle from shore. They were soft pictures to wake up to and I didn't notice anything else happening, so I went back to sleep.

In the afternoon, the rains came. I saw them a mile ahead, a gray wave rushing at us. The rain was almost solid and coming fast and it was enough to get your blood moving. I watched from the bow and saw a bright light above the water, then the sky cracked and a rainbow began to form and I felt things moving around inside. The rainbow arced over the clouds and the rain and the river and things began jumping inside and everything began to shimmer and I yelled for Tano.

Time must have stopped because I don't know where Tano was or how long it took him to get to the bow, but suddenly we were side by side and we passed through a seam. The boat disappeared, but the rain and the clouds caught us and we floated.

As far as I could see, the rainbow came from the beginning, out past the jungle, even from out past where I sat with Tano on the beach in San Diego and told him I had a plan, past where we were on the sand dune in Florida and howling at the moon, past where I had met him and he told me it was going to be Columbus Day and I hit the road and stuck my thumb out in the snow,

367

past the bird singing by himself in the tree in the Great Swamp, past the baseball games and looking at Winslow Homer's *Gulf Stream* and *Prisoners from the Front* with my grandfather, out way past all that, way back over the jungle, the rainbow rose. It lifted and turned like a great sky river carrying all those stories and all those beginnings, pulling them all together until they were one, then sliding down a ridge of clouds until they found us and poured highways of colors at our feet.

"The end of the rainbow ... The end of the rainbow ... " I whispered and shook Tano.

We washed in it and in a few seconds it disappeared and the skies broke with black rain and the deckhands raced around the boat and pulled down the flaps and I knew nothing ever would be quite the same.

XLVII

FOR a few days that stretched into a few weeks after the end of the rainbow, I was hot. It was something like a gambler's hot, but it had more to do with a seeing that was reading. People and events connected and there were intimations of other things.

Our second night in Manaus, when Tano and I were red-hot, I took him out to dinner, fulfilling the first half of the promise I made upriver about getting back alive and celebrating.

The night before, we had gone out with Melnick and he got us drunk and stuffed us with fish stew and we told him stories about "Hello, the boat is gone," and getting lost, and he told us stories about his coming to the jungle and about Glück and Brazil.

We had seen Glück in the afternoon and half heartedly asked if he wanted to go to lunch with us, but he excused himself, then said good-bye for the last time and tagged on an "I'm sorry we got lost."

All that was over with the second night when Tano and I went to the café behind the market, where we had a well-lit table above the river, with a tablecloth and a dinner that went by the name of gaucho-something-or-other.

369

We didn't talk much, just sat above the river and watched passing boats with kerosene lanterns that made them look like jack-o'-lanterns. Through most of dinner, the restaurant radio played Brazilian music, but near the end it stopped, and on came Bob Dylan's "Like a Rolling Stone."

> When you got nothing, you got nothing to lose
> You're invisible now, you got no secrets to conceal.

Yeah, we knew.

Ten years and more ended with that trip and that night, but we were mostly quiet about it, and if it wasn't me, it was Tano who said, "Now ain't the time to be talkin' about it."

XLVIII

I kept the second half of my promise in New York. When I
was on the river, and I was hungry and tired and unable to think,
I told myself that if I got back OK, I would treat myself to a
Scotch at the Oak Room of the Plaza Hotel in New York.

I arrived in New York on a Friday night, the day before a
horse, a filly I had heard about in Brazil, was running in the Belmont Stakes. The horse had won the Kentucky Derby and
finished second in the Preakness and her name was Genuine Risk.

I started late and took a bus and subway to get to Belmont
Park. I didn't get there until the end of the seventh race, which
was just in time, and I ran to the paddock and found her through
the whispers.

When she came round my side of the rail, she looked at me,
a quick, big, brown stare that opened into flesh and muscle and
heart, the kind of look bad horseplayers look for and see all the
time.

I bet everything I had on her, except $5 I had kept in my
pocket for the drink at the Plaza, then in a moment of weakness,
I spotted a South of the Border horse, and for old times' sake, I
put the $5 on Pikotazo to show.

371

I watched the race from the grandstand, through a hole in a wall of people at the rail.

It had rained that day and the night before, and the track was sloppy. Genuine Risk broke well, but stayed in the pack through the backstretch, then, coming into the home turn, she made her move, splitting horses and rounding into a brief lead. It was a big move, one you could have been blind and still knew happened, you could hear eighty thousand gasps and feel a flutter of hearts. When Risk made that turn, I knew even if she didn't win, she was a game horse and I loved her.

She finished second to a 53–1 shot, Temperance Hill, who refused to give ground in the stretch. Still, after Risk crossed the finish line, people were on their feet cheering her, which was something I never had seen happen for a horse that didn't quite make it.

My Plaza-drink money also went down, but not so majestically, finishing last, only slightly diminishing the sense that I thought I still was hot.

I finished business a few days later, when I put on a corduroy jacket and a white shirt and went to town.

I wanted to sit at the bar, but it was full and the maitre d' at the Oak Room said there was one free table. It was the same table I had sat at with the woman from San Diego and San Francisco and Hoboken, two Christmases earlier, when things were going well. We drank martinis then and she told me secrets and for a moment, I had thought things were not going to stop.

The night I went by myself, I took the seat against the window, across from the one I'd had before.

From one side of my table, I overheard a conversation between a man I gathered was an editor for the *New York Times* and a woman who was talking about Brazil and sounding as if she was coming on to him. On the other side of me, there was a rock and roll producer and a so-so looking woman whom the producer might have been shaping into a queen. Across the room, a woman sat by herself at the bar. The place was packed, but we were the only people alone, and I had the feeling because of that, loose forces in the room expected us to get together. Once, a waiter looked at me, then at her, and back at me, but that was as far as it went.

372

There was only one other group I noticed, five women at a middle table, who occasionally looked over their shoulders.

I ordered Scotch, smoked cigarettes, and drank slowly. I was nervous, but not sure why, and at one point had to concentrate on keeping my head straight because I felt dizzy and it was hard to breathe, which I combated by ordering another Scotch.

Just after my drink arrived, one of the women from the middle table came over to me. She had auburn hair, dark eyes, and a white dress.

"Why do you look so glum?" she said in an airy voice.

"I'm not glum. I'm very happy."

"Are you getting married?"

"No, not that." I smiled.

"You got the job?"

"No, no, nothing like that."

"What is it? Can you tell me?"

I smiled again. For a moment, I thought I would tell her something, but I got a knot in my throat and I felt like I was choking, then I steadied and mumbled, "No, I'd rather not."

She had been smiling and the lines around her mouth disappeared.

I told her thanks for coming to talk, and she walked away.

I finished my Scotch and tried to gather myself, smoked another cigarette and waved to the waiter for my bill.

When I left, I stopped at her table, leaned over her shoulder, and said I was sorry, "But, this is the truth, I was on a trip in the Amazon and when things got bad, and when I thought I might not return, I promised myself that if I did, I'd come here and buy myself a drink. I tried to tell you, but I got knotted up," then stumbling around, I didn't know what else to say. "Thanks, it was nice to meet you."

I walked out the door and down a hallway, past the Palm Court, when I heard her call.

"Can you tell me any more?" she said.

"I can't."

"Where are you going now?"

I paused and thought about half the truth and then about sometime in the future.

"I think I have someone to go home to."

373

She half smiled and seemed embarrassed.

"What's your name?"

I told her. "And yours?"

"Dorothy."

"Thanks . . . Thanks for your interest."

I started walking, but in a step everything exploded white.

"Dorothy"—I spun around—"my being here had a lot to do with rainbows."

She smiled, then whispered, "I'm so glad."

For a moment, I saw her years ago, as a child who thought about another Dorothy going to Oz. Maybe, too, I had finished a story for her.

I kissed her hand, said good-bye, and she walked down a hallway, turned a corner, and was gone.

Rivers never end. They struggle with the earth and flow to a place where they can no longer be seen, then empty and wait for the sky to bring the end back to the beginning. Their journeys are perpetual.

Once in a bending of light, I saw rivers set free.

December 31, 1982
Mexico